Finn Boerner

C000098346

WATSON-GANDY ON
CORPORATE INSOLVENCY PRACTICE

WATSON-GANDY ON CORPORATE INSOLVENCY PRACTICE

LITIGATION PROCEDURE AND PRECEDENTS

Professor Mark Watson-Gandy
Barrister, Thirteen Old Square Chambers

With thanks to
David Perry, Solicitor, Wortley Redmayne & Kershaw
Damon Watt, Solicitor, EMW Picton Howell LLP

Wildy, Simmonds & Hill Publishing

Copyright © 2010 Wildy, Simmonds & Hill Publishing
Crown copyright – extracts of Insolvency Act 1986, Insolvency Rules 1986, statutory forms

Watson-Gandy on Corporate Insolvency Practice
Litigation Procedure and Precedents

British Library Cataloguing in Publication Data
A catalogue record for this book is available from the British Library

ISBN 9780854900466

Typeset in Times New Roman by Cornubia Press Ltd
Printed and bound in the United Kingdom by CPI Antony Rowe, Chippenham, Wiltshire

First published in 2010 by
Wildy, Simmonds & Hill Publishing
58 Carey Street
London WC2A 2JF
England

Contents

Preface

In 1733 Samuel Madden, an Irish writer and cleric, published a pamphlet, *Memories of the Twentieth Century: Being Original Letters of State under George VI*, in which he predicted a dystopian world dominated by two gigantic and powerful corporations, the Royal Fishery Company and the Plantation Company (to be incorporated by Frederick I and George III respectively). It was to be another century before the modern corporation began to appear, but Madden's vision of a world in thrall to corporate forms was prescient.

The late twentieth century saw a period of buccaneering corporate growth and enormous prosperity which, however, culminated in serious reverses in 2007–2009, the effects of which we are still coming to terms with. Books such as Roger Bootle's *The Trouble with Markets* and Graham Turner's *No Way to Run an Economy* and many others raise serious questions about the way in which global corporate life has been regulated (or not).

A by-product of corporate growth, by which I mean not just the increase in the number of companies but the reach of corporate structures in their many forms, has been a greater emphasis on insolvency, which has moved from the edges of legal practice to its core. No self-respecting law firm can now afford to be ignorant of what was once regarded as an arcane specialism but is now seen as an important check on the less creditable aspects of corporate business dealings.

Mark Watson-Gandy's *Corporate Insolvency Practice* is the latest of a burgeoning number of text books devoted to aspects of insolvency. What is the justification for yet another addition? The answer lies in the approach the author takes to his subject and the market to which he directs himself. Any practitioner will welcome a practical guide to practice and procedure; the non-specialist will, however, be especially grateful for Watson-Gandy's clear and concise introduction to 30 of the most common insolvency procedures affecting companies. Each is dealt with systematically by reference to what the procedure in question is designed to achieve, the statutory form, the key statutory provisions and a variety of precedents.

Watson-Gandy on Corporate Insolvency Practice will fill a gap on many shelves; and in many practitioners' knowledge.

Stephen Baister
Chief Bankruptcy Registrar of the High Court
Royal Courts of Justice, London
January 2010

CHAPTER 1

STATUTORY DEMAND

OBJECTIVE

A company is deemed unable to pay its debts[1] if a creditor (by assignment or otherwise) to whom the company is indebted in a sum exceeding £750 then due has served on the company's registered office a statutory demand in the prescribed form requiring the company to pay the sum so due and the company has for 3 weeks thereafter neglected to pay the sum or to secure or compound for it to the reasonable satisfaction of the creditor.

STATUTORY FORM

Form 4.1. The statutory demand must set out:

- the amount of the debt;
- the consideration for the debt or, if none, how it arises;
- any charge by way of interest not previously notified to the company as included in its liability that has accrued at the date of the demand;
- any other charge accruing from time to time that has accrued at the date of the demand;
- the amount or rate of the charge;
- the grounds on which payment of any charge is claimed;
- the purpose of the demand, and the fact that, if the demand is not complied with, proceedings may be instituted for the winding up of the company;
- the time within which it must be complied with, if that consequence is to be avoided;
- the methods of compliance which are open to the company;

---

[1]   Section 123 of the Insolvency Act 1986.

- contact information for the creditor to enable the company to communicate with him, with a view to securing or compounding for the debt to the creditor's satisfaction. This must include:
    - a named contact accrued at the date of the demand;
    - the contact's address;
    - the contact's telephone number.

The statutory demand must be dated and signed.

SERVICE

The statutory demand can only be served by leaving it at the company's registered office. It is not sufficient to send the demand by post. Nor is it sufficient to serve the demand at a trading address which is not the company's registered office.

EVIDENCE

A witness statement should be prepared proving service. The deponent should be the process server who effected service.

This should address:

- how the deponent effected service of the demand, where he did it and on whom;
- the date and time of service;
- the reaction (if any) to service.

This should exhibit:

- the statutory demand.

NOTES

Unlike a statutory demand presented against a private individual, there is no procedure to set aside statutory demands against a company. Instead, the company has to obtain an injunction to restrain the advertisement of the petition or further proceedings on it or even strike it out.

KEY STATUTORY PROVISIONS

Rules 4.4 to 4.6 of the Insolvency Rules 1986

4.4 Preliminary

(1) This Chapter does not apply where a petition for the winding up of a company is presented under section 124 on or after the date on which the Rules come into force and the petition is based on failure to comply with a written demand served on the company before that date.

(2) A written demand served by a creditor on a company under section 123(1)(a) (registered companies) or 222(1)(a) (unregistered companies) is known in winding-up proceedings as 'the statutory demand'.

(3)   The statutory demand must be dated, and be signed either by the creditor himself or by a person stating himself to be authorized to make the demand on the creditor's behalf.

4.5 Form and content of statutory demand

(1)   The statutory demand must state the amount of the debt and the consideration for it (or, if there is no consideration, the way in which it arises).

(2)   If the amount claimed in the demand includes—

    (a)   any charge by way of interest not previously notified to the company as included in its liability, or

    (b)   any other charge accruing from time to time,

the amount or rate of the charge must be separately identified, and the grounds on which payment of it is claimed must be stated.

In either case the amount claimed must be limited to that which has accrued due at the date of the demand.

4.6 Information to be given in statutory demand

(1)   The statutory demand must include an explanation to the company of the following matters—

    (a)   the purpose of the demand, and the fact that, if the demand is not complied with, proceedings may be instituted for the winding up of the company;

    (b)   the time within which it must be complied with, if that consequence is to be avoided; and

    (c)   the methods of compliance which are open to the company.

(2)   Information must be provided for the company as to how an officer or representative of it may enter into communication with one or more named individuals, with a view to securing or compounding for the debt to the creditor's satisfaction.
In the case of any individual so named in the demand, his address and telephone number (if any) must be given.

Section 123(1)(a) of the Insolvency Act 1986

123 Definition of inability to pay debts

(1)   A company is deemed unable to pay its debts—

    (a)   if a creditor (by assignment or otherwise) to whom the company is indebted in a sum exceeding £750 then due has served on the company, by leaving it at the company's registered office, a written demand (in the prescribed form) requiring the company to pay the sum so due and the company has for 3 weeks thereafter neglected to pay the sum or to secure or compound for it to the reasonable satisfaction of the creditor ...

1.1   CREDITOR'S STATUTORY DEMAND

Rule 4.5
Statutory demand under section 123(1)(a) of the Insolvency Act 1986

Warning

THIS IS AN IMPORTANT DOCUMENT.

THIS DEMAND MUST BE DEALT WITH WITHIN 21 DAYS AFTER ITS SERVICE UPON THE COMPANY OR A WINDING-UP ORDER COULD BE MADE IN RESPECT OF THE COMPANY.

PLEASE READ THE DEMAND AND NOTES CAREFULLY.

Notes for Creditor

If the creditor is entitled to the debt by way of assignment, details of the original creditor and any intermediary assignees should be given in part B on page 3.

If the amount of debt includes interest not previously notified to the company as included in its liability, details should be given, including the grounds upon which interest is charged. The amount of interest must be shown separately.

Any other charge accruing due from time to time may be claimed. The amount or rate of the charge must be identified and the grounds on which it is claimed must be stated.

In either case the amount claimed must be limited to that which has accrued due at the date of the demand.

If signatory of the demand is a solicitor or other agent of the creditor the name of his/her firm should be given.

Demand

To BUSTCO LIMITED
Address Suite 1, 1 Poor Street, London

This demand is served on you by the creditor.

Name ANGRY LIMITED
Address 1 Unpaid Bill Street, London

The creditor claims that the company owes the sum of £2,045,687.50 full particulars of which are set out on page 2.

The creditor demands that the company do pay the above debt or secure or compound for it to the creditor's satisfaction.

Signature of individual ....

Name CLIVE CRABBY (BLOCK LETTERS)

Date 25 December 2007

(Delete if signed by the creditor himself)
Position with or relationship to creditor: SOLICITOR

(Delete if signed by the creditor himself)
I am authorised to make this demand on the creditor's behalf.

Address
WIGG & CO
I LAW STREET
LONDON
Tel. No. 0207 666 6666
Ref CC/Angry/1234

NB The person making this demand must complete the whole of this page, page 2 and parts A and B (as applicable) on page 3.

Particulars of Debt

(These particulars must include (a) when the debt was incurred, (b) the consideration for the debt (or if there is no consideration the way in which it arose) and (c) the amount due as the date of this demand.)

Notes for Creditor

Please make sure that you have read the notes on page I before completing this page.

Note: If space is insufficient continue on reverse of page 3 and clearly indicate on this page that you are doing so.

The Debtor is indebted to the Creditor:

(a)   in the sum of £1,000,000 in respect of a consignment of widgets sold and delivered by the Petitioner to the Company under a contract dated 17th December 2007 under invoice reference 0010

(b)   in the sum of £1,000,000 in respect of a consignments of widgets sold and delivered by the Petitioner to the Company under contracts dated 10th May 2007 under invoice reference 0011

(c)   together with £45,687.50 in contractual interest calculated at a rate of 13.1% per day from the date of delivery of the invoice to the date of this demand.

TOTAL £2,045,687.50

PART A

The individual or individuals to whom any communication regarding this demand may be addressed is/are:

Name
WIGG & CO

Address
1 LAW STREET
LONDON
Tel. No. 0207 666 6666
Ref CC/Angry/1234

PART B

For completion if the creditor is entitled to the debt by way of assignment

Name [ ]
Date(s) of Assignment [ ]
Original creditor [ ]
Assignees [ ]

How to comply with a statutory demand

If the company wishes to avoid a winding-up petition being presented it must pay the debt shown on page 1, particulars of which are set out on page 2 of this notice, within the period of 21 days after its service upon the company. Alternatively, the company can attempt to come to a settlement with the creditor. To do this the company should:

- inform the individual (or one of the individuals) named in part A above immediately that it is willing and able to offer security for the debt to the creditor's satisfaction; or
- inform the individual (or one of the individuals) named in part A immediately that it is willing and able to compound for the debt to the creditor's satisfaction.

If the company disputes the demand in whole or in part it should:

- contact the individual (or one of the individuals) named in part A immediately.

Remember: The Company has only 21 days after the date of service on it of this document before the creditor may present a winding-up petition.

CHAPTER 2

CREDITOR'S WINDING UP PETITION AGAINST A UK REGISTERED COMPANY

OBJECTIVE

A petition to wind up a company can be presented if you can show that one of the statutory grounds under section 122(1) of the Insolvency Act 1986 are made out, for example, that the company is unable to pay its debts as they fall due.[1]

A company is deemed unable to pay its debts:[2]

- if a creditor (by assignment or otherwise) to whom the company is indebted in a sum exceeding £750 then due has served on the company's registered office a statutory demand in the prescribed form requiring the company to pay the sum so due and the company has for 3 weeks thereafter neglected to pay the sum or to secure or compound for it to the reasonable satisfaction of the creditor; or

---

[1] Section 122(1)(g) of the Insolvency Act 1986.

[2] Section 123 of the Insolvency Act 1986.

- if execution or other process issued on a judgment, decree or order of any court in favour of a creditor of the company is returned unsatisfied in whole or in part; or
- if it is proved to the satisfaction of the court that the company is unable to pay its debts as they fall due;
- if it is proved to the satisfaction of the court that the value of the company's assets is less than the amount of its liabilities, taking into account its contingent and prospective liabilities.

It is possible to prove a company is unable to pay its debts without recourse to a statutory demand. This can be satisfied if the company admits it is unable to pay its debts[3] or has a receiver appointed. It has been held that evidence of a failure to pay a debt that is due and not disputed is of itself evidence of insolvency even though there is other evidence of substantial surplus of assets over liabilities[4] even though a statutory demand has not been served.[5]

A debt is undisputed unless there is a dispute on a substantial ground.

PETITION

The petition needs to be in the statutory form. It must contain:

- the name and number of the company to be wound up;
- the date when the company was incorporated and under which companies act;
- the address of the registered office;
- the nominal capital of the company;
- the issued capital of the company;
- the principal objects for which the company was established;
- particulars of the debt owed to the petitioner including the amount;
- particulars of the facts which the petitioner relies on to show that the company is insolvent;[6]
- that the company is insolvent and unable to pay its debts;
- particulars of whether the company is an insurance undertaking; a credit institution; an investment undertaking providing services involving the holding of funds or securities for third parties; a collective investment undertaking;[7]
- particulars of whether the EC Regulation applies;
- particulars of whether these proceedings will be main proceedings;[8]
- a statement that it is just and equitable that the company should be wound up.

The petition needs to be presented at or posted to the Chambers of the Registrar of the Companies Court, Royal Courts of Justice, Thomas More Building, Strand, London or at a Chancery District Registry or at a county court with insolvency jurisdiction for the area in which the company has its registered office.[9]

---

[3] *Re Douglas Griggs* [1963] Ch 19.

[4] *Cornhill Insurance plc v Improvement Services Ltd* [1986] 1 WLR 114.

[5] *Re Taylor Industrial Flooring Ltd* [1990] BCLC 216.

[6] For example that despite being served with a statutory demand, over 3 weeks have now elapsed without the Company paying or satisfying the debt or to making any offer to the Petitioner to secure or compound the same.

[7] Article 1(2) of Council Regulation (EC) No 1346/2000 of 29 May 2000 on insolvency proceedings.

[8] As defined in Article 3 of Council Regulation (EC) No 1346/2000 of 29 May 2000 on insolvency proceedings.

[9] For further discussion of the county court's jurisdiction, see below and Chapter 30 'Toolkit'.

Before the petition is presented the central index of winding up petitions at TM2.09 of Thomas More Building should be checked. If an existing petition is already current against the company, the creditor should not lodge a second petition but simply support the existing petition.

The county court has jurisdiction to wind up a company where the company's paid up or credited as paid up does not exceed £120,000 and the county court is in the district in which the company's registered office is situated.[10] The registered office is the place which is the place which has been the longest been the registered office during the 6 months immediately preceeding the presentation of the petition to wind up.[11]

EVIDENCE

The petition needs to be verified by affidavit which should be field at the same time sworn by the petitioner (or one of its officers if the petitioner is a company) or his solicitor.

The affidavit should address:

- the capacity in which the deponent makes the affidavit;
- the authority the deponent has to make the affidavit;
- that the deponent has the requisite knowledge of the matters referred to in the petition;
- how that knowledge was obtained;
- that the statements in the petition are true or true to the best of the deponent's knowledge, information or belief;[12]
- where the company's centre of main interest is considered to be;
- whether in the opinion of the deponent the ec regulation applies;
- whether the winding-up proceedings will be main or territorial proceedings.

And exhibit:

- the petition.[13]

COURT FEES

The court fee is £190[14] but one needs to also pay a deposit of £715[15] which will be used to pay the official receiver if the company goes into liquidation. There is a further court fee of £5 for the search of the central index of winding up petitions.

---

[10]   Section 117(2) of the Insolvency Act 1986.
[11]   Section 117(6) of the Insolvency Act 1986.
[12]   Rule 4.12(1) of the Insolvency Rules 1986 (SI 1986/1925).
[13]   Rule 4.12(3) of the Insolvency Rules 1986.
[14]   Paragraph 3.3 of Schedule 1 to the Civil Proceedings Fees Order 2008 (SI 2008/1053).
[15]   Insolvency Proceedings (Fees) (Amendment) Order 2009 (SI 2009/645).

SERVICE

A sealed copy of the petition should be served at the company's registered office at least 7 business days before it is advertised in the *London Gazette* and evidence of both service and advertisement needs to be filed in court. Service is by delivery to a director, officer or employee or other person who acknowledges himself authorised to accept service on behalf of the company or, in the absence of the same, by depositing at the registered office in such a way that it is likely to come to the attention of a person attending the office.[16] Where service on the registered office is not practicable, the petition may be served by depositing at the company's last known principal place of business in such a way that it is likely to come to the attention of a person attending there or by delivering it to the company's secretary, director, manager or principal officer.[17]

Where service is not practicable in this way an application should be made for substituted service.

A sealed copy of the petition should also be served, if applicable to the company, on any liquidator appointed in an existing voluntary liquidation, any administrator appointed in an existing administration order, any supervisor of a voluntary arrangement, any administrative receiver, any member state liquidator who has been appointed and the Financial Services Authority if the company is or was an authorised institution.[18]

An affidavit should be prepared proving service. The deponent should be the process server who effected service.

This should address:

- how the deponent effected service of the petition;
- the place where service was effected;
- the date and time of service;
- if the service was effected on an individual, the name of that individual, their relationship to the debtor company and whether they acknowledged himself authorised to accept service on behalf of the company;
- if service was not on an individual, how service of the petition would have been brought to the attention of a person attending the office;
- the reaction (if any) to service.

This should exhibit:

- a sealed copy of the petition;
- a sealed copy of any order for substituted service.

---

[16]   Rule 4.8(3) of the Insolvency Rules 1986.

[17]   Rule 4.8(4) of the Insolvency Rules 1986.

[18]   Rules 4.7 and 4.10 of the Insolvency Rules 1986.

Any creditor, director, contributory or member of the debtor company is entitled, on request and on payment of the statutory fee, to be provided by the petitioner or his solicitor within 2 days of making the request with a copy of the petition.[19]

ADVERTISEMENT

The petition must be advertised once in the *London Gazette*, unless the court otherwise directs, not less than 7 business days *after* the date of service but not less than 7 business days *before* the day fixed for the hearing.[20] For the computation of business days Saturdays, Sundays, Good Friday, Christmas Day and bank holidays are excluded.

Failure to comply with the rule, without good reason accepted by the court, may lead to the summary dismissal of the petition on the return date.[21] If the court, in its discretion, grants an adjournment, this will be on condition that the petition is advertised in due time for the adjourned hearing. No further adjournments for the purpose of advertisement will normally be granted.[22]

If the time limits have not been complied with the petitioner should make an application to extend the date for hearing of the petition or to abridge the time for the advertisement as appropriate.

The advertisement must state:

- the company's name and registered number;
- the company's registered office;
- the name of the petitioner;
- the address of the petitioner;
- the date of presentation of the petition;
- that date and place of hearing of the petition;
- the name and address of the petitioner's solicitors if instructed;
- that any person intending to appear at the hearing must give notice of his intention to do so in accordance with rule 4.16.[23]

It is necessary that a copy of every advertisement published must be lodged with the court as soon as possible after publication and in any event not later than the day appointed by the registrar.[24] This is so even if the advertisement is defective (eg is published at a date not in accordance with Insolvency Rules 1986, or omits or misprints some important words) or if the petitioner decides not to pursue the petition (eg on receiving payment).[25]

---

[19] Rule 4.13 of the Insolvency Rules 1986.

[20] Rule 4.11(4) of the Insolvency Rules 1986.

[21] Rule 4.11(6) of the Insolvency Rules 1986.

[22] Paragraph 2.1 of the CPR Practice Direction – Insolvency Proceedings.

[23] Rule 4.11 of the Insolvency Rules 1986.

[24] Rule 4.14(2) of the Insolvency Rules 1986.

[25] Paragraph 2.2 of the CPR Practice Direction – Insolvency Proceedings.

CERTIFICATE OF COMPLIANCE

At least 5 days before the hearing of the petition the petitioner must file in court a certificate of compliance.

This needs to state:

- the date of presentation of the petition;
- the date fixed for the hearing; and
- the date or dates on which the petition was served and advertised in compliance with the Insolvency Rules 1986.

This certificate should annexe:

- a copy of the advertisement of the petition.

The rules on procedure and timing are strict and the petition could potentially be struck out if they are not followed.

THE HEARING

At the day of the hearing but before the petition is heard, the petitioner will need to file with the clerk of the court a list of names and addresses of people who intend to appear on the petition and whether they intend to support or oppose it.[26] If no notice of intention to appear has been given then the notice should state so.

The hearing is in open court before the Companies Court registrar or district judge. Advocates are expected to robe. The parties should expect the hearing to be dealt with a summary fashion and if the petition is opposed, for the petition to be adjourned for a contested hearing before the registrar or judge.

KEY STATUTORY PROVISIONS

Paragraphs 2 to 4 of Part Two of the CPR Practice Direction – Insolvency Proceedings

Part Two
Companies

2 Advertisement of winding up petition

2.1　Insolvency Rule 4.11(2)(b) is mandatory, and designed to ensure that the class remedy of winding up by the court is made available to all creditors, and is not used as a means of putting pressure on the company to pay the petitioner's debt. Failure to comply with the rule, without good reason accepted by the court, may lead to the summary dismissal of the petition on the return date (Insolvency Rule 4.11(5)). If the court, in its discretion, grants an adjournment, this

---

[26]　Rule 4.17 of the Insolvency Rules 1986.

will be on condition that the petition is advertised in due time for the adjourned hearing. No further adjournment for the purpose of advertisement will normally be granted.

2.2 Copies of every advertisement published in connection with a winding up petition must be lodged with the Court as soon as possible after publication and in any event not later than the day specified in Insolvency Rule 4.14 of the Insolvency Rules 1986. This direction applies even if the advertisement is defective in any way (e.g. is published at a date not in accordance with the Insolvency Rules, or omits or misprints some important words) or if the petitioner decides not to pursue the petition (e.g. on receiving payment).

3 Certificate of compliance – time for filing

3.1 In the High Court in order to assist practitioners and the Court the time laid down by Insolvency Rule 4.14 of the Insolvency Rules 1986, for filing a certificate of compliance and a copy of the advertisement, is hereby extended to not later than 4.30 pm on the Friday preceding the day on which the petition is to be heard. Applications to file the certificate and the copy advertisement after 4.30 pm on the Friday will only be allowed if some good reason is shown for the delay.

4 Errors in petitions

4.1 Applications for leave to amend errors in petitions which are discovered subsequent to a winding up order being made should be made to the Court Manager in the High Court and to the District Judge in the county court.

4.2 Where the error is an error in the name of the company, the Court Manager in the High Court and the District Judge in the county court may make any necessary amendments to ensure that the winding up order is drawn with the correct name of the company inserted. If there is any doubt, e.g. where there might be another company in existence which could be confused with the company to be wound up, the Court Manager will refer the application to the Registrar and the District Judge may refer it to the Judge.

4.3 Where an error is an error in the registered office of the company and any director or member of the company claims that the company was unaware of the petition by reason of it having been served at the wrong registered office, it will be open to them to apply to rescind the winding up order in the usual way.

4.4 Where it is discovered that the company had been struck off the Register of Companies prior to the winding up order being made, the matter must be restored to the list before the order is entered to enable an order for the restoration of the name to be made as well as the order to wind up.

Rules 4.7 to 4.14 of the Insolvency Rules 1986

4.7 Presentation and filing of petition

(1) The petition, verified by affidavit in accordance with Rule 4.12 below, shall be filed in court.

(2) No petition shall be filed unless there is produced on presentation of the petition a receipt for the deposit payable or paragraph (2A) applies.

(2A) This paragraph applies in any case where the Secretary of State has given written notice to the court that the petitioner has made suitable alternative arrangements for the payment of the deposit to the official receiver and such notice has not been revoked in relation to the petitioner in accordance with paragraph (2B).

(2B) A notice of the kind referred to in paragraph (2A) may be revoked in relation to the petitioner in whose favour it is given by a further notice in writing to the court stating that the earlier notice is revoked in relation to the petitioner.

(3) If the petitioner is other than the company itself, there shall be delivered with the petition—

    (a) one copy for service on the company, and

    (b) one copy to be exhibited to the affidavit verifying service.

(4) There shall in any case be delivered with the petition—

    (a) if the company is in course of being wound up voluntarily, and a liquidator has been appointed, one copy of the petition to be sent to him;

    (b) if the company is in administration, one copy to be sent to the administrator;

    (c) if an administrative receiver has been appointed in relation to the company, one copy to be sent to him;

    (d) if there is in force for the company a voluntary arrangement under Part I of the Act, one copy for the supervisor of the arrangement; ...

    (da) if a member State liquidator has been appointed in main proceedings in relation to the company, one copy to be sent to him; and

    (e) if the company is an authorized deposit-taker or a former authorized deposit-taker and the petitioner is not the Financial Services Authority, one copy to be sent to the Authority.

(5) Each of the copies delivered shall have applied to it the seal of the court, and shall be issued to the petitioner.

(6) The court shall fix a venue for the hearing of the petition; and this shall be endorsed on any copy issued to the petitioner under paragraph (5).

(7) Where a petition is filed at the instance of a company's administrator the petition shall—

    (a) be expressed to be the petition of the company by its administrator,

    (b) state the name of the administrator, [the court case number and the date that the company entered administration], and

(c) where applicable, contain an application under paragraph 79 of Schedule B1, requesting that the appointment of the administrator shall cease to have effect.

(8) Any petition filed in relation to a company in respect of which there is in force a voluntary arrangement under Part I of the Act or which is in administration shall be presented to the court to which the nominee's report under section 2 was submitted or the court having jurisdiction for the administration.

(9) Any petition such as is mentioned in paragraph (7) above or presented by the supervisor of a voluntary arrangement under Part I of the Act in force for the company shall be treated as if it were a petition filed by contributories, and Chapter 4 in this Part of the Rules shall apply accordingly.

(10) Where a petition contains a request for the appointment of a person as liquidator in accordance with section 140 (appointment of former administrator or supervisor as liquidator) the person whose appointment is sought shall, not less than 2 days before the return day for the petition, file in court a report including particulars of—

(a) a date on which he notified creditors of the company, either in writing or at a meeting of creditors, of the intention to seek his appointment as liquidator, such date to be at least 10 days before the day on which the report under this paragraph is filed, and

(b) details of any response from creditors to that notification, including any objections to his appointment.

4.8 Service of petition

(1) The following paragraphs apply as regards service of the petition on the company (where the petitioner is other than the company itself); and references to the petition are to a copy of the petition bearing the seal of the court in which it is presented.

(2) Subject as follows, the petition shall be served at the company's registered office, that is to say—

(a) the place which is specified, in the company's statement delivered under section 9 of the Companies Act as the intended situation of its registered office on incorporation, or

(b) if notice has been given by the company to the registrar of companies under section 87 of that Act (change of registered office), the place specified in that notice or, as the case may be, in the last such notice.

(3) Service of the petition at the registered office may be effected in any of the following ways—

(a) it may be handed to a person who there and then acknowledges himself to be, or to the best of the server's knowledge, information and belief is, a director or other officer, or employee, of the company; or

(b) it may be handed to a person who there and then acknowledges himself to be authorized to accept service of documents on the company's behalf; or

(c) in the absence of any such person as is mentioned in sub-paragraph (a) or (b), it may be deposited at or about the registered office in such a way that it is likely to come to the notice of a person attending at the office.

(4) If for any reason service at the registered office is not practicable, or the company has no registered office or is an unregistered company, the petition may be served on the company by leaving it at the company's last known principal place of business in such a way that it is likely to come to the attention of a person attending there, or by delivering it to the secretary or some director, manager or principal officer of the company, wherever that person may be found.

(5) In the case of an oversea company, service may be effected in any manner provided for by section 1139(2) of the Companies Act.

(6) If for any reason it is impracticable to effect service as provided by paragraphs (2) to (5), the petition may be served in such other manner as the court may approve or direct.

(7) Application for leave of the court under paragraph (6) may be made ex parte, on affidavit stating what steps have been taken to comply with paragraphs (2) to (5), and the reasons why it is impracticable to effect service as there provided.

4.9 Proof of service

(1) Service of the petition shall be proved by affidavit, specifying the manner of service.

(2) The affidavit shall have exhibited to it—

(a) a sealed copy of the petition, and

(b) if substituted service has been ordered, a sealed copy of the order;

and it shall be filed in court immediately after service.

4.10 Other persons to receive copies of petition

(1) If to the petitioner's knowledge the company is in course of being wound up voluntarily, a copy of the petition shall be sent by him to the liquidator.

(2) If to the petitioner's knowledge an administrative receiver has been appointed in relation to the company, or the company is in administration, a copy of the petition shall be sent by him to the receiver or, as the case may be, the administrator.

(3) If to the petitioner's knowledge there is in force for the company a voluntary arrangement under Part I of the Act, a copy of the petition shall be sent by him to the supervisor of the voluntary arrangement.

(3A) If to the petitioner's knowledge, there is a member State liquidator appointed in main proceedings in relation to the company, a copy of the petition shall be sent by him to that person.

This does not apply if the petitioner referred to in this paragraph is a member State liquidator.

(4)   If the company is an authorized institution or former authorized institution within the meaning of the Banking Act 1987 a copy of the petition shall be sent by the petitioner to the Financial Services Authority.

This does not apply if the petitioner is the Financial Services Authority itself.

(5)   A copy of the petition which is required by this Rule to be sent shall be dispatched on the next business day after the day on which the petition is served on the company.

4.11 Advertisement of petition

(1)   Unless the court otherwise directs, the petitioner shall give notice of the petition.

(2)   The notice shall be gazetted.

(3)   Where compliance with paragraph (2) is not reasonably practicable, the court may direct that instead of the notice being gazetted, it shall be given in such other manner as the court thinks fit.

(4)   The notice must be made to appear—

    (a)   if the petitioner is the company itself, not less than 7 business days before the day appointed for the hearing; and

    (b)   otherwise, not less than 7 business days after service of the petition on the company, nor less than 7 business days before the day so appointed.

(5)   The notice must state—

    (a)   the name, registered number of the company and the address of its registered office, or—

        (i)   in the case of an unregistered company, the address of its principal place of business;

        (ii)   in the case of an [overseas] company, the address at which service of the petition was effected;

    (b)   the name and address of the petitioner;

    (c)   where the petitioner is the company itself, the address of its registered office or, in the case of an unregistered company, of its principal place of business;

    (d)   the date on which the petition was presented;

   (e)   the venue fixed for the hearing of the petition;

   (f)   the name and address of the petitioner's solicitor (if any); and

   (g)   that any person intending to appear at the hearing (whether to support or oppose the petition) must give notice of his intention in accordance with Rule 4.16.

(6)   If notice of the petition is not given in accordance with this Rule, the court may dismiss it.

4.12 Verification of petition

(1)   The petition shall be verified by an affidavit that the statements in the petition are true, or are true to the best of the deponent's knowledge, information and belief.

(2)   If the petition is in respect of debts due to different creditors, the debts to each creditor must be separately verified.

(3)   The petition shall be exhibited to the affidavit verifying it.

(4)   The affidavit shall be made—

   (a)   by the petitioner (or if there are two or more petitioners, any one of them), or

   (b)   by some person such as a director, company secretary or similar company officer, or a solicitor, who has been concerned in the matters giving rise to the presentation of the petition, or

   (c)   by some responsible person who is duly authorized to make the affidavit and has the requisite knowledge of those matters.

(5)   Where the deponent is not the petitioner himself, or one of the petitioners, he must in the affidavit identify himself and state—

   (a)   the capacity in which, and the authority by which, he makes it, and

   (b)   the means of his knowledge of the matters sworn to in the affidavit.

(6)   The affidavit is prima facie evidence of the statements in the petition to which it relates.

(7)   An affidavit verifying more than one petition shall include in its title the names of the companies to which it relates and shall set out, in respect of each company, the statements relied on by the petitioner; and a clear and legible photocopy of the affidavit shall be filed with each petition which it verifies.

(8)   The affidavit shall state whether, in the opinion of the person making the application, (i) the EC Regulation will apply and (ii) if so, whether the proceedings will be main proceedings or territorial proceedings.

4.13 Persons entitled to copy of petition

Every director, contributory or creditor of the company is entitled to be furnished by the solicitor for the petitioner (or by the petitioner himself, if acting in person) with a copy of the petition within 2 days after requiring it, on payment of the appropriate fee.

4.14 Certificate of compliance

(1)   The petitioner or his solicitor shall, at least 5 days before the hearing of the petition, file in court a certificate of compliance with the Rules relating to service and advertisement.

(2)   The certificate shall show—

(a)   the date of presentation of the petition,

(b)   the date fixed for the hearing, and

(c)   the date or dates on which the petition was served and advertised in compliance with the Rules.

A copy of the advertisement of the petition shall be filed in court with the certificate.

(3)   Non-compliance with this Rule is a ground on which the court may, if it thinks fit, dismiss the petition.

Sections 7(4), 122 to 125 of the Insolvency Act 1986

7 Implementation of proposal

(4)   The supervisor—

(a)   may apply to the court for directions in relation to any particular matter arising under the voluntary arrangement, and

(b)   is included among the persons who may apply to the court for the winding up of the company or for an administration order to be made in relation to it.

122 Circumstances in which company may be wound up by the court

(1)   A company may be wound up by the court if—

(a)   the company has by special resolution resolved that the company be wound up by the court,

(b)   being a public company which was registered as such on its original incorporation, the company has not been issued with a trading certificate under section 761 of the Companies Act 2006 (requirement as to minimum share capital)[27] and more than a year has expired since it was so registered,

---

[27]   This was the certificate under section 117 of the Companies Act 1985 (on public company share capital requirements).

(c) it is an old public company, within the meaning of the Consequential Provisions Act,

(d) the company does not commence its business within a year from its incorporation or suspends its business for a whole year,

(e) except in the case of a private company limited by shares or by guarantee, the number of members is reduced below 2,

(f) the company is unable to pay its debts,

(fa) at the time at which a moratorium for the company under section 1A comes to an end, no voluntary arrangement approved under Part I has effect in relation to the company,

(g) the court is of the opinion that it is just and equitable that the company should be wound up.

(2) In Scotland, a company which the Court of Session has jurisdiction to wind up may be wound up by the Court if there is subsisting a floating charge over property comprised in the company's property and undertaking, and the court is satisfied that the security of the creditor entitled to the benefit of the floating charge is in jeopardy.

For this purpose a creditor's security is deemed to be in jeopardy if the Court is satisfied that events have occurred or are about to occur which render it unreasonable in the creditor's interests that the company should retain power to dispose of the property which is subject to the floating charge.

123 Definition of inability to pay debts
(1) A company is deemed unable to pay its debts—

(a) if a creditor (by assignment or otherwise) to whom the company is indebted in a sum exceeding £750 then due has served on the company, by leaving it at the company's registered office, a written demand (in the prescribed form) requiring the company to pay the sum so due and the company has for 3 weeks thereafter neglected to pay the sum or to secure or compound for it to the reasonable satisfaction of the creditor, or

(b) if, in England and Wales, execution or other process issued on a judgment, decree or order of any court in favour of a creditor of the company is returned unsatisfied in whole or in part, or

(c) if, in Scotland, the induciae of a charge for payment on an extract decree, or an extract registered bond, or an extract registered protest, have expired without payment being made, or

(d) if, in Northern Ireland, a certificate of unenforceability has been granted in respect of a judgment against the company, or

(e)   if it is proved to the satisfaction of the court that the company is unable to pay its debts as they fall due.

(2)   A company is also deemed unable to pay its debts if it is proved to the satisfaction of the court that the value of the company's assets is less than the amount of its liabilities, taking into account its contingent and prospective liabilities.

(3)   The money sum for the time being specified in subsection (1) (a) is subject to increase or reduction by order under section 416 in Part XV.

124 Application for winding up

(1)   Subject to the provisions of this section, an application to the court for the winding up of a company shall be by petition presented either by the company, or the directors, or by any creditor or creditors (including any contingent or prospective creditor or creditors), contributory or contributories, or by a liquidator (within the meaning of Article 2(b) of the EC Regulation) appointed in proceedings by virtue of Article 3(1) of the EC Regulation or a temporary administrator (within the meaning of Article 38 of the EC Regulation) or by the designated officer for a magistrates' court in the exercise of the power conferred by section 87A of the Magistrates' Courts Act 1980 (enforcement of fines imposed on companies), or by all or any of those parties, together or separately.

(2)   Except as mentioned below, a contributory is not entitled to present a winding-up petition unless either—

(a)   the number of members is reduced below 2, or

(b)   the shares in respect of which he is a contributory, or some of them, either were originally allotted to him, or have been held by him, and registered in his name, for at least 6 months during the 18 months before the commencement of the winding up, or have devolved on him through the death of a former holder.

(3)   A person who is liable under section 76 to contribute to a company's assets in the event of its being wound up may petition on either of the grounds set out in section 122(1) (f) and (g), and subsection (2) above does not then apply; but unless the person is a contributory otherwise than under section 76, he may not in his character as contributory petition on any other ground.

(3A) A winding-up petition on the ground set out in section 122(1) (fa) may only be presented by one or more creditors.

(4)   A winding-up petition may be presented by the Secretary of State—

(a)   if the ground of the petition is that in section 122(1) (b) or (c), or

(b)   in a case falling within section 124A or 124B below.

(4AA) A winding up petition may be presented by the Financial Services Authority in a case falling within section 124C (1) or (2).

(4A) A winding-up petition may be presented by the Regulator of Community Interest Companies in a case falling within section 50 of the Companies (Audit, Investigations and Community Enterprise) Act 2004.

(5)   Where a company is being wound up voluntarily in England and Wales, a winding-up petition may be presented by the official receiver attached to the court as well as by any other person authorized in that behalf under the other provisions of this section; but the court shall not make a winding-up order on the petition unless it is satisfied that the voluntary winding up cannot be continued with due regard to the interests of the creditors or contributories.

124B Petition for winding up of SE
(1)   Where—

    (a)   an SE whose registered office is in Great Britain is not in compliance with Article 7 of Council Regulation (EC) No 2157/2001 on the Statute for a European company (the 'EC Regulation') (location of head office and registered office), and

    (b)   it appears to the Secretary of State that the SE should be wound up, he may present a petition for it to be wound up if the court thinks it is just and equitable for it to be so.

(2)   This section does not apply if the SE is already being wound up by the court.

(3)   In this section 'SE' has the same meaning as in the EC Regulation.

124C Petition for winding up of SCE
(1)   Where, in the case of an SCE whose registered office is in Great Britain—

    (a)   there has been such a breach as is mentioned in Article 73(1) of Council Regulation (EC) No 1435/2003 on the Statute for a European Cooperative Society (SCE) (the 'European Cooperative Society Regulation') (winding up by the court or other competent authority), and

    (b)   it appears to the Financial Services Authority that the SCE should be wound up,

the Authority may present a petition for the SCE to be wound up if the court thinks it is just and equitable for it to be so.

(2)   Where, in the case of an SCE whose registered office is in Great Britain—

    (a)   the SCE is not in compliance with Article 6 of the European Cooperative Society Regulation (location of head office and registered office, and

    (b)   it appears to the Financial Service Authority that the SCE should be wound up,

the Authority may present a petition for the SCE to be wound up if the court thinks it is just and equitable for it to be so.

(3)   This section does not apply if the SCE is already being wound up by the court.

(4)   In this section 'SCE' has the same meaning as in the European Cooperative Society Regulation.

125 Powers of court on hearing of petition

(1)   On hearing a winding-up petition the court may dismiss it, or adjourn the hearing conditionally or unconditionally, or make an interim order, or any other order that it thinks fit; but the court shall not refuse to make a winding-up order on the ground only that the company's assets have been mortgaged to an amount equal to or in excess of those assets, or that the company has no assets.

(2)   If the petition is presented by members of the company as contributories on the ground that it is just and equitable that the company should be wound up, the court, if it is of opinion—

(a)   that the petitioners are entitled to relief either by winding up the company or by some other means, and

(b)   that in the absence of any other remedy it would be just and equitable that the company should be wound up,

shall make a winding-up order; but this does not apply if the court is also of the opinion both that some other remedy is available to the petitioners and that they are acting unreasonably in seeking to have the company wound up instead of pursuing that other remedy.

2.1 CREDITOR'S WINDING UP PETITION

IN THE HIGH COURT OF JUSTICE
CHANCERY DIVISION
COMPANIES COURT

NO: [ ] OF 20[ ]

IN THE MATTER OF BUSTCO LIMITED, REGISTERED NUMBER 011111
AND IN THE MATTER OF THE INSOLVENCY ACT 1986

To the High Court of Justice

The Petition of Angry Ltd of 1 Unpaid Bill Street, London

1. Bustco Limited ('the Company') was incorporated on 30th October 1996 under the Companies Act 1985.

2. The registered office of the Company is at Suite 1, 1 Poor Street, London.

3. The nominal capital of the Company is £1000 divided into 1000 shares of £1 each. The amount of the capital paid up or credited as paid up is £2.

4. The principal objects for which the Company was established are as follows: to carry on business as a general trading company and other objects stated in the memorandum of association of the Company.

5. The Company is indebted to the Petitioner in the sum of £2,045,687.50 in respect of the goods sold and delivered by the Petitioner to the Company under contracts dated 17th December 2007 and 10th May 2007.

6. On 25th December 2007 the Petitioner served on the Company by leaving it at the Company's registered office a demand under his hand requiring the Company to pay the said sum, which demand was in the prescribed form.

7. Over 3 weeks have now elapsed since the Petitioner served the said demand, but the Company has neglected to pay or satisfy the said sum or any part thereof or to make any offer to the Petitioner to secure or compound the same.

8. The Company is insolvent and unable to pay its debts.

9. The Company is not an insurance undertaking; a credit institution; an investment undertaking providing services involving the holding of funds or securities for third parties; a collective investment undertaking as referred to in Article 1(2) of the EC Regulation.

10.   For the reasons stated in the affidavit of H Wigg filed in support hereof it is considered that the EC Regulation will apply and that these proceedings will be main proceedings as defined in Article 3 of the EC Regulation.

11.   In the circumstances it is just and equitable that the Company should be wound up.

The Petitioner therefore prays as follows:

(1)   That BUSTCO LIMITED, registered number 011111, may be wound up by the Court under the provisions of the Insolvency Act 1986; or

(2)   That such other order may be made as the Court thinks fit.

Note: It is intended to serve this Petition on BUSTCO LIMITED.

ENDORSEMENT

This Petition having been presented to the Court on [ ] 20[ ] will be heard at the Royal Courts of Justice, Strand, London WC2A 2LL on:

Date: [ ] 20[ ]
Time: [ ] am/pm

(or as soon thereafter as the Petition can be heard)

The Solicitor to the Petitioner is:

WIGG & CO
1 LAW STREET
LONDON

2.2   WITNESS STATEMENT VERIFYING THE WINDING UP PETITION

Petitioner: AH Wigg: 1st: HW1: [ ] 20[ ]

IN THE HIGH COURT OF JUSTICE
CHANCERY DIVISION
COMPANIES COURT

PETITION NO: [ ] OF 20[ ]

IN THE MATTER OF BUSTCO LIMITED
COMPANY NUMBER 011111
AND IN THE MATTER OF THE INSOLVENCY ACT 1986

_____

1st WITNESS STATEMENT OF HARRY WIGG

_____

I, Harry Wigg of 1 Wigg Street, London, Solicitor of the Supreme Court, state as follows:

1.   I am the solicitor with care and conduct of this petition on behalf of the Petitioner. I am authorised to make this witness statement on its behalf. The statements in the petition now produced and shown to me marked 'HW1' are made from my own knowledge except where otherwise indicated, in which case I have explained the source of my information or belief.

2.   I have been concerned in the matters giving rise to the Petition and have the requisite knowledge of the matters referred to in the Petition because I have inspected the terms and conditions of business and related correspondence and invoice giving rise to the debt upon which the Petition is founded and undertaken a search on the Company at Companies House.

3.   The statements in the Petition are true to the best of my knowledge, information and belief.

4   The Company's centre of main interest is considered to be Suite 1, 1 Poor Street, London. Consequently, the winding-up proceedings will be affected by the EC Regulation and will be main proceedings.

STATEMENT OF TRUTH

I believe that the facts stated in this Witness Statement are true.

Signed [ ]
Full name [*HARRY WIGG*]
Dated [ ] 20[ ]

2.3   ADVERTISEMENT OF A WINDING UP PETITION

THE HIGH COURT OF JUSTICE
CHANCERY DIVISION

NO: [ ] OF 20[ ]

IN THE MATTER OF BUSTCO LIMITED
COMPANY NUMBER 0111111
AND IN THE MATTER OF THE INSOLVENCY ACT 1986

A Petition to wind up the above-named Company number 01111 of Suite 1, 1 Poor Street, London presented on [ ] 20[ ] by Angry Ltd of 1 Unpaid Bill Street, London, claiming to be a creditor of the Company, will be heard at the Royal Courts of Justice, Strand, London WC2A 2LL on:

Date: [ ] 20[ ]
Time: [ ] am/pm

(or as soon thereafter as the Petition can be heard).

Any person intending to appear on the hearing of the Petition (whether to support or oppose it) must give notice of intention to do so to the Petitioner or his/its Solicitor in accordance with Rule 4.16 by [ ] hours on [ ] 20[ ].

The Petitioner's Solicitor is WIGG & CO of 1 LAW STREET, LONDON

Dated [ ] 20[ ]

2.4   CERTIFICATE OF COMPLIANCE

Certificate of compliance

THE HIGH COURT OF JUSTICE
CHANCERY DIVISION

NO: [ ] OF 20[ ]

IN THE MATTER OF BUSTCO LIMITED
COMPANY NUMBER 0111111
AND IN THE MATTER OF THE INSOLVENCY ACT 1986

ANGRY LTD

<u>Petitioning Creditor</u>

-and-

BUSTCO LIMITED

<u>Debtor</u>

Winding-up Petition presented to the Court on [ ] 20[ ]

I certify that the above-mentioned Petition which will be heard on [ ] 20[ ] was served in accordance with the provisions of Rule 4.8 on [ ] 20[ ] and advertised in accordance with the provisions of Rule 4.11 on [ ] 20[ ] in the London Gazette.

....

(Signature)
Partner in the firm of
WIGG & CO
Dated [ ] 20[ ]
Name in block letters [ ]

Note: A copy of the advertisement must be filed in Court with this certificate.

CHAPTER 3

RESPONDING TO A CREDITOR'S PETITION: NOTICE TO ATTEND AT THE HEARING OF A PETITION

OBJECTIVE

At the day of the hearing but before the petition is heard, the petitioner will need to file with the clerk of the court a list of names and addresses of people who intend to appear on the petition and whether they intend to support or oppose it.[1] Provided a notice has been served, the debtor company, contributories and creditors can be heard on the petition. If no notice of intention to appear has been given then the notice should state so and the court will be entitled to proceed as if the petition is unopposed and a person who has failed to give notice of his intention to appear will not be heard without the court's permission.[2]

NOTICE OF INTENTION TO APPEAR

Form 4.9. The notice must set out:[3]

- the name of the party on behalf of whom it is to be filed;
- the address of the party on behalf of whom it is to be filed;
- the telephone number of the party on behalf of whom it is to be filed;
- the reference of the party on behalf of whom it is to be filed;
- the name of any other person authorised to speak on his behalf;

---

[1]   Rule 4.17 of the Insolvency Rules 1986.

[2]   Rule 4.16(5) of the Insolvency Rules 1986.

[3]   Rule 4.16(2) of the Insolvency Rules 1986.

- whether they intend to support or oppose the petition;
- the amount and nature of his debt (if any).

SERVICE

The notice of intention to appear must be sent so as to reach the petitioner not later than 4pm on the business day before the hearing. For the computation of business days Saturdays, Sundays, Good Friday, Christmas Day and bank holidays are excluded.

EVIDENCE

The debtor company should file and serve his witness statement in opposition to the petition not less than 7 days before the hearing.[4]

This will need to address:

- the relationship between creditor and debtor;
- particulars of why the debt is disputed or of any set off or cross claim;[5]
- particulars of any other grounds upon which the petition is opposed;
- details of any litigation on the debt;
- evidence of the solvency of the company.

And exhibit:

- the demand;
- the petition;
- the evidence showing the dispute or set off;
- any correspondence on the threatened petition, including any letter telling the creditor that the debt is disputed;
- documentary evidence of the solvency of the company, eg management accounts, letter from auditors, bank statement showing credit balances.

Creditors and contributories are not expected to play a prominent role in the hearing and need not file evidence unless directed by the court. A creditor supporting the petition may apply to be substituted where it appears that the petitioner is not able or willing to progress his petition.

---

[4]   Rule 4.18 of the Insolvency Rules 1986.

[5]   Counterclaims may be relied on: *Re Wanda Modes* [2002] 1 BCLC 289, Park J.

KEY STATUTORY PROVISIONS

Rules 4.16 to 4.19 of the Insolvency Rules 1986

4.16 Notice of appearance

(1)   Every person who intends to appear on the hearing of the petition shall give to the petitioner notice of his intention in accordance with this Rule.

(2)   The notice shall specify—

(a)   the name and address of the person giving it, and any telephone number and reference which may be required for communication with him or with any other person (to be also specified in the notice) authorized to speak or act on his behalf;

(b)   whether his intention is to support or oppose the petition; and

(c)   the amount and nature of his debt.

(3)   The notice shall be sent to the petitioner at the address shown for him in the court records, or in the advertisement of the petition required by Rule 4.11; or it may be sent to his solicitor.

(4)   The notice shall be sent so as to reach the addressee not later than 16.00 hours on the business day before that which is appointed for the hearing (or, where the hearing has been adjourned, for the adjourned hearing).

(5)   A person failing to comply with this Rule may appear on the hearing of the petition only with the leave of the court.

4.17 List of appearances

(1)   The petitioner shall prepare for the court a list of the persons (if any) who have given notice under Rule 4.16, specifying their names and addresses and (if known to him) their respective solicitors.

(2)   Against the name of each creditor in the list it shall be stated whether his intention is to support the petition, or to oppose it.

(3)   On the day appointed for the hearing of the petition, a copy of the list shall be handed to the court before the commencement of the hearing.

(4)   If any leave is given under Rule 4.16(5), the petitioner shall add to the list the same particulars in respect of the person to whom leave has been given.

4.18 Affidavit in opposition

(1)   If the company intends to oppose the petition, its affidavit in opposition shall be filed in court not less than 7 days before the date fixed for the hearing.

(2)　A copy of the affidavit shall be sent by the company to the petitioner, forthwith after filing.

4.19 Substitution of creditor or contributory for petitioner

(1)　This Rule applies where a person petitions and is subsequently found not entitled to do so, or where the petitioner—

    (a)　fails to advertise his petition within the time prescribed by the Rules or such extended time as the court may allow, or

    (b)　consents to withdraw his petition, or to allow it to be dismissed, consents to an adjournment, or fails to appear in support of his petition when it is called on in court on the day originally fixed for the hearing, or on a day to which it is adjourned, or

    (c)　appears, but does not apply for an order in the terms of the prayer of his petition.

(2)　The court may, on such terms as it thinks just, substitute as petitioner any creditor or contributory who in its opinion would have a right to present a petition, and who is desirous of prosecuting it.

(2A)　Where a member State liquidator has been appointed in main proceedings in relation to the company, without prejudice to paragraph (2), the court may, on such terms as it thinks just, substitute the member State liquidator as petitioner, where he is desirous of prosecuting the petition.

(3)　An order of the court under this Rule may, where a petitioner fails to advertise his petition within the time prescribed by these Rules, or consents to withdraw his petition, be made at any time.

3.1 SUPPORTING CREDITOR'S NOTICE OF INTENTION TO APPEAR

Rule 4.16
Notice of Intention to Appear on Petition

THE HIGH COURT OF JUSTICE
CHANCERY DIVISION

NO: [ ] OF 20[ ]

IN THE MATTER OF BUSTCO LIMITED
COMPANY NUMBER 0111111
AND IN THE MATTER OF THE INSOLVENCY ACT 1986

Winding Up Petition presented on [ ] 20[ ]
To be heard on [ ] 20[ ]

TAKE NOTICE that Furious plc of 2 Unpaid Bill Street, London a creditor of the above named Company for £2,463.07 intends to appear on the hearing of the above mentioned Petition to support it.

Signed [ ]
Dated [ ] 20[ ]
Position to the Creditor: [*Director*]

Name address and reference of the Creditors Solicitors: [ ]
Tel: [ ]
Reference: [ ]

To the Petitioner's Solicitors: WIGG & CO of 1 LAW STREET, LONDON
Tel: [ ]
Reference: [ ]

3.2   SUPPORTING CREDITOR'S APPLICATION TO BE SUBSTITUTED AS PETITIONER

THE HIGH COURT OF JUSTICE
CHANCERY DIVISION

NO: [ ] OF 20[ ]

IN THE MATTER OF BUSTCO LIMITED
COMPANY NUMBER 0111111
AND IN THE MATTER OF THE INSOLVENCY ACT 1986

TAKE NOTICE that Furious plc of 2 Unpaid Bill Street, London intend to apply to the Registrar on:

Date: [ ] 20[ ]
Time: [ ] am/pm
Place: [ ]

For an order that the Applicant may be substituted as petitioner in the petition to wind up the above named Company presented by the Respondent on 1st April 2009.

Signed [ ]
Solicitor for the Applicant
Dated [ ] 20[ ]

Our address for service is:

SNARKY & SNIDE
5 ACTION PARADE
LONDON

To the Petitioner's Solicitor:
WIGG & CO of 1 LAW STREET, LONDON

To the Respondent's Solicitor:
SILK & CO, 2 LAW STREET, LONDON

If you do not attend the Court may make such order as it think fit.

CHAPTER 4

RESPONDING TO A STATUTORY DEMAND: APPLICATION TO RESTRAIN THE PRESENTATION OF A PETITION

OBJECTIVE

Given that there is no formal procedure to set aside a statutory demand presented against a company and the serious consequences of the presentation or advertisement of a petition against a company,[1] a debtor will often wish to seek an injunction to restrain presentation of a petition if suitable undertakings are not received from the creditor serving the demand.

WARNING LETTER

Before an application is made for an injunction a warning letter should be sent to the other side inviting them to give an undertaking not to present a winding up petition based upon it.

This should be sent in an open letter:

- setting out why the debt is disputed;
- stating that the threat of winding up proceedings is inappropriate;
- requiring solicitor's undertaking not to present and advertise the petition;

---

[1] Most noticeably under section 127 of the Insolvency Act 1986.

- requiring a solicitor's undertaking to give 3 days' notice prior to presenting the petition;
- giving a costs warning.

The need for the costs warning arises because a wasted costs order may be made against a solicitor who presents petition knowing it is bona fide contested and fails to advise client that the petition is an abuse of process.[2]

APPLICATION

The company should apply on notice by originating application against the creditor to a High Court judge to restrain presentation of the winding up petition. The application can be made ex parte if urgent. Three copies of the application are needed.

COURT FEES

Where the application is made by originating application a court fee of £130 is payable.[3] Where the application is made by consent a court fee of £30 is payable.[4]

SERVICE

The application and evidence will need to be filed at court and served on the respondent as soon as practicable after it is filed and in any event, unless it is necessary to apply ex parte or on short notice, at least 3 days before the hearing date.[5]

EVIDENCE

The application should be supported by a witness statement. This will need to address:

- the relationship between creditor and debtor;
- details of why the debt is disputed or of any set off or cross claim;
- details of any litigation on the debt;
- particulars of any evidence of the solvency of the company.

And exhibit:

- the demand;
- the evidence showing the dispute or set off;
- any letter telling the creditor that the debt is disputed;
- any correspondence on the threatened petition;
- documentary evidence of the solvency of the company, eg management accounts, letter from auditors, bank statement showing credit balances.

---

[2]   *Philex v Golban* [1994] BCC 390.

[3]   Paragraph 3.5 of Schedule 1 to the Civil Proceedings Fees Order 2008.

[4]   Paragraph 3.11 of Schedule 1 to the Civil Proceedings Fees Order 2008.

[5]   Rule 23.7 of the Civil Procedure Rules 1998 (SI 1998/3132) (hereafter CPR).

Care should be taken to ensure that the evidence filed is sufficient to establish the defence, set off or cross claim is genuine, serious and of substance.[6]

KEY STATUTORY PROVISIONS

Paragraph 8.1 of the CPR Practice Direction – Insolvency Proceedings

Restraint of presentation of a winding-up petition
8.1   An application to restrain presentation of a Winding-up petition must be made to the Judge by the issue of an Originating Application (Form 7.1).

Rules 7.3 to 7.8 and 7.57 of the Insolvency Rules 1986

7.3 Form and contents of application
(1)   Each application shall be in writing and shall state—

  (a)   the names of the parties;

  (b)   the nature of the relief or order applied for or the directions sought from the court;

  (c)   the names and addresses of the persons (if any) on whom it is intended to serve the application or that no person is intended to be served;

  (d)   where the Act or Rules require that notice of the application is to be given to specified persons, the names and addresses of all those persons (so far as known to the applicant); and

  (e)   the applicant's address for service.

(2)   An originating application shall set out the grounds on which the applicant claims to be entitled to the relief or order sought.

(3)   The application must be signed by the applicant if he is acting in person or, when he is not so acting, by or on behalf of his solicitor.

7.4 Filing and service of application
(1)   The application shall be filed in court, accompanied by one copy and a number of additional copies equal to the number of persons who are to be served with the application.

(2)   Subject as follows in this Rule and the next, or unless the Rule under which the application is brought provides otherwise, or the court otherwise orders, upon the presentation of the documents mentioned in paragraph (1) above, the court shall fix a venue for the application to be heard.

(3)   Unless the court otherwise directs, the applicant shall serve a sealed copy of the application, endorsed with the venue for the hearing, on the respondent named in the application (or on each respondent if more than one).

---

[6]   *Orion Media v Media Brook* [2002] 1 BCLC 184, Laddie J.

(4)   The court may give any of the following directions—

(a)   that the application be served upon persons other than those specified by the relevant provision of the Act or Rules;

(b)   that the giving of notice to any person may be dispensed with;

(c)   that notice be given in some way other than that specified in paragraph (3).

(5)   Unless the provision of the Act or Rules under which the application is made provides otherwise, and subject to the next paragraph, the application must be served at least 14 days before the date fixed for the hearing.

(6)   Where the case is one of urgency, the court may (without prejudice to its general power to extend or abridge time limits)—

(a)   hear the application immediately, either with or without notice to, or the attendance of, other parties, or

(b)   authorize a shorter period of service than that provided for by paragraph (5);

and any such application may be heard on terms providing for the filing or service of documents, or the carrying out of other formalities, as the court thinks fit.

7.5 Other hearings ex parte

(1)   Where the relevant provisions of the Act or Rules do not require service of the application on, or notice of it to be given to, any person, the court may hear the application *ex parte*.

(2)   Where the application is properly made *ex parte*, the court may hear it forthwith, without fixing a venue as required by Rule 7.4(2).

(3)   Alternatively, the court may fix a venue for the application to be heard, in which case Rule 7.4 applies (so far as relevant).

7.6 Hearing of application

(1)   Unless allowed or authorized to be made otherwise, every application before the registrar shall, and every application before the judge may, be heard in chambers.

(2)   Unless either—

(a)   the judge has given a general or special direction to the contrary, or

(b)   it is not within the registrar's power to make the order required,
the jurisdiction of the court to hear and determine the application may be exercised by the registrar, and the application shall be made to the registrar in the first instance.

(3)   Where the application is made to the registrar he may refer to the judge any matter which he thinks should properly be decided by the judge, and the judge may either dispose of the matter or refer it back to the registrar with such directions as he thinks fit.

(4)   Nothing in this Rule precludes an application being made directly to the judge in a proper case.

7.7 Use of affidavit evidence

(1)   In any proceedings evidence may be given by affidavit unless by any provision of the Rules it is otherwise provided or the court otherwise directs; but the court may, on the application of any party, order the attendance for cross-examination of the person making the affidavit.

(2)   Where, after such an order has been made, the person in question does not attend, his affidavit shall not be used in evidence without the leave of the court.

7.8 Filing and service of affidavits

(1)   Unless the provision of the Act or Rules under which the application is made provides otherwise, or the court otherwise allows—

   (a)   if the applicant intends to rely at the first hearing on affidavit evidence, he shall file the affidavit or affidavits (if more than one) in court and serve a copy or copies on the respondent, not less than 14 days before the date fixed for the hearing, and

   (b)   where a respondent to an application intends to oppose it and to rely for that purpose on affidavit evidence, he shall file the affidavit or affidavits (if more than one) in court and serve a copy or copies on the applicant, not less than 7 days before the date fixed for the hearing.

(2)   Any affidavit may be sworn by the applicant or by the respondent or by some other person possessing direct knowledge of the subject matter of the application.

7.57 Affidavits

(1)   Subject to the following paragraphs of this Rule the practice and procedure of the High Court with regard to affidavits, their form and contents and the procedure governing their use are to apply to all insolvency proceedings.

(2)   Where, in insolvency proceedings, an affidavit is made by the official receiver or the responsible insolvency practitioner, the deponent shall state the capacity in which he makes it, the position which he holds, and the address at which he works.

(3)   A creditor's affidavit of debt may be sworn before his own solicitor.

(4)   The official receiver, any deputy official receiver, or any officer of the court duly authorized in that behalf, may take affidavits and declarations.

(5)   Subject to paragraph (6), where the Rules provide for the use of an affidavit, a witness statement verified by a statement of truth may be used as an alternative.

(6)   Paragraph (5) does not apply to Rules ... 3.4, 4.33, 6.60 (statement of affairs), 4.42, 6.66, 6.72 (further disclosure), 4.39, 4.40, 6.65; 6.70 (accounts), 4.73, 4.77, 6.96; 6.99 (claims) and 9.3, 9.4 (examinations).

(7)   Where paragraph (5) applies any form prescribed by Rule 12.7 of these Rules shall be modified as necessary.

4.1 ORIGINATING APPLICATION FOR AN ORDER RESTRAINING THE PRESENTATION OF A WINDING UP PETITION

Rule 7.2
Originating Application

IN THE HIGH COURT OF JUSTICE
CHANCERY DIVISION
COMPANIES COURT

NO: [ ] OF 20[ ]

IN THE MATTER OF BUSTCO LIMITED, REGISTERED NUMBER 011111
AND IN THE MATTER OF THE INSOLVENCY ACT 1986

BETWEEN:-

BUSTCO LIMITED

<u>Applicant</u>

-and-

ANGRY LIMITED

<u>Respondent</u>

LET Angry Ltd of 1 Unpaid Bill Street, London attend before the Judge on:

Date: [ ] 20[ ]
Time: [ ] am/pm
Place: Royal Courts of Justice, Strand, London WC2A 2LL

On the hearing of an application by BUSTCO LIMITED, the Applicant, for an Order in the following terms:

1. That the Respondent be restrained, whether by itself, or by its employees or agents or otherwise howsoever, from presenting any petition to this Honourable Court or any court for the winding up of the above named Applicant, BUSTCO LIMITED based on the debt of £2,045,687.50 claimed in the statutory demand dated 24th December 2007 and served on the Applicant on 25th December 2007.

2. And/or such other order as to this Honourable Court may seem fit.

3. That the costs of this application be paid by the Respondent to the Applicant.

The grounds upon which the Applicant claims to be entitled to the order sought herein are set out in the witness statement of IAN FLAKEY made on [ ] 20[ ] and filed herein and true copy of which is filed herewith.

The names and addresses of the persons upon whom it is intended to serve this application are:

ANGRY LIMITED, 1 Unpaid Bill Street, London

The Applicant's address for service is:

SILK & CO
2 LAW STREET
LONDON

Signed [ ]
Solicitor for the Applicant [ ]
Dated [ ] 20[ ]

If you do not attend, the Court may make such order as it thinks fit.

4.2   WITNESS STATEMENT IN SUPPORT OF AN APPLICATION FOR AN ORDER RESTRAINING THE PRESENTATION OF A WINDING UP PETITION

Applicant: I Flakey: 1st: IF1: [ ] 20[ ]

IN THE HIGH COURT OF JUSTICE
CHANCERY DIVISION
COMPANIES COURT

NO: [ ] OF 20[ ]

IN THE MATTER OF BUSTCO LIMITED, REGISTERED NUMBER 011111
AND IN THE MATTER OF THE INSOLVENCY ACT 1986

BETWEEN:-

BUSTCO LIMITED

Applicant

-and-

ANGRY LIMITED

Respondent

1st WITNESS STATEMENT OF IAN FLAKEY

I, Ian Flakey, 1 Geranium Cottage, London, Company Director, state as follows:

1.   I am the managing director of the Applicant Company and I am authorised to make this witness statement on its behalf.

2.   The matters set out in this witness statement are true and within my own knowledge except where otherwise indicated, in which case I have explained the source of my information or belief.

3.   There is now produced and shown to me a bundle consisting of true copies of the documents I will refer to in my witness statements marked 'IF1'.

4.   I make the application in support of the company's application to restrain the presentation of a winding up petition against it.

5.   On 25th December 2007 my company was served at its registered office with a statutory demand by Angry Limited claiming £2,045,687.50 based on an invoice for goods they say were sold and delivered to my company. I refer to page [ ] of 'IF1' which is a true copy of the statutory demand.

6. The Applicant Company made no such order and was never delivered any such goods. I refer to page [ ] of 'IF1' which is a true copy of the Applicant's records for purchases and deliveries for the periods alluded to by Angry Limited.

7. On 26th December 2007 my solicitors, Silk & Co, wrote to Angry Limited explaining the basis on which the alleged debt is disputed and inviting them to give appropriate undertakings not to present a petition against my company. They warned that any petition would be an abuse of process as the debt was disputed. I refer to page [ ] of 'IF1' which is a true copy of my solicitor's letter.

8. On 27th December 2007 Gustav Grim of Angry Limited telephoned me and said 'You're a bunch of crooks. Your solicitors don't scare me. If you don't pay me immediately, I'm going to wind your company up'. I refer to page [ ] of 'IF1' which is a true copy of my note of this conversation.

9. Bustco Limited is a profitable company and is able to pay its debts as they fall due. I refer to page [ ] of 'IF1' which is a true copy of a letter from my company's accountant, Derrick Devious, setting out the company's latest accounts and confirming the company's solvency.

10. Bustco Limited operating in a small marketplace in which having a reputation for financial stability is of crucial importance. Presentation of a winding up petition would cause irreparable damage to our reputation and our ability to trade. I fear that unless restrained by this Honourable Court, Angry Limited intends to present a winding up petition against my company.

STATEMENT OF TRUTH

I believe that the facts stated in this Witness Statement are true.

Signed [ ]
Full name [*IAN FLAKEY*]
Dated [ ] 20[ ]

4.3   DRAFT MINUTE OF AN ORDER MADE WITHOUT NOTICE[7] RESTRAINING THE PRESENTATION OF A WINDING UP PETITION

Injunction

IN THE HIGH COURT OF JUSTICE
CHANCERY DIVISION
COMPANIES COURT

NO: [ ] OF 20[ ]

IN THE MATTER OF BUSTCO LIMITED, REGISTERED NUMBER 011111
AND IN THE MATTER OF THE INSOLVENCY ACT 1986

BEFORE THE HONOURABLE MR JUSTICE [ ]
DATED: [ ] 20[ ]

<u>Applicant</u>

BUSTCO LIMITED

<u>Respondent</u>

ANGRY LIMITED

Name, address and reference of the Respondent:
Angry Ltd of 1 Unpaid Bill Street, London

<u>PENAL NOTICE</u>

IF YOU XAVIER MINUS, DISOBEY THIS ORDER YOU MAY BE HELD IN CONTEMPT OF COURT AND MAY BE IMPRISONED, FINED OR HAVE YOUR ASSETS SEIZED.

ANY PERSON WHO KNOWS OF THIS ORDER AND DOES ANYTHING WHICH HELPS OR PERMITS THE RESPONDENT TO BREACH THE TERMS OF THIS ORDER MAY ALSO BE HELD IN CONTEMPT OF COURT AND MAY BE IMPRISONED, FINED OR HAVE THEIR ASSETS SEIZED.

---

[7]   The application should only be made on an ex parte basis is cases of great urgency. The court will usually only grant a temporary injunction until an inter partes hearing can be heard however and the applicant will be required to make full and frank disclosure in his evidence. This precedent may be conveniently adjusted for an inter partes hearing. In such cases the requirements for undertakings will be less stringent.

ORDER

UPON HEARING Counsel for the Applicant without notice on [ ] 20[ ]

UPON READING the Witness Statement of Ian Flakey dated [ ] 20[ ]

AND UPON the Judge accepting the Undertakings in the Schedule at the end of this Order

IT IS ORDERED:

1. That the Respondent be restrained until further order of this Honourable Court, whether by itself, or by its employees or agents or otherwise howsoever, from presenting any petition to this Honourable Court or any court for the winding up of the above named Applicant, BUSTCO LIMITED based on the debt of £2,045,687.50 claimed in the statutory demand dated 24th December 2007 and served on the Applicant on 25th December 2007.

2. That the Respondent may apply on giving 24 hours notice in writing to the Applicant's legal representatives to vary or discharge this order.

3. Costs reserved.

Communications with the Court

All communications to the court about this order should be sent to:

Room TM 505, Royal Courts of Justice, Strand, London WC2A 2LL quoting the case number. The telephone number is 0207 947 6754.

The offices are open between 10 am and 4.30 pm Monday to Friday.

SCHEDULE 1
Undertakings given to the Court by the Applicant

1   If the Court later finds that this Order has caused loss to the Respondent and decides that the Respondent should be compensated for that loss, the Applicant will comply with any Order the Court may make; and

2   The Applicant will cause a Witness Statement to be filed confirming the substance of what was said to the Court by the Applicant's Counsel; and

3   As soon as practicable the Applicant will serve on the Respondent an application for a return date together with a copy of the Witness Statements and exhibits containing the evidence relied on by the Applicant.

4   Anyone notified of this Order will be given a copy of it by the Applicant's legal representatives.

CHAPTER 5

RESPONDING TO A PETITION: APPLICATION TO RESTRAIN THE ADVERTISEMENT OF A PETITION

OBJECTIVE

Given the serious financial and reputational consequences of presentation and advertisement of a petition against a company,[1] a debtor will often wish to seek an injunction restrain advertisement of a petition if suitable undertakings are not received from the creditor serving the demand.

The purpose of advertisement is twofold: (1) to give notice of the petition to those who are entitled to be heard on it, namely the creditors – whether actual, contingent or prospective – and contributories of the company; and (2) to give notice to those who might trade with the company during the period between the presentation of the petition and its final determination and who might thus be adversely affected by the provisions of section 127 of the Insolvency Act 1986.[2]

Since rule 4.11(1) requires advertisement unless the court otherwise directs, it is for the company to show sufficient reason for the judge to exercise his discretion and depart from the normal practice.[3]

---

[1]   Most noticeably under section 127 of the Insolvency Act 1986.

[2]   *In re A Company* [1995] 1 WLR 959.

[3]   Ibid.

The application needs to be made promptly given that the petitioner must advertise the petition, unless the court otherwise directs, not less than 7 business days after the date of service but not less than 7 business days before the day fixed for the hearing.[4]

WARNING LETTER

Before an application is made for an injunction, a warning letter should be sent to the other side inviting them to give an undertaking not to advertise and proceed further on their winding up petition.

This should be sent in an open letter:

- setting out why the debt is disputed;
- stating that winding up proceedings are inappropriate;
- requiring solicitor's undertaking not to proceed further and advertise the petition;
- requiring a solicitor's undertaking to take steps to withdraw the petition;
- giving a costs warning;
- stating that if the solicitor, is not prepared to give the undertaking it will be the company's intention to apply for an injunction in those terms;
- requiring, if those circumstances apply, a solicitor's undertaking not to proceed further and advertise the petition until that hearing takes place.

The need for the costs warning arises because a wasted costs order may be made against a solicitor who presents petition knowing it is bona fide contested and fails to advise client that the petition is an abuse of process.[5]

APPLICATION

The company applies on notice by ordinary application against the creditor to the judge to restrain presentation of the winding up petition. The application can be made ex parte if urgent. Three copies of the application are needed.

COURT FEES

Where the application is made by ordinary application on notice to other parties, a court fee of £60 is payable.[6] Where the application is made by consent or without notice in existing proceedings a court fee of £30 is payable.[7]

---

[4] Rule 4.11(1) of the Insolvency Rules 1986.
[5] *Philex v Golban* [1994] BCC 390.
[6] Paragraph 3.12 of Schedule 1 to the Civil Proceedings Fees Order 2008.
[7] Paragraph 3.11 of Schedule 1 to the Civil Proceedings Fees Order 2008.

SERVICE

The application and evidence will need to be filed at court and served on the respondent as soon as practicable after it is filed and in any event, unless it is necessary to apply ex parte or on short notice, at least 14 days before the date fixed for the hearing.[8]

Given that advertisement may take place any time after the 7th day after service, an undertaking should immediately be sought not to advertise the petition until the application is heard. If the petitioner fails to give this undertaking the application should be made ex parte.

EVIDENCE

The application should be supported by a witness statement.

This will need to address:

- the relationship between creditor and debtor;
- details of why the debt is disputed or of any set off or cross claim;
- details of any litigation on the debt;
- any other grounds and evidence upon which company would succeed in establishing that the proceedings sought to be restrained would constitute an abuse of process;[9]
- particulars of any evidence of the solvency of the company;
- whether there is any risk of prejudice to the creditors or contributories of the company from not being given notice of the petition and from the company being permitted to continue to trade with third parties who would be in ignorance of the petition in the light of section 127 of the Insolvency Act 1986;[10]
- the explanation why no application was made to restrain presentation of the petition;
- the grounds for the deponent's belief that advertisement may cause serious damage to the reputation and financial stability of the companies.[11]

And exhibit:

- the petition;
- the evidence showing the dispute or set off or cross claim;
- any letter telling the creditor that the debt is disputed;
- any correspondence on the threatened petition;
- documentary evidence of the solvency of the company, eg management accounts, letter from auditors, bank statement showing credit balances.

Care should be taken to ensure that the evidence filed is sufficient to establish the defence or cross claim or set off is genuine, serious and of substance.[12]

---

[8]   Rule 7.4(5) of the Insolvency Rules 1986.

[9]   *Coulson Sanderson & Ward Ltd v Ward* (1986) 2 BCC 99 at 207.

[10]   This is usually addressed by the grant of a validation order and an undertaking by the directors not to trade outside its terms.

[11]   *In re A Company* [1995] 1 WLR 959.

KEY STATUTORY PROVISIONS

Rules 7.3 to 7.8 and 7.57 of the Insolvency Rules 1986

7.3 Form and contents of application

(1)   Each application shall be in writing and shall state—

  (a)   the names of the parties;

  (b)   the nature of the relief or order applied for or the directions sought from the court;

  (c)   the names and addresses of the persons (if any) on whom it is intended to serve the application or that no person is intended to be served;

  (d)   where the Act or Rules require that notice of the application is to be given to specified persons, the names and addresses of all those persons (so far as known to the applicant); and

  (e)   the applicant's address for service.

(2)   An originating application shall set out the grounds on which the applicant claims to be entitled to the relief or order sought.

(3)   The application must be signed by the applicant if he is acting in person or, when he is not so acting, by or on behalf of his solicitor.

7.4 Filing and service of application

(1)   The application shall be filed in court, accompanied by one copy and a number of additional copies equal to the number of persons who are to be served with the application.

(2)   Subject as follows in this Rule and the next, or unless the Rule under which the application is brought provides otherwise, or the court otherwise orders, upon the presentation of the documents mentioned in paragraph (1) above, the court shall fix a venue for the application to be heard.

(3)   Unless the court otherwise directs, the applicant shall serve a sealed copy of the application, endorsed with the venue for the hearing, on the respondent named in the application (or on each respondent if more than one).

(4)   The court may give any of the following directions—

  (a)   that the application be served upon persons other than those specified by the relevant provision of the Act or Rules;
  (b)   that the giving of notice to any person may be dispensed with;

  (c)   that notice be given in some way other than that specified in paragraph (3).

---

[12]   *Orion Media v Media Brook* [2002] 1 BCLC 184, Laddie J.

(5)   Unless the provision of the Act or Rules under which the application is made provides otherwise, and subject to the next paragraph, the application must be served at least 14 days before the date fixed for the hearing.

(6)   Where the case is one of urgency, the court may (without prejudice to its general power to extend or abridge time limits)—

(a)   hear the application immediately, either with or without notice to, or the attendance of, other parties, or

(b)   authorize a shorter period of service than that provided for by paragraph (5);

and any such application may be heard on terms providing for the filing or service of documents, or the carrying out of other formalities, as the court thinks fit.

7.5 Other hearings ex parte

(1)   Where the relevant provisions of the Act or Rules do not require service of the application on, or notice of it to be given to, any person, the court may hear the application *ex parte*.

(2)   Where the application is properly made *ex parte*, the court may hear it forthwith, without fixing a venue as required by Rule 7.4(2).

(3)   Alternatively, the court may fix a venue for the application to be heard, in which case Rule 7.4 applies (so far as relevant).

7.6 Hearing of application

(1)   Unless allowed or authorized to be made otherwise, every application before the registrar shall, and every application before the judge may, be heard in chambers.

(2)   Unless either—

(a)   the judge has given a general or special direction to the contrary, or

(b)   it is not within the registrar's power to make the order required,

the jurisdiction of the court to hear and determine the application may be exercised by the registrar, and the application shall be made to the registrar in the first instance.

(3)   Where the application is made to the registrar he may refer to the judge any matter which he thinks should properly be decided by the judge, and the judge may either dispose of the matter or refer it back to the registrar with such directions as he thinks fit.

(4)   Nothing in this Rule precludes an application being made directly to the judge in a proper case.

7.7 Use of affidavit evidence

(1)   In any proceedings evidence may be given by affidavit unless by any provision of the Rules it is otherwise provided or the court otherwise directs; but the court may, on the application of any party, order the attendance for cross-examination of the person making the affidavit.

(2)   Where, after such an order has been made, the person in question does not attend, his affidavit shall not be used in evidence without the leave of the court.

7.8 Filing and service of affidavits

(1)   Unless the provision of the Act or Rules under which the application is made provides otherwise, or the court otherwise allows—

   (a)   if the applicant intends to rely at the first hearing on affidavit evidence, he shall file the affidavit or affidavits (if more than one) in court and serve a copy or copies on the respondent, not less than 14 days before the date fixed for the hearing, and

   (b)   where a respondent to an application intends to oppose it and to rely for that purpose on affidavit evidence, he shall file the affidavit or affidavits (if more than one) in court and serve a copy or copies on the applicant, not less than 7 days before the date fixed for the hearing.

(2)   Any affidavit may be sworn by the applicant or by the respondent or by some other person possessing direct knowledge of the subject matter of the application.

7.57 Affidavits

[(1)   Subject to the following paragraphs of this Rule the practice and procedure of the High Court with regard to affidavits, their form and contents and the procedure governing their use are to apply to all insolvency proceedings.

(2)   Where, in insolvency proceedings, an affidavit is made by the official receiver or the responsible insolvency practitioner, the deponent shall state the capacity in which he makes it, the position which he holds, and the address at which he works.

(3)   A creditor's affidavit of debt may be sworn before his own solicitor.

(4)   The official receiver, any deputy official receiver, or any officer of the court duly authorized in that behalf, may take affidavits and declarations.

(5)   Subject to paragraph (6), where the Rules provide for the use of an affidavit, a witness statement verified by a statement of truth may be used as an alternative.

(6)   Paragraph (5) does not apply to Rules ... 3.4, 4.33, 6.60 (statement of affairs), 4.42, 6.66, 6.72 (further disclosure), 4.39, 4.40, 6.65; 6.70 (accounts), 4.73, 4.77, 6.96; 6.99 (claims) and 9.3, 9.4 (examinations).

(7)   Where paragraph (5) applies any form prescribed by Rule 12.7 of these Rules shall be modified as necessary.

5.1 ORDINARY APPLICATION FOR AN ORDER TO RESTRAIN ADVERTISEMENT

Rule 7.2
Ordinary Application

IN THE HIGH COURT OF JUSTICE
CHANCERY DIVISION
COMPANIES COURT

NO: [ ] OF 20[ ]

IN THE MATTER OF BUSTCO LIMITED, REGISTERED NUMBER 011111
AND IN THE MATTER OF THE INSOLVENCY ACT 1986

BETWEEN:-

ANGRY LIMITED

Petitioner

-and-

BUSTCO LIMITED

Respondent

TAKE NOTICE that BUSTCO LIMITED intends to apply to the Judge on:

Date: [ ] 20[ ]
Time: [ ] am/pm
Place: Royal Courts of Justice, Strand, London WC2A 2LL

For an Order in the following terms:

1. That ANGRY LIMITED, the Petitioner named in a petition presented to this Honourable Court on [ ] be restrained from proceeding further upon the Petition whether by advertising the same or otherwise.

2. That the Petition be removed from the file of proceedings.

3. That the costs of this application be paid by the Petitioner.

Signed [ ]
Solicitor for the Applicant
Dated [ ] 20[ ]

The Applicant's address for service is:

SILK & CO
2 LAW STREET
LONDON

To:
ANGRY LIMITED, I Unpaid Bill Street, London

If you do not attend, the Court may make such order as it thinks fit.

5.2 WITNESS STATEMENT IN SUPPORT OF AN APPLICATION FOR AN ORDER TO RESTRAIN ADVERTISEMENT

Applicant: I Flakey: Ist: IFI: [ ] 20[ ]

IN THE HIGH COURT OF JUSTICE
CHANCERY DIVISION
COMPANIES COURT

NO: [ ] OF 20[ ]

IN THE MATTER OF BUSTCO LIMITED, REGISTERED NUMBER 011111
AND IN THE MATTER OF THE INSOLVENCY ACT 1986

BUSTCO LIMITED

<u>Applicant</u>

-and-

ANGRY LIMITED

<u>Respondent</u>

Ist WITNESS STATEMENT OF IAN FLAKEY

I, Ian Flakey, I Geranium Cottage, London, Company Director, state as follows:

1. I am the managing director of the Applicant Company and I am authorised to make this witness statement on its behalf.

2. The matters set out in this witness statement are true and within my own knowledge except where otherwise indicated, in which case I have explained the source of my information or belief.

3. There is now produced and shown to me a bundle consisting of true copies of the documents I will refer to in my witness statements marked 'IFI'.

4. I make the application in support of the company's application to restrain the Respondent from advertising the winding up petition it has presented against it.

5. On 25th December 2007 my company was served at its registered office with a statutory demand by Angry Limited claiming £2,045,687.50 based on an invoice for goods they say were sold and delivered to my company. I refer to page [ ] of 'IFI' which is a true copy of the statutory demand.

6. The Applicant Company made no such order and was never delivered any such goods. I refer to page [ ] of 'IF1' which is a true copy of the Applicant's records for purchases and deliveries for the periods alluded to by Angry Limited.

7. Upon discovering the statutory demand on my return from the Christmas vacation on 5th January 2008 I instructed my solicitors, Silk & Co, write to Angry Limited to explain that the debt was disputed.

8. On 5th January 2008 my solicitors, Silk & Co, wrote to Angry Limited explaining that my company had first seen the statutory demand today, the basis on which the alleged debt is disputed and inviting them to give appropriate undertakings not to present a petition against my company. They warned that any petition would be an abuse of process as the debt was disputed. I refer to page [ ] of 'IF1' which is a true copy of my solicitor's letter.

9. Instead of replying to my solicitor's letter or waiting for the period allowed for payment under the statutory demand to elapse, on 6th January 2008 Gustav Grim of Angry Limited served us with a winding up petition.. I refer to page [ ] of 'IF1' which is a true copy of the petition.

10. In the circumstances, Bustco had no proper opportunity to make an application to the Court to restrain the presentation.

11. On 6th January 2008 my solicitors, Silk & Co, wrote to Angry Limited explaining the basis on which the alleged debt is disputed and inviting them to give appropriate undertakings not to advertise a petition against my company. They warned that any petition would be an abuse of process as the debt was disputed. They stated that if there was no reply to the letter by return they would be making an application to the court to restrain advertisement and suggested that an undertaking be given by Angry Limited not to advertise until the application could be heard. I refer to page [ ] of 'IF1' which is a true copy of my solicitor's letter.

12. There has been no reply to that letter to date.

13. Bustco Limited is a profitable company and is able to pay its debts as they fall due. I refer to page [ ] of 'IF1' which is a true copy of a letter from my company's accountant, Derrick Devious, setting out the company's latest accounts and confirming the company's solvency.

14. Bustco Limited operating in a small marketplace in which having a reputation for financial stability is of crucial importance. Presentation of a winding up petition would cause irreparable damage to our reputation and our ability to trade. I fear that unless restrained by this Honourable Court, Angry Limited intends to advertise its winding up petition against my company.

STATEMENT OF TRUTH

I believe that the facts stated in this Witness Statement are true.

Signed [ ]
Full name [*IAN FLAKEY*]
Dated [ ] 20[ ]

5.3 DRAFT MINUTE OF AN ORDER MADE WITHOUT NOTICE RESTRAINING THE PRESENTATION OF A WINDING UP PETITION

Injunction

IN THE HIGH COURT OF JUSTICE
CHANCERY DIVISION
COMPANIES COURT

NO: [ ] OF 20[ ]

IN THE MATTER OF BUSTCO LIMITED, REGISTERED NUMBER 011111
AND IN THE MATTER OF THE INSOLVENCY ACT 1986

BEFORE THE HONOURABLE MR JUSTICE [ ]
DATED: [ ] 20[ ]

Applicant

BUSTCO LIMITED

Respondent

ANGRY LIMITED

Name, address and reference of the Respondent:
Angry Ltd of 1 Unpaid Bill Street, London

PENAL NOTICE

IF YOU XAVIER MINUS, DISOBEY THIS ORDER YOU MAY BE HELD IN CONTEMPT OF COURT AND MAY BE IMPRISONED, FINED OR HAVE YOUR ASSETS SEIZED.

ANY PERSON WHO KNOWS OF THIS ORDER AND DOES ANYTHING WHICH HELPS OR PERMITS THE RESPONDENT TO BREACH THE TERMS OF THIS ORDER MAY ALSO BE HELD IN CONTEMPT OF COURT AND MAY BE IMPRISONED, FINED OR HAVE THEIR ASSETS SEIZED.

ORDER

UPON HEARING Counsel for the Applicant without notice on [ ] 20[ ]

UPON READING the Witness Statement of Ian Flakey dated [ ] 20[ ]

AND UPON the Judge accepting the Undertakings in the Schedule at the end of this Order

IT IS ORDERED:

1. That the Respondent be restrained until further order of this Honourable Court, whether by itself, or by its employees or agents or otherwise howsoever, from presenting any petition to this Honourable Court or any court for the winding up of the above named Applicant, BUSTCO LIMITED based on the debt of £2,045,687.50 claimed in the statutory demand dated 24th December 2007 and served on the Applicant on 25th December 2007.

2. The Respondent may apply on giving 24 hours notice in writing to the Applicant's legal representatives vary or discharge this order.

3. Costs reserved.

Communications with the Court

All communications to the court about this order should be sent to:

Room TM 505, Royal Courts of Justice, Strand, London WC2A 2LL quoting the case number. The telephone number is 0207 947 6754.

The offices are open between 10 am and 4.30 pm Monday to Friday.

SCHEDULE 1
Undertakings given to the Court by the Applicant

1   If the Court later finds that this Order has caused loss to the Respondent and decides that the Respondent should be compensated for that loss, the Applicant will comply with any Order the Court may make; and

2   The Applicant will cause an Witness Statement to be filed confirming the substance of what was said to the Court by the Applicant's Counsel; and

3   As soon as practicable the Applicant will serve on the Respondent an application for a return date together with a copy of the Witness Statements and exhibits containing the evidence relied on by the Applicant.

4   Anyone notified of this Order will be given a copy of it by the Applicant's legal representatives.

5.4   DRAFT MINUTE OF AN ORDER MADE ON NOTICE RESTRAINING THE ADVERTISEMENT OF A WINDING UP PETITION

Injunction

IN THE HIGH COURT OF JUSTICE
CHANCERY DIVISION
COMPANIES COURT

NO: [ ] OF 20[ ]

IN THE MATTER OF BUSTCO LIMITED, REGISTERED NUMBER 011111
AND IN THE MATTER OF THE INSOLVENCY ACT 1986

BEFORE THE HONOURABLE MR JUSTICE [ ]
DATED: [ ] 20[ ]

<u>Applicant</u>

BUSTCO LIMITED

<u>Respondent</u>

ANGRY LIMITED

Name, address and reference of the Respondent:
Angry Ltd of 1 Unpaid Bill Street, London

<u>PENAL NOTICE</u>

IF YOU XAVIER MINUS, DISOBEY THIS ORDER YOU MAY BE HELD IN CONTEMPT OF COURT AND MAY BE IMPRISONED, FINED OR HAVE YOUR ASSETS SEIZED.

ANY PERSON WHO KNOWS OF THIS ORDER AND DOES ANYTHING WHICH HELPS OR PERMITS THE RESPONDENT TO BREACH THE TERMS OF THIS ORDER MAY ALSO BE HELD IN CONTEMPT OF COURT AND MAY BE IMPRISONED, FINED OR HAVE THEIR ASSETS SEIZED.

ORDER

UPON HEARING Counsel for the Applicant and the Respondent

UPON READING the Witness Statement of Ian Flakey dated [ ] 20[ ]

IT IS ORDERED:

1. That ANGRY LIMITED, the Petitioner named in a petition presented to this Honourable Court [ ] be restrained from proceeding further upon the Petition whether by advertising the same or otherwise.

2. That the Petition be removed from the file of proceedings.

3. That the costs of and occasioned by this application summarily assessed in the sum of £24,000 be paid by the Petitioner by [ ] 20[ ].

Communications with the Court

All communications to the court about this order should be sent to:

Room TM 505, Royal Courts of Justice, Strand, London WC2A 2LL quoting the case number. The telephone number is 0207 947 6754.

The offices are open between 10 am and 4.30 pm Monday to Friday.

CHAPTER 6

RESPONDING TO A PETITION: APPLICATION FOR A VALIDATION ORDER

OBJECTIVE

In a winding up by the court, any disposition of the company's property, and any transfer of shares, or alteration in the status of the company's members, made after the commencement of the winding up is, unless the court otherwise orders, void.[1]

Unless the court makes a winding up order on an administration application[2] or a prior resolution has been made for a voluntary winding up,[3] the winding up of a company by the court is deemed to commence at the time of the presentation of the petition for winding up.[4]

---

[1]   Section 127 of the Insolvency Act 1986.

[2]   Where the court makes a winding-up order by virtue of paragraph 13(1)(e) of Schedule B1 to the Insolvency Act 1986 the winding up is deemed to commence on the making of the order: section 129(1A) of the Insolvency Act 1986.

[3]   In circumstances where a resolution for voluntary winding up is passed before the petition for winding up has been heard by the court, winding up commences when the resolution was passed by the company for voluntary winding up: section 129(1) of the Insolvency Act 1986.

[4]   Section 129(2) of the Insolvency Act 1986.

The effect of this is in practice to sterilise the company's ability to trade or make payments and its bankers, as soon as they become aware of the winding up petition, will freeze the bank account. This is because payments into or out of the company's bank account are dispositions of property, irrespective of whether the account is in credit or overdrawn.[5]

The company may apply to the court for a validation order which operates to allow the company to continue to trade by:

- validating dispositions of property in the company's ordinary course of business;
- validating payments to and from the company's bank account in the ordinary course of business;
- validating specific isolated transactions beneficial to the company.

The court is cautious about making such an order and credible evidence needs to be shown that it would benefit all creditors.[6] The court will seek to ensure the interests of unsecured creditors are not prejudiced.[7] Transactions which have the effect of reducing the assets available to creditors will not be validated.

APPLICATION

Any person interested in the transaction (in practice, the application is usually made by the company) may apply on notice by ordinary application made to the registrar or district judge. An application should be made to the judge only: (1) where it is urgent and no registrar or district judge is available to hear it; or (2) where it is complex or raises new or controversial points of law; or (3) is estimated to last longer than 30 minutes. The application can be made ex parte if urgent. Three copies of application are needed.

COURT FEES

Where the application is made by ordinary application on notice to other parties, a court fee of £60 is payable.[8] Where the application is made by consent or without notice in existing proceedings a court fee of £30 is payable.[9]

EVIDENCE

The application should be supported by a witness statement by the company's director. This will need to address:

- the company's registered office;
- the company's nominal and paid up share capital;
- details of the circumstances leading to presentation of the petition;
- how the company became aware of presentation of the petition;

---

[5] *Re Tain Construction Ltd, Rose v AIB Group (UK) plc* [2003] 1 WLR 2791, *Re McGuinness Bros (UK) Ltd* (1987) 3 BCC 571.

[6] *Fairways Graphics* [1991] BCLC 468.

[7] *Re Gray's Inn Construction Co* [1980] 1 WLR 711.

[8] Paragraph 3.12 of Schedule 1 to the Civil Proceedings Fees Order 2008.

[9] Paragraph 3.11 of Schedule 1 to the Civil Proceedings Fees Order 2008.

- whether the petition has been advertised;[10]
- whether the bank or the payee was aware the petition has been presented;[11]
- whether the petition debt is admitted or disputed and, if the latter, brief details of the basis on which the debt is disputed;
- full details of the company's financial position including details of its assets;
- the effect on the company's financial position if the transaction goes ahead;
- details of the dispositions or payments in respect of which an order is sought;
- the reasons relied on in support of the need for such dispositions or payments to be made;
- details of any consents obtained from the persons affected by the transaction;
- details of the property of any property to be disposed of (including its title number if the property is land) and evidence that any proposed disposal will be at a proper value;
- whether the proposed transactions were in good faith and in the ordinary course of business;[12]
- that there was no basis for considering that the transaction might operate to prefer a creditor or guarantor;[13]
- any facts demonstrating the benefit of the transaction to creditors as a whole;
- any facts demonstrating that there is no prejudice to the creditors as a whole by the transaction taking place;
- the detail of the company's financial position showing the company's trading is profitable.

And exhibit:

- evidence of the companies assets (including details of any security and the amounts secured) and liabilities, eg the latest filed accounts, any draft audited accounts, management accounts or estimated statement of affairs);
- a cash flow forecast and profit and loss projection for the period for which the order is sought;
- any draft agreement for any proposed transactions;
- an independent valuation of the property to be disposed of.

This should be supported by an affidavit from the company's accountant. This should confirm:

- the financial information given by the director;
- the company is solvent and able to pay its debts as they fall due;[14]
- the proposed transaction or series of transactions in respect of which the order is sought will be beneficial to or will not prejudice the interests of all the unsecured creditors as a class;[15]
- the effect of the transaction on the company's financial position.

---

[10] *Re Tain Construction Ltd, Rose v AIB Group (UK) plc* [2003] 1 WLR 2791.

[11] Ibid.

[12] Ibid.

[13] Ibid.

[14] *Denney v John Hudson & Co Ltd* [1992] BCLC 901, [1992] BCC 503, CA; *Re Fairway Graphics Ltd* [1991] BCLC 468.

[15] Ibid.

And exhibit:

- evidence of the company's assets (including details of any security and the amounts secured) and liabilities, eg the latest filed accounts, any draft audited accounts, management accounts or estimated statement of affairs);
- a cash flow forecast and profit and loss projection for the period for which the order is sought.

SERVICE

The application and evidence will need to be filed and court and served on the respondent as soon as practicable after it is filed and in any event, unless it is necessary to apply ex parte or on short notice, at least 14 days before the date fixed for the hearing.[16] The application should be served on:

- the petitioning creditor;
- any liquidator appointed in an existing voluntary liquidation;
- any administrator appointed in an existing administration order;
- any supervisor of a voluntary arrangement;
- any administrative receiver;
- any member state liquidator who has been appointed;
- the Financial Services Authority if the company is or was an authorised institution;
- any creditor who has given notice to the petitioner of his intention to appear on the hearing of the petition pursuant to rule 4.16 of the Insolvency Rules 1986; and
- any creditor who has been substituted as petitioner pursuant to rule 4.19 of the Insolvency Rules 1986.

The court does have power, in cases of urgency, to hear an application immediately with or without notice to the other parties.[17]

Service may be effected by post provided it is addressed to the person it is to be served on and prepaid for either first or second class post.[18] It may be sent to the last known address of the person to be served.[19]

A document sent by first class post is treated as being served on the 2nd business day after posting, unless the contrary is shown.[20] A document sent by second class post is treated as being served on the 4th business day after posting, unless the contrary is shown.[21] The date of posting is presumed to be the date postmarked on the envelope, unless the contrary is shown.[22]

---

[16]   Rule 7.4(5) of the Insolvency Rules 1986.
[17]   Rule 7.4(6) of the Insolvency Rules 1986.
[18]   Rule 12.10(1) of the Insolvency Rules 1986.
[19]   Rule 12.10(1A) of the Insolvency Rules 1986.
[20]   Rule 12.10(2) of the Insolvency Rules 1986.
[21]   Rule 12.10(3) of the Insolvency Rules 1986.
[22]   Rule 12.10(4) of the Insolvency Rules 1986.

Where service of any application or any order of the court is to be made to a person outside England and Wales an application must be made to the registrar for directions as to the manner, timing and proof of service.[23]

The application needs to be supported by a witness statement stating:[24]

- the grounds upon which the application is made;
- in what place the person to be served is either to be found or presumed to be found.

Subject to these provisions, Part 6 of the CPR is deemed to apply under the Insolvency Rules 1986.[25]

KEY STATUTORY PROVISIONS

Practice Note – Validation Orders (sections 127 and 284 of the Insolvency Act 1986)

The following Practice Note was issued by the Chancellor of the High Court. Companies

1. Section 127(1) Insolvency Act 1986 provides, 'In a winding up by the court, any disposition of the company's property, and any transfer of shares, or alteration in the status of the company's members, made after the commencement of the winding up is, unless the court otherwise orders, void'. Section 129(2) Insolvency Act 1986 provides that, 'the winding up of a company by the court is deemed to commence at the time of the presentation of the petition for winding up'.

2. A company against which a winding up petition has been presented ('the company') may apply to the court after presentation of the petition for relief from the effects of the foregoing provisions by seeking an order that a disposition or dispositions of its property, including payments out of its bank account (whether such account is in credit or overdrawn), shall not be void in the event of a winding up order being made on the hearing of the petition (a 'validation order').

3. In accordance with the *Practice Note on the Hearing of Insolvency Proceedings of 23 May 2005* [2005] BCC 456, [2005] BPIR 688 an application for a validation order should generally be made to the registrar or district judge. An application should be made to the judge only (a) where it is urgent and no registrar or district judge is available to hear it, or (b) where it is complex or raises new or controversial points of law, or (c) is estimated to last longer than 30 minutes.

4. Save in exceptional circumstances, notice of the making of the application should be given to (a) the petitioning creditor, (b) any person entitled to receive a copy of the petition pursuant to r. 4.10 Insolvency Rules 1986, (c) any creditor who has given notice to the petitioner of his

---

[23] Rule 12.12(3) of the Insolvency Rules 1986.

[24] Rule 12.12(4) of the Insolvency Rules 1986.

[25] Rule 12.11 of the Insolvency Rules 1986.

intention to appear on the hearing of the petition pursuant to r. 4.16 Insolvency Rules 1986 and (d) any creditor who has been substituted as petitioner pursuant to r. 4.19 Insolvency Rules 1986.

5. The application should be supported by written evidence in the form of an affidavit or witness statement which, save in exceptional circumstances, should be made by a director or officer of the company who is intimately acquainted with the company's affairs and financial circumstances. If appropriate, supporting evidence in the form of an affidavit or witness statement from the company's accountant should also be produced.

6. The extent and contents of the evidence will vary according to the circumstances and the nature of the relief sought, but in the majority of cases it should include, as a minimum, the following information: when and to whom notice has been given in accordance with paragraph 4 above; the company's registered office; company's nominal and paid up capital; details of the circumstances leading to presentation of the petition; how the company became aware of presentation of the petition; whether the petition debt is admitted or disputed and, if the latter, brief details of the basis on which the debt is disputed; full details of the company's financial position including details of its assets (including details of any security and the amount(s) secured) and liabilities, which should be supported, as far as possible, by documentary evidence, e.g. the latest filed accounts, any draft audited accounts, management accounts or estimated statement of affairs; a cash flow forecast and profit and loss projection for the period for which the order is sought; details of the dispositions or payments in respect of which an order is sought; the reasons relied on in support of the need for such dispositions or payments to be made; other information relevant to the exercise of the court's discretion; details of any consents obtained from the persons mentioned in paragraph 4 above (supported by documentary evidence where appropriate).

7. Where an application is made urgently to enable payments to be made which are essential to continued trading (e.g. wages) and it is not possible to assemble all the evidence listed above, the court may consider granting limited relief for a short period, but there should be sufficient evidence to satisfy the court that the interests of creditors are unlikely to be prejudiced.

8. Where the application involves a disposition of property the court will need details of the property (including its title number if the property is land) and to be satisfied that any proposed disposal will be at a proper value. Accordingly an independent valuation should be obtained and exhibited to the evidence.

9. The court will need to be satisfied by credible evidence that the company is solvent and able to pay its debts as they fall due or that a particular transaction or series of transactions in respect of which the order is sought will be beneficial to or will not prejudice the interests of all the unsecured creditors as a class (*Denney v John Hudson & Co Ltd* [1992] BCLC 901, [1992] BCC 503, CA; *Re Fairway Graphics Ltd* [1991] BCLC 468).

10. A draft of the order sought should be attached to the application.

Sections 127 to 129 of the Insolvency Act 1986

127 Avoidance of property dispositions, etc

(1) In a winding up by the court, any disposition of the company's property, and any transfer of shares, or alteration in the status of the company's members, made after the commencement of the winding up is, unless the court otherwise orders, void.

(2) This section has no effect in respect of anything done by an administrator of a company while a winding-up petition is suspended under paragraph 40 of Schedule B1.

128 Avoidance of attachments, etc

(1) Where a company registered in England and Wales is being wound up by the court, any attachment, sequestration, distress or execution put in force against the estate or effects of the company after the commencement of the winding up is void.

(2) This section, so far as relates to any estate or effects of the company situated in England and Wales, applies in the case of a company registered in Scotland as it applies in the case of a company registered in England and Wales.

129 Commencement of winding up by the court

(1) If, before the presentation of a petition for the winding up of a company by the court, a resolution has been passed by the company for voluntary winding up, the winding up of the company is deemed to have commenced at the time of the passing of the resolution; and unless the court, on proof of fraud or mistake, directs otherwise, all proceedings taken in the voluntary winding up are deemed to have been validly taken.

(1A) Where the court makes a winding-up order by virtue of paragraph 13(1) (e) of Schedule B1, the winding up is deemed to commence on the making of the order.

(2) In any other case, the winding up of a company by the court is deemed to commence at the time of the presentation of the petition for winding up.

Practice Direction – Order under section 127 of the Insolvency Act 1986

This Practice Direction supplements Part 49 of the CPR.

1. Attention is drawn to the undesirability of asking as a matter of course for a winding up order as an alternative to an order under s.459 Companies Act 1985. The petition should not ask for a winding up order unless that is the remedy which the petitioner prefers or it is thought that it may be the only remedy to which the petitioner is entitled.

2. Whenever a winding up order is asked for in a contributory's petition, the petition must state whether the petitioner consents or objects to an order under s.127 of the Insolvency Act 1986 ('a s.127 order') in the standard form. If he objects, the written evidence in support must contain a short statement of his reasons.

3.   If the petitioner objects to a s.127 order in the standard form but consents to such an order in a modified form, the petition must set out in the form of order to which he consents, and the written evidence in support must contain a short statement of his reasons for seeking the modification.

4.   If the petition contains a statement that the petitioner consents to a s.127 order, whether in the standard or a modified form, but the petitioner changes his mind before the first hearing of the petition, he must notify the respondents and may apply on notice to a Judge for an order directing that no s.127 order or a modified order only (as the case may be) shall be made by the Registrar, but validating dispositions made without notice of the order made by the Judge.

5.   If the petition contains a statement that the petitioner consents to a s.127 order, whether in the standard or a modified form, the Registrar shall without further enquiry make an order in such form at the first hearing unless an order to the contrary has been made by the Judge in the meantime.

6.   If the petition contains a statement that the petitioner objects to a s.127 order in the standard form, the company may apply (in the case of urgency, without notice) to the Judge for an order.

7.   Section 127 Order – Standard Form:

      (Title etc.)
      ORDER
      That notwithstanding the presentation of the said Petition

      (1)   payments made into or out of the bank accounts of the Company in the ordinary course of business of the Company and

      (2)   dispositions of the property of the Company made in the ordinary course of its business for proper value between the date of presentation of the Petition and the date of judgment on the Petition or further order in the meantime shall not be void by virtue of the provisions of section 127 of the Insolvency Act 1986 in the event of an Order for the winding up of the Company being made on the said Petition provided that (the relevant bank) shall be under no obligation to verify for itself whether any transaction through the company's bank accounts is in the ordinary course of business, or that it represents full market value for the relevant transaction.

      This form of Order may be departed from where the circumstances of the case require.

6.1   ORDINARY APPLICATION FOR A VALIDATION ORDER

Rule 7.2
Ordinary Application

IN THE HIGH COURT OF JUSTICE
CHANCERY DIVISION
COMPANIES COURT

NO: [ ] OF 20[ ]

IN THE MATTER OF BUSTCO LIMITED, REGISTERED NUMBER 011111
AND IN THE MATTER OF THE INSOLVENCY ACT 1986

BETWEEN:-

ANGRY LIMITED

Petitioner

-and-

BUSTCO LIMITED

Respondent

TAKE NOTICE that BUSTCO LIMITED intends to apply to the Judge on:

Date: [ ] 20[ ]
Time: [ ] am/pm
Place: Royal Courts of Justice, Strand, London WC2A 2LL

For an Order in the following terms:

(1)   That notwithstanding the presentation of the said Petition:

a.   payments made into or out of the bank accounts of the Company in the ordinary course of business of the Company, and

b.   dispositions of the property of the Company made in the ordinary course of its business for proper value (for the avoidance of doubt, including the proposed sale of the company van, registration mark 'REK 1' to Foxy Motors Limited for £2,000),

between the date of presentation of the Petition and the date of judgment on the Petition or further order in the meantime shall not be void by virtue of the provisions of section 127 of the Insolvency Act 1986 in the event of an Order for the winding up of the Company being made on the said Petition provided that (the relevant bank) shall be under no obligation to verify for itself whether any transaction through the company's bank accounts is in the ordinary course of business, or that it represents full market value for the relevant transaction.

(2)   That the costs of this application be paid by the Petitioner.

Signed [ ]
Solicitor for the Applicant
Dated [ ] 20[ ]

The Applicant's address for service is:

SILK & CO
2 LAW STREET
LONDON

To:
ANGRY LIMITED, 1 UNPAID BILL STREET, LONDON

If you do not attend, the Court may make such order as it thinks fit.

6.2   DRAFT VALIDATION ORDER

IN THE HIGH COURT OF JUSTICE
CHANCERY DIVISION
COMPANIES COURT

NO: [ ] OF 20[ ]

IN THE MATTER OF BUSTCO LIMITED, REGISTERED NUMBER 011111
AND IN THE MATTER OF THE INSOLVENCY ACT 1986

BEFORE MR REGISTRAR WISE

ANGRY LIMITED

<u>Petitioner</u>

-and-

BUSTCO LIMITED

<u>Respondent</u>

DRAFT MINUTE OF ORDER

UPON the Respondent's application dated [ ] 20[ ]

AND UPON HEARING Counsel for the Petitioner and the Respondent

AND UPON READING the evidence noted as having been read

IT IS ORDERED:

(1)   That notwithstanding the presentation of the said Petition:

   (a)   payments made into or out of the bank accounts of the Company in the ordinary course of business of the Company, and

   (b)   dispositions of the property of the Company made in the ordinary course of its business for proper value (including the proposed sale of the company van, registration mark 'REK 1' to Foxy Motors Limited for £2,000),

between the date of presentation of the Petition and the date of judgment on the Petition or further order in the meantime shall not be void by virtue of the provisions of section 127 of the Insolvency Act 1986 in the event of an Order for the winding up of the Company being made on the said Petition provided that (the relevant bank) shall be under no obligation to verify for itself whether any transaction through the company's bank accounts is in the ordinary course of business, or that it represents full market value for the relevant transaction.

(2)   [*Provision for costs*]

Dated [ ] 20[ ]

6.3 WITNESS STATEMENT IN SUPPORT OF AN APPLICATION FOR A VALIDATION ORDER

Applicant: I Flakey: 1st: IF1: [ ] 20[ ]

IN THE HIGH COURT OF JUSTICE
CHANCERY DIVISION
COMPANIES COURT

NO: [ ] OF 20[ ]

IN THE MATTER OF BUSTCO LIMITED, REGISTERED NUMBER 011111
AND IN THE MATTER OF THE INSOLVENCY ACT 1986

BUSTCO LIMITED

<u>Applicant</u>

-and-

ANGRY LIMITED

<u>Respondent</u>

1st WITNESS STATEMENT OF IAN FLAKEY

I, Ian Flakey, I Geranium Cottage, London, Company Director, state as follows:

1. I am the managing director of the Applicant Company and I am authorised to make this witness statement on its behalf.

2. The matters set out in this witness statement are true and within my own knowledge except where otherwise indicated, in which case I have explained the source of my information or belief.

3. There is now produced and shown to me a bundle consisting of true copies of the documents I will refer to in my witness statements marked 'IF1'.

4. I make the application in support of the company's application for an order that notwithstanding the presentation of the said Petition:

    (a) payments made into or out of the bank accounts of the Company in the ordinary course of business of the Company, and

    (b) dispositions of the property of the Company made in the ordinary course of its business for proper value (including the proposed sale of the company van, registration mark 'REK 1' to Foxy Motors Limited for £2,000),

between the date of presentation of the Petition and the date of judgment on the Petition or further order in the meantime shall not be void by virtue of the provisions of section 127 of the Insolvency Act 1986 in the event of an Order for the winding up of the Company being made on the said Petition provided that (the relevant bank) shall be under no obligation to verify for itself whether any transaction through the company's bank accounts is in the ordinary course of business, or that it represents full market value for the relevant transaction.

5.   Bustco Limited was incorporated on 30th October 1996 under the Companies Act 1985.

6.   The registered office of the Company is at Suite 1, 1 Poor Street, London.

7.   The nominal capital of the Company is £1000 divided into 1000 shares of £1 each. The amount of the capital paid up or credited as paid up is £2.

8.   The principal objects for which the Company was established are to carry on business as a general trading company and other objects stated in the memorandum of association of the Company.

9.   On 25th December 2007 my company was served at its registered office with a statutory demand by Angry Limited claiming £2,045,687.50 based on an invoice for goods they say were sold and delivered to my company. I refer to page [ ] of 'IF1' which is a true copy of the statutory demand.

10. The Applicant Company made no such order and was never delivered any such goods. I refer to page [ ] of 'IF1' which is a true copy of the Applicant's records for purchases and deliveries for the periods alluded to by Angry Limited.

11. Upon discovering the statutory demand on my return from the Christmas vacation on 5th January 2008 I instructed my solicitors, Silk & Co, write to Angry Limited to explain that the debt was disputed.

12. On 5th January 2008 my solicitors, Silk & Co, wrote to Angry Limited explaining that my company had first seen the statutory demand today, the basis on which the alleged debt is disputed and inviting them to give appropriate undertakings not to present a petition against my company. They warned that any petition would be an abuse of process as the debt was disputed. I refer to page [ ] of 'IF1' which is a true copy of my solicitor's letter.

13. Instead of replying to my solicitor's letter or of waiting for the period allowed for payment under the statutory demand to elapse, on 6th January 2008, Gustav Grim of Angry Limited served us with a winding up petition.. I refer to page [ ] of 'IF1' which is a true copy of the petition.

14. The winding up petition has not been advertised and Bustco has made an application to the Court to restrain the presentation which is due to be heard on [ ] 20[ ]. Angry Limited appears to have told our bank about the winding up petition and our bank has frozen our account and refused either to accept our customer's money or pay out on our cheques.

15. Bustco Limited is a profitable company and is able to pay its debts as they fall due. I refer to page [ ] of 'IF1' which is a true copy of a letter from my company's accountant, Derrick Devious, setting out

the company's latest accounts and confirming the company's solvency and setting out of list of the company's principal assets and their book valuations.

16. Bustco Limited presently holds £50,000 in credit in its bank account and a further £20,000 in cheques it has been unable to present at the Bank because of the petition.

17. But for the presentation of the winding up order it would have paid £10,000 this month in wages, national insurance contributions and PAYE for its employees. It has the same liability each month it trades. It would also have wished to pay a further £5,000 to its suppliers and £1,000 in business rates, electricity and water (it has no obligation to pay rent as it owns its own premises). As with the wage cost, these are monthly outgoings. Next month the VAT quarter falls due and Bustco will have to pay an additional £9,000 to Her Majesty's Revenue and Customs. I refer to page [ ] of 'IF1' which is a true copy of a list of payments we would wish to make each month for the next three months.

18. Whilst this would in theory diminish the amount available in the bank account, it would allow the company to continue to trade. As I have said the company is profitable and allowing the company to continue to trade would (even were the company to be wound up) swell the resources available to any creditors. I refer to page [ ] of 'IF1' which is a true copy of projections prepared by my company's accountant, Derrick Devious, showing the monthly projected profit and loss of Bustco if the company was allowed to trade over the next quarter.

19. Before the petition was presented Bustco Limited had agreed to sell its Nogo van, registration mark 'REK 1' to Foxy Motors Limited for £2,000. I refer to page [ ] of 'IF1' which is a true copy of the proposed sale agreement. We had proposed to make the sale because we had discovered it was more cost effective to outsource our deliveries. I refer to page [ ] of 'IF1' which is a true copy of I refer to page [ ] of 'IF1' which is a true copy of the extract from the current edition of Glassers Guide which shows Nogo vans of the age and condition of ours have a resale value of £2000. We are anxious to resell the van now because Foxy may withdraw from the sale if we do not complete it soon and if we retain it much longer we will have to be put to the extra expense of an MOT and new tax disk as these fall due next month. In short the sale benefits not only Bustco but any creditors we may have.

20. The proposed transactions and payments are made in good faith and in the ordinary course of Bustco's business. There is no basis for considering that the payments or transaction might operate to prefer some creditor or guarantor over any others. Indeed this Honourable Court will appreciate that there is no prejudice to the creditors as a whole by the order being granted.

STATEMENT OF TRUTH

I believe that the facts stated in this Witness Statement are true.

Signed [ ]
Full name [*IAN FLAKEY*]
Dated [ ] 20[ ]

CHAPTER 7

APPLICATION TO RESCIND A WINDING UP ORDER

OBJECTIVE

Every court which has the jurisdiction to wind up companies may review, rescind or vary any order made by it the exercise of that jurisdiction.[1] The applicant does not need to demonstrate that the court erred in making the order nor that there are grounds for appeal.[2] The making of winding up order affects all the creditors and the court will be cautious about exercising its discretion to rescind the winding up order.

In the case of an unsuccessful application the costs of the petitioning creditor, the supporting creditors and of the Official Receiver will normally be ordered to be paid by the creditor or the contributory making or joining in the application. The reason for this is that if the costs of an unsuccessful application are made payable by the company, they fall unfairly on the general body of creditors.[3]

Applications to rescind must be made within 7 days of the winding up order. The court does however have the power to extend time.[4]

---

[1]   Rule 7.47(1) of the Insolvency Rules 1986.

[2]   *Re Dollar Land (Feltham) Ltd* [1995] BCC 740.

[3]   Paragraph 7.3 of the CPR Practice Direction – Insolvency Proceedings.

[4]   Rule 12.9(2) of the Insolvency Rules 1986.

APPLICATION

Any application for the rescission of a winding up order shall be made to the High Court[5] within 7 days after the date on which the order was made.[6] Applications will only be entertained if made: (1) by a creditor; or (2) by a contributory; or (3) by the company jointly with a creditor or with a contributory.[7]

There is no need to issue a form of application[8] (Form 7.2) as the petition is restored before the court.[9] Notice of any such proposed application and a copy of the evidence relied on must be given to:

- the court;
- the Official Receiver;[10]
- the petitioner;
- any supporting creditors who were heard on the petition.

However, an application will need to be made by ordinary application to extend time if the application is made outside the 7-day period. The respondents would be the Official Receiver and the petitioner.

COURT FEES

Where the application is made by ordinary application on notice to other parties, a court fee of £60 is payable.[11] Where the application is made by consent a court fee of £30 is payable.[12]

EVIDENCE

The application should be supported by a witness statement by the company's director. This will need to address:

- who makes the application;[13]
- the deponent's capacity to speak for them;
- the company's nominal and paid up share capital;
- details of the circumstances leading to the winding up order;
- how the company became aware of the winding up order;
- that there has been some change of circumstances or new evidence justifying the rescission;[14]
- the circumstances are exceptional;[15]

---

5   *Re Calahurst Ltd* (1989) 5 BCC 318.

6   Rule 7.47(4) of the Insolvency Rules 1986, para 7.1 of the CPR Practice Direction – Insolvency Proceedings.

7   Paragraph 7.2 of the CPR Practice Direction – Insolvency Proceedings.

8   Although a court fee will still need to be paid.

9   Paragraph 7.5 of the CPR Practice Direction – Insolvency Proceedings.

10   Paragraph 7.1 of the CPR Practice Direction – Insolvency Proceedings.

11   Paragraph 3.12 of Schedule 1 to the Civil Proceedings Fees Order 2008.

12   Paragraph 3.11 of Schedule 1 to the Civil Proceedings Fees Order 2008.

13   Paragraph 7.2 of the CPR Practice Direction – Insolvency Proceedings.

14   *Papanicola v Humphreys* [2005] 2 All ER 418.

15   Ibid.

- that these matters demonstrate a material difference to the position before the court when the winding up order was made;[16]
- the explanation of the effect of the evidence of the company's assets;[17]
- the explanation of the evidence of the company's liabilities;[18]
- if the application is made outside the 7-day period, the explanation and justification for the delay;[19]
- that the liquidator has (as yet) not incurred expenses in investigating the company's insolvency.[20]

And exhibit:

- the petition;
- the winding up order;
- any material demonstrating the new circumstances or new evidence;
- written evidence of the company's assets;[21]
- written evidence of the company's liabilities.[22]

INTERIM RELIEF

Making an application to rescind or indeed lodging an appeal of the winding up order does not operate to stay the winding up. Whilst the court has power to order a stay of a winding up petition,[23] in practice, it is never granted.[24] The court may however be prepared instead to grant a stay of the advertisement of proceedings.[25] The application must be made to the judge.

KEY STATUTORY PROVISIONS

Paragraph 7 of the CPR Practice Direction – Insolvency Proceedings

Rescission of a winding up order

7.1 Any application for the rescission of a winding up order shall be made within seven days after the date on which the order was made (Insolvency Rule 7.47(4)). Notice of any such application must be given to the Official Receiver.

---

[16] Ibid.

[17] Paragraph 7.2 of the CPR Practice Direction – Insolvency Proceedings.

[18] Ibid.

[19] *Wilson v The Specter Partnership* [2007] BPIR 654.

[20] *Re Mid East Trading Ltd* [1997] 3 All ER 481, 489.

[21] Paragraph 7.2 of the CPR Practice Direction – Insolvency Proceedings.

[22] Ibid.

[23] Paragraph 7.14 of the CPR Practice Direction – Insolvency Proceedings.

[24] *Re A & BC Chewing Gum* [1975] 1 WLR 579.

[25] Rule 4.21(4) of the Insolvency Rules 1986, paragraph 17.25 of the CPR Practice Direction – Insolvency Proceedings.

7.2   Applications will only be entertained if made (a) by a creditor, or (b) by a contributory, or (c) by the company jointly with a creditor or with a contributory. The application must be supported by written evidence of assets and liabilities.

7.3   In the case of an unsuccessful application the costs of the petitioning creditor, the supporting creditors and of the Official Receiver will normally be ordered to be paid by the creditor or the contributory making or joining in the application. The reason for this is that if the costs of an unsuccessful application are made payable by the company, they fall unfairly on the general body of creditors.

7.4   Cases in which the making of the winding up order has not been opposed may, if the application is made promptly, be dealt with on a statement by the applicant's legal representative of the circumstances; but apart from such cases, the court will normally require any application to be supported by written evidence.

7.5   There is no need to issue a form of application (Form 7.2) as the petition is restored before the Court.

Rules 7.47 and 12.9 of the Insolvency Rules 1986

7.47 Appeals and reviews of court orders (winding up)
(1)   Every court having jurisdiction under the Act to wind up companies may review, rescind or vary any order made by it in the exercise of that jurisdiction.

(2)   An appeal from a decision made in the exercise of that jurisdiction by a county court or by a registrar of the High Court lies to a single judge of the High Court; and an appeal from a decision of that judge on such an appeal lies, with the leave of that judge or the Court of Appeal, to the Court of Appeal.

(3)   A county court is not, in the exercise of its jurisdiction to wind up companies, subject to be restrained by the order of any other court, and no appeal lies from its decision in the exercise of that jurisdiction except as provided by this Rule.

(4)   Any application for the rescission of a winding-up order shall be made within 7 days after the date on which the order was made.

12.9 Time-Limits
(1)   The provisions of CPR rule 2.8 (time) apply, as regards computation of time, to anything required or authorised to be done by the Rules.

(2)   The provisions of CPR rule 3.1(2)(a) (the court's general powers of management) apply so as to enable the court to extend or shorten the time for compliance with anything required or authorised to be done by the Rules.

7.1 ORDINARY APPLICATION TO EXTEND TIME AND RESCIND THE WINDING UP

Rule 7.2
Ordinary Application

IN THE HIGH COURT OF JUSTICE
CHANCERY DIVISION
COMPANIES COURT

NO: [ ] OF 20[ ]

IN THE MATTER OF BUSTCO LIMITED, REGISTERED NUMBER 011111
AND IN THE MATTER OF THE INSOLVENCY ACT 1986

BETWEEN:-

(1) IAN FLAKEY
(2) BUSTCO LIMITED

Applicant

-and-

(1) THE OFFICIAL RECEIVER
(2) ANGRY LIMITED

Respondent

TAKE NOTICE that BUSTCO LIMITED intends to apply to the Registrar on:

Date: [ ] 20[ ]
Time: [ ] am/pm
Place: Royal Courts of Justice, Strand, London WC2A 2LL

For an Order in the following terms:

(1) To extend time to the 1st and 2nd Applicant to make and file an application to rescind the winding up order made against the 2nd Applicant.

(2) To rescind the winding up order made against the 2nd Applicant.

(3) That the costs of this application be provided for.

Signed [ ]
Solicitor for the Applicant
Dated [ ] 20[ ]

The Applicant's address for service is:

SILK & CO
2 LAW STREET
LONDON

To:
ANGRY LIMITED, I UNPAID BILL STREET, LONDON
THE OFFICIAL RECEIVER

If you do not attend, the Court may make such order as it thinks fit.

7.2 WITNESS STATEMENT IN SUPPORT OF AN APPLICATION TO EXTEND TIME AND RESCIND THE WINDING UP

Applicant: I Flakey: Ist: IFI: [ ] 20[ ]

IN THE HIGH COURT OF JUSTICE
CHANCERY DIVISION
COMPANIES COURT

NO: [ ] OF 20[ ]

IN THE MATTER OF BUSTCO LIMITED, REGISTERED NUMBER 011111
AND IN THE MATTER OF THE INSOLVENCY ACT 1986

BETWEEN:-

(1) IAN FLAKEY
(2) BUSTCO LIMITED

<u>Applicant</u>

-and-

(1) THE OFFICIAL RECEIVER
(2) ANGRY LIMITED

<u>Respondent</u>

1st WITNESS STATEMENT OF IAN FLAKEY

I, Ian Flakey, I Geranium Cottage, London, Director of the Bustco Limited, state as follows:

1. I am the managing director of the Applicant Company. I am authorised to make this witness statement on its behalf. I am also a creditor of the company in the sum of £1.

2. The matters deposed to in this witness statement are within my own knowledge except where otherwise indicated, in which case I have explained the source of my information or belief.

3. I make the application in support of my and the company's application to rescind the winding up order made against the company and for an order extending the time in which to make this application.

4. The company has a share capital of 100 shares all of which have been issued to and fully paid up by me.

5.   On 25th June 2008 a winding up order was made against my company based on a petition filed by Angry Limited claiming £2,045,687.50.

6.   Both I and the company were wholly unaware of the petition or the making of the order until we were contacted by the Official Receiver. It was never served on the company or on me. Obviously I had no opportunity to attend and resist the petition on the hearing at which the winding up order was made.

7.   Had I or the company known of this we could have simply paid this sum by return.

8.   I refer to my exhibit 'IF1' which sets out my accountant's report of the assets and liabilities of Bustco Limited. This Honourable Court will note at page [ ] that the assets include a bank account which showed £4 million in credit.

9.   Plainly these are exceptional circumstances and no doubt had the Honourable Court had the benefit of this information or indeed had the company had any opportunity to be represented before it, it is likely that a different order would have been made.

10. Whilst this application is made outside the 7-day period, I and the company were first made aware of the winding up order yesterday. We immediately sought advice and took steps to lodge this application today. The Official Receiver has only recently opened the file on the Company and I understand from him has not incurred yet any expenses in investigating the company's insolvency.

STATEMENT OF TRUTH

I believe that the facts stated in this Witness Statement are true.

Signed [ ]
Full name [*IAN FLAKEY*]
Dated [ ] 20[ ]

CHAPTER 8

WINDING UP PETITION ON JUST AND EQUITABLE GROUNDS

OBJECTIVE

A petition to wind up a company can be presented if you can show that it is just and equitable to wind up the company under section 122(1)(g) of the Insolvency Act 1986.

Circumstances in which it might be just and equitable to wind up the company include:

- Where the affairs of the company are deadlocked.[1]
- Where the principal objects of the company can no longer be achieved.[2]
- Where the petitioner is excluded or expelled from the management of the company where the company was formed on the basis of an agreement that the petitioner would participate in the management of the company[3] or other oppressive conduct to the shareholders in their capacity as members.[4]

---

[1] *Re Yenidje Tobacco* [1916] 2 Ch 426.

[2] *Re Perfectair Holdings Ltd* [1990] BCLC 423.

[3] *Re Westbourne Galleries* [1973] AC 360.

[4] *Scottish Co-operative Society v Meyer* [1959] AC 324.

- Where there has been a proven lack of probity on the part of those running the company in the conduct of its affairs.[5]

A petition may only be presented by the company, its directors, a creditor (including a contingent or prospective creditor), contributory,[6] liquidator or by a designated officer of the magistrates' court seeking to enforce fines.[7] A contributory is only entitled to present a petition if the members are reduced below two or if he has held his shares for at least 6 months before commencement of winding up or they have devolved to him on death.[8] The holder of a fully paid share is a contributory to the extent that he can show that he will have a tangible interest in the company being wound up.[9]

PETITION

The petition needs to be in the statutory form. It must contain:

- the name and number of the company to be wound up;
- the date the company was incorporated and under which Companies Act;
- the address of the registered office;
- the nominal capital of the company;
- the issued capital of the company;
- the petitioner's shareholding;
- the facts upon which demonstrate that the petitioner has locus to present the petition. For example that the petitioner holds shares in the company and that they either were originally allotted to him, or have been held by him, and registered in his name, for at least 6 months during the 18 months before the commencement of the winding up, or have devolved on him through the death of a former holder;
- the principal objects for which the company was established;
- that there will be a surplus of assets or some form of tangible interest on winding up or that winding up will minimise some disadvantage he is suffering as a shareholder;
- that the conduct of the respondents has caused the petitioner to lose all trust and confidence in the management of the respondents;
- particulars of the facts which the petitioner relies on to show that it is just an equitable that the company be wound up;
- that it is just and equitable that the company should be wound up;
- whether the petitioner consents to an order under section 127 of the Insolvency Act 1986;
- a prayer that the company be wound up under the Insolvency Act 1986 and such other order as the court thinks fit.

The respondent should be the company and, where the petition is presented against a private limited company, all the shareholders. Where a petition is presented against a public company, it is acceptable practice to make only the alleged wrongdoers respondents and defer joining other shareholders until later.

---

5   *Re Neath Harbour Smelting and Rolling Works Ltd* (1887) 2 TLR 336.

6   Section 79 of the Insolvency Act 1986.

7   Section 124(1) of the Insolvency Act 1986.

8   Section 124(2) of the Insolvency Act 1986.

9   *Re Chesterfield Catering Co Ltd* [1977] Ch 373.

Whilst the company is a necessary respondent to the petition, it is wrong for the company's money to be spent on disputes between shareholders and the court will, in an appropriate case, grant an injunction to prevent the company spending money on the litigation or dispensing with the need for its being represented.[10]

The petition needs to be presented at or posted to the Chambers of the Registrar of the Companies Court, Royal Courts of Justice, Thomas More Building, Strand, London or at a Chancery District Registry. Before the petition is presented the central index of winding up petitions at TM2.09 of Thomas More Building should be checked. If an existing petition is already current against the company, the petitioner should not lodge a second petition. Sufficient supplementary copies should be also lodged to allow for service on each respondent. The petitions will be stamped with a return date.

EVIDENCE

The petition does not need to be verified by affidavit at the time when it is lodged. Directions as to evidence will be given at the first hearing. Evidence will be required at this stage however if no or a modified form of the section 127 order is sought.

COURT FEES

The court fee is £190[11] but one needs to also pay a deposit of £715[12] which will be used to pay the official receiver if the company goes into liquidation.

SERVICE

A sealed copy of the petition should be served on each respondent and at the company's registered office at least 14 days before the return date. Service is by delivery to a director, officer or employee or other person who acknowledges himself authorised to accept service on behalf of the company or, in the absence of the same, by depositing at the registered office in such a way that it is likely to come to the attention of a person attending the office.[13] Where service on the registered office is not practicable, the petition may be served by depositing at the company's last known principal place of business in such a way that it is likely to come to the attention of a person attending there or by delivering it to the company's secretary, director, manager or principal officer.[14]

Where service is not practicable in this way an application should be made for substituted service.

A sealed copy of the petition should also be served, if applicable on the company, on any liquidator appointed in an existing voluntary liquidation, any administrator appointed under an existing administration order, any supervisor of a voluntary arrangement, any administrative receiver, any member

---

[10]   *Re Milgate Developments Ltd* [1993] BCLC 291.

[11]   Paragraph 3.3 of Schedule 1 to the Civil Proceedings Fees Order 2008.

[12]   Insolvency Proceedings (Fees) (Amendment) Order 2009.

[13]   Rule 4.8(3) of the Insolvency Rules 1986.

[14]   Rule 4.8(4) of the Insolvency Rules 1986.

state liquidator who has been appointed and the Financial Services Authority if the company is or was an authorised institution.[15]

An affidavit should be prepared proving service. The deponent should be the process server who effected service.

This should address:

- how the deponent effected service of the petition;
- the place where service was effected;
- the date and time of service;
- if the service was effected on an individual, the name of that individual, their relationship to the debtor company and whether they acknowledged himself authorised to accept service on behalf of the company;
- if service was not on an individual, how service of the petition would have been brought to the attention of a person attending the office;
- the reaction (if any) to service.

This should exhibit:

- a sealed copy of the petition;
- a sealed copy of any order for substituted service.

Any creditor, director, contributory or member of the debtor company is entitled, on request and on payment of the statutory fee, to be provided by the petitioner or his solicitor within 2 days of making the request with a copy of the petition.[16]

ADVERTISEMENT

No attempt should be made to advertise the petition before directions have been given on this issue by the Registrar. A prematurely advertised petition is likely to be struck out as an abuse of process.[17] The Registrar will usually only order the advertisement of the petition at a very late stage. This is because the petition is likely to damage the value and business of the company and, being a dispute between shareholders of a solvent company, it is unlikely to concern creditors.

At the return date the registrar will usually direct that there be no advertisement of the petition until further hearing. The petition should thereafter be referred to by number and disclosures about the petition to third parties may cause the petition to be struck out as an abuse of process.[18]

---

[15]   Rule 4.7 of the Insolvency Rules 1986.

[16]   Rule 4.13 of the Insolvency Rules 1986.

[17]   *Re Doreen Boards Ltd* [1996] 1 BCLC 501.

[18]   *Re a Company (no 0013925 of 1992)* [1992] BCLC 562.

THE HEARING

The hearing is in open court before the Companies Court registrar or district judge. Advocates are not expected to robe. The parties should expect the hearing to deal with directions for the petition and are well advised to attempt to agree a proposed timetable in advance. The registrar will usually wish to consider whether points of claim and defence should be ordered or whether the issue on the petition is simple and the petition and further evidence will suffice. He may also wish to address any issues of service of the petition, make a section 127 order and direct that there be no advertisement of the petition until further hearing and give directions on discovery, inspection and interrogatories.

KEY STATUTORY PROVISIONS

Paragraphs 2.2 and 3.1 of the CPR Practice Direction – Insolvency Proceedings

2.2 Copies of every advertisement published in connection with a winding up petition must be lodged with the Court as soon as possible after publication and in any event not later than the day specified in Insolvency Rule 4.14 of the Insolvency Rules 1986. This direction applies even if the advertisement is defective in any way (e.g. is published at a date not in accordance with the Insolvency Rules, or omits or misprints some important words) or if the petitioner decides not to pursue the petition (e.g. on receiving payment).

Certificate of compliance—time for filing

3.1 In the High Court in order to assist practitioners and the Court the time laid down by Insolvency Rule 4.14 of the Insolvency Rules 1986, for filing a certificate of compliance and a copy of the advertisement, is hereby extended to not later than 4.30 pm on the Friday preceding the day on which the petition is to be heard. Applications to file the certificate and the copy advertisement after 4.30 pm on the Friday will only be allowed if some good reason is shown for the delay.

Rules 4.7 to 4.14 of the Insolvency Rules 1986

4.7 Presentation and filing of petition

(1) The petition, verified by affidavit in accordance with Rule 4.12 below, shall be filed in court.

(2) No petition shall be filed unless there is produced on presentation of the petition a receipt for the deposit payable or paragraph (2A) applies.

(2A) This paragraph applies in any case where the Secretary of State has given written notice to the court that the petitioner has made suitable alternative arrangements for the payment of the deposit to the official receiver and such notice has not been revoked in relation to the petitioner in accordance with paragraph (2B).

(2B) A notice of the kind referred to in paragraph (2A) may be revoked in relation to the petitioner in whose favour it is given by a further notice in writing to the court stating that the earlier notice is revoked in relation to the petitioner.

(3)   If the petitioner is other than the company itself, there shall be delivered with the petition—

    (a)   one copy for service on the company, and

    (b)   one copy to be exhibited to the affidavit verifying service.

(4)   There shall in any case be delivered with the petition—

    (a)   if the company is in course of being wound up voluntarily, and a liquidator has been appointed, one copy of the petition to be sent to him;

    (b)   if the company is in administration, one copy to be sent to the administrator;

    (c)   if an administrative receiver has been appointed in relation to the company, one copy to be sent to him;

    (d)   if there is in force for the company a voluntary arrangement under Part I of the Act, one copy for the supervisor of the arrangement; ...

    (da) if a member State liquidator has been appointed in main proceedings in relation to the company, one copy to be sent to him; and

    (e)   if the company is an authorized deposit-taker or a former authorized deposit-taker and the petitioner is not the Financial Services Authority, one copy to be sent to the Authority.

(5)   Each of the copies delivered shall have applied to it the seal of the court, and shall be issued to the petitioner.

(6)   The court shall fix a venue for the hearing of the petition; and this shall be endorsed on any copy issued to the petitioner under paragraph (5).

(7)   Where a petition is filed at the instance of a company's administrator the petition shall—

    (a)   be expressed to be the petition of the company by its administrator,

    (b)   state the name of the administrator, [the court case number and the date that the company entered administration], and

    (c)   where applicable, contain an application under paragraph 79 of Schedule B1, requesting that the appointment of the administrator shall cease to have effect.

(8)   Any petition filed in relation to a company in respect of which there is in force a voluntary arrangement under Part I of the Act or which is in administration shall be presented to the court to which the nominee's report under section 2 was submitted or the court having jurisdiction for the administration.

(9) Any petition such as is mentioned in paragraph (7) above or presented by the supervisor of a voluntary arrangement under Part I of the Act in force for the company shall be treated as if it were a petition filed by contributories, and Chapter 4 in this Part of the Rules shall apply accordingly.

(10) Where a petition contains a request for the appointment of a person as liquidator in accordance with section 140 (appointment of former administrator or supervisor as liquidator) the person whose appointment is sought shall, not less than 2 days before the return day for the petition, file in court a report including particulars of—

(a) a date on which he notified creditors of the company, either in writing or at a meeting of creditors, of the intention to seek his appointment as liquidator, such date to be at least 10 days before the day on which the report under this paragraph is filed, and

(b) details of any response from creditors to that notification, including any objections to his appointment.

4.8 Service of petition

(1) The following paragraphs apply as regards service of the petition on the company (where the petitioner is other than the company itself); and references to the petition are to a copy of the petition bearing the seal of the court in which it is presented.

(2) Subject as follows, the petition shall be served at the company's registered office, that is to say—

(a) the place which is specified, in the company's statement delivered under section 9 of the Companies Act as the intended situation of its registered office on incorporation, or

(b) if notice has been given by the company to the registrar of companies under section 87 of that Act (change of registered office), the place specified in that notice or, as the case may be, in the last such notice.

(3) Service of the petition at the registered office may be effected in any of the following ways—

(a) it may be handed to a person who there and then acknowledges himself to be, or to the best of the server's knowledge, information and belief is, a director or other officer, or employee, of the company; or

(b) it may be handed to a person who there and then acknowledges himself to be authorized to accept service of documents on the company's behalf; or

(c) in the absence of any such person as is mentioned in sub-paragraph (a) or (b), it may be deposited at or about the registered office in such a way that it is likely to come to the notice of a person attending at the office.

(4) If for any reason service at the registered office is not practicable, or the company has no registered office or is an unregistered company, the petition may be served on the company by

leaving it at the company's last known principal place of business in such a way that it is likely to come to the attention of a person attending there, or by delivering it to the secretary or some director, manager or principal officer of the company, wherever that person may be found.

(5)   In the case of an oversea company, service may be effected in any manner provided for by section 1139(2) of the Companies Act.

(6)   If for any reason it is impracticable to effect service as provided by paragraphs (2) to (5), the petition may be served in such other manner as the court may [approve or] direct.

(7)   Application for leave of the court under paragraph (6) may be made *ex parte*, on affidavit stating what steps have been taken to comply with paragraphs (2) to (5), and the reasons why it is impracticable to effect service as there provided.

4.9 Proof of service

(1)   Service of the petition shall be proved by affidavit, specifying the manner of service.

(2)   The affidavit shall have exhibited to it—

(a)   a sealed copy of the petition, and

(b)   if substituted service has been ordered, a sealed copy of the order;

and it shall be filed in court immediately after service.

4.10 Other persons to receive copies of petition

(1)   If to the petitioner's knowledge the company is in course of being wound up voluntarily, a copy of the petition shall be sent by him to the liquidator.

(2)   If to the petitioner's knowledge an administrative receiver has been appointed in relation to the company, or [the company is in administration], a copy of the petition shall be sent by him to the receiver or, as the case may be, the administrator.

(3)   If to the petitioner's knowledge there is in force for the company a voluntary arrangement under Part I of the Act, a copy of the petition shall be sent by him to the supervisor of the voluntary arrangement.

(3A) If to the petitioner's knowledge, there is a member State liquidator appointed in main proceedings in relation to the company, a copy of the petition shall be sent by him to that person.

This does not apply if the petitioner referred to in this paragraph is a member State liquidator.

(4)   If the company is an authorized institution or former authorized institution within the meaning of the Banking Act 1987 a copy of the petition shall be sent by the petitioner to the Financial Services Authority.

This does not apply if the petitioner is the Financial Services Authority itself.

(5) A copy of the petition which is required by this Rule to be sent shall be dispatched on the next business day after the day on which the petition is served on the company.

4.11 Advertisement of petition

(1) Unless the court otherwise directs, the petitioner shall give notice of the petition.

(2) The notice shall be gazetted.

(3) Where compliance with paragraph (2) is not reasonably practicable, the court may direct that instead of the notice being gazetted, it shall be given in such other manner as the court thinks fit.

(4) The notice must be made to appear—

    (a) if the petitioner is the company itself, not less than 7 business days before the day appointed for the hearing; and

    (b) otherwise, not less than 7 business days after service of the petition on the company, nor less than 7 business days before the day so appointed.

(5) The notice must state—

    (a) the name, registered number of the company and the address of its registered office, or—

        (i) in the case of an unregistered company, the address of its principal place of business;

        (ii) in the case of an [overseas] company, the address at which service of the petition was effected;

    (b) the name and address of the petitioner;

    (c) where the petitioner is the company itself, the address of its registered office or, in the case of an unregistered company, of its principal place of business;

    (d) the date on which the petition was presented;

    (e) the venue fixed for the hearing of the petition;

    (f) the name and address of the petitioner's solicitor (if any); and

    (g) that any person intending to appear at the hearing (whether to support or oppose the petition) must give notice of his intention in accordance with Rule 4.16.

(6) If notice of the petition is not given in accordance with this Rule, the court may dismiss it.

4.12 Verification of petition

(1) The petition shall be verified by an affidavit that the statements in the petition are true, or are true to the best of the deponent's knowledge, information and belief.

(2) If the petition is in respect of debts due to different creditors, the debts to each creditor must be separately verified.

(3) The petition shall be exhibited to the affidavit verifying it.

(4) The affidavit shall be made—

    (a) by the petitioner (or if there are two or more petitioners, any one of them), or

    (b) by some person such as a director, company secretary or similar company officer, or a solicitor, who has been concerned in the matters giving rise to the presentation of the petition, or

    (c) by some responsible person who is duly authorized to make the affidavit and has the requisite knowledge of those matters.

(5) Where the deponent is not the petitioner himself, or one of the petitioners, he must in the affidavit identify himself and state—

    (a) the capacity in which, and the authority by which, he makes it, and

    (b) the means of his knowledge of the matters sworn to in the affidavit.

(6) The affidavit is prima facie evidence of the statements in the petition to which it relates.

(7) An affidavit verifying more than one petition shall include in its title the names of the companies to which it relates and shall set out, in respect of each company, the statements relied on by the petitioner; and a clear and legible photocopy of the affidavit shall be filed with each petition which it verifies.

(8) The affidavit shall state whether, in the opinion of the person making the application, (i) the EC Regulation will apply and (ii) if so, whether the proceedings will be main proceedings or territorial proceedings.

4.13 Persons entitled to copy of petition

Every director, contributory or creditor of the company is entitled to be furnished by the solicitor for the petitioner (or by the petitioner himself, if acting in person) with a copy of the petition within 2 days after requiring it, on payment of the appropriate fee.

4.14 Certificate of compliance

(1) The petitioner or his solicitor shall, at least 5 days before the hearing of the petition, file in court a certificate of compliance with the Rules relating to service and advertisement.

(2) The certificate shall show—

   (a) the date of presentation of the petition,

   (b) the date fixed for the hearing, and

   (c) the date or dates on which the petition was served and advertised in compliance with the Rules.

   A copy of the advertisement of the petition shall be filed in court with the certificate.

(3) Non-compliance with this Rule is a ground on which the court may, if it thinks fit, dismiss the petition.

Sections 7(4), 122(1), 123 and 124(1) of the Insolvency Act 1986

7 Implementation of proposal
(4) The supervisor—

   (a) may apply to the court for directions in relation to any particular matter arising under the voluntary arrangement, and

   (b) is included among the persons who may apply to the court for the winding up of the company or for an administration order to be made in relation to it.

122 Circumstances in which company may be wound up by the court
(1) A company may be wound up by the court if—

   (a) the company has by special resolution resolved that the company be wound up by the court,

   (b) being a public company which was registered as such on its original incorporation, the company has not been issued with a trading certificate under section 761 of the Companies Act 2006 (requirement as to minimum share capital) and more than a year has expired since it was so registered,

   (c) it is an old public company, within the meaning of the Consequential Provisions Act,

   (d) the company does not commence its business within a year from its incorporation or suspends its business for a whole year,

   (e) except in the case of a private company limited by shares or by guarantee, the number of members is reduced below 2,

   (f) the company is unable to pay its debts,

(fa) at the time at which a moratorium for the company under section 1A comes to an end, no voluntary arrangement approved under Part I has effect in relation to the company,

(g) the court is of the opinion that it is just and equitable that the company should be wound up.

(2) In Scotland, a company which the Court of Session has jurisdiction to wind up may be wound up by the Court if there is subsisting a floating charge over property comprised in the company's property and undertaking, and the court is satisfied that the security of the creditor entitled to the benefit of the floating charge is in jeopardy.

For this purpose a creditor's security is deemed to be in jeopardy if the Court is satisfied that events have occurred or are about to occur which render it unreasonable in the creditor's interests that the company should retain power to dispose of the property which is subject to the floating charge.

124 Application for winding up

(1) Subject to the provisions of this section, an application to the court for the winding up of a company shall be by petition presented either by the company, or the directors, or by any creditor or creditors (including any contingent or prospective creditor or creditors), contributory or contributories[, or by a liquidator (within the meaning of Article 2(b) of the EC Regulation) appointed in proceedings by virtue of Article 3(1) of the EC Regulation or a temporary administrator (within the meaning of Article 38 of the EC Regulation) or by the designated officer for a magistrates' court] in the exercise of the power conferred by section 87A of the Magistrates' Courts Act 1980 (enforcement of fines imposed on companies), or by all or any of those parties, together or separately.

(2) Except as mentioned below, a contributory is not entitled to present a winding-up petition unless either—

(a) the number of members is reduced below 2, or

(b) the shares in respect of which he is a contributory, or some of them, either were originally allotted to him, or have been held by him, and registered in his name, for at least 6 months during the 18 months before the commencement of the winding up, or have devolved on him through the death of a former holder.

(3) A person who is liable under section 76 to contribute to a company's assets in the event of its being wound up may petition on either of the grounds set out in section 122(1)(f) and (g), and subsection (2) above does not then apply; but unless the person is a contributory otherwise than under section 76, he may not in his character as contributory petition on any other ground.

(3A) A winding-up petition on the ground set out in section 122(1)(fa) may only be presented by one or more creditors.

(4) A winding-up petition may be presented by the Secretary of State—

(a)   if the ground of the petition is that in section 122(1)(b) or (c), or

(b)   in a case falling within section 124A or 124B below.

(4AA)   A winding up petition may be presented by the Financial Services Authority in a case falling within section 124C(1) or (2).

(4A) A winding-up petition may be presented by the Regulator of Community Interest Companies in a case falling within section 50 of the Companies (Audit, Investigations and Community Enterprise) Act 2004.

(5)   Where a company is being wound up voluntarily in England and Wales, a winding-up petition may be presented by the official receiver attached to the court as well as by any other person authorized in that behalf under the other provisions of this section; but the court shall not make a winding-up order on the petition unless it is satisfied that the voluntary winding up cannot be continued with due regard to the interests of the creditors or contributories.

124B Petition for winding up of SE
(1)   Where—

(a)   an SE whose registered office is in Great Britain is not in compliance with Article 7 of Council Regulation (EC) No 2157/2001 on the Statute for a European company (the 'EC Regulation') (location of head office and registered office), and

(b)   it appears to the Secretary of State that the SE should be wound up, he may present a petition for it to be wound up if the court thinks it is just and equitable for it to be so.

(2)   This section does not apply if the SE is already being wound up by the court.

(3)   In this section 'SE' has the same meaning as in the EC Regulation.

124C Petition for winding up of SCE
(1)   Where, in the case of an SCE whose registered office is in Great Britain—

(a)   there has been such a breach as is mentioned in Article 73(1) of Council Regulation (EC) No 1435/2003 on the Statute for a European Cooperative Society (SCE) (the 'European Cooperative Society Regulation') (winding up by the court or other competent authority), and

(b)   it appears to the Financial Services Authority that the SCE should be wound up,

the Authority may present a petition for the SCE to be wound up if the court thinks it is just and equitable for it to be so.

(2)   Where, in the case of an SCE whose registered office is in Great Britain—

(a)   the SCE is not in compliance with Article 6 of the European Cooperative Society Regulation (location of head office and registered office, and

(b)   it appears to the Financial Service Authority that the SCE should be wound up,

the Authority may present a petition for the SCE to be wound up if the court thinks it is just and equitable for it to be so.

(3)   This section does not apply if the SCE is already being wound up by the court.

(4)   In this section 'SCE' has the same meaning as in the European Cooperative Society Regulation.

125 Powers of court on hearing of petition

(1)   On hearing a winding-up petition the court may dismiss it, or adjourn the hearing conditionally or unconditionally, or make an interim order, or any other order that it thinks fit; but the court shall not refuse to make a winding-up order on the ground only that the company's assets have been mortgaged to an amount equal to or in excess of those assets, or that the company has no assets.

(2)   If the petition is presented by members of the company as contributories on the ground that it is just and equitable that the company should be wound up, the court, if it is of opinion—

(a)   that the petitioners are entitled to relief either by winding up the company or by some other means, and

(b)   that in the absence of any other remedy it would be just and equitable that the company should be wound up,

shall make a winding-up order; but this does not apply if the court is also of the opinion both that some other remedy is available to the petitioners and that they are acting unreasonably in seeking to have the company wound up instead of pursuing that other remedy.

8.1   WINDING UP PETITION ON JUST AND EQUITABLE GROUNDS

IN THE HIGH COURT OF JUSTICE
CHANCERY DIVISION
COMPANIES COURT

NO: [ ] OF 20[ ]

IN THE MATTER OF BUSTCO LIMITED, REGISTERED NUMBER 011111
AND IN THE MATTER OF THE INSOLVENCY ACT 1986

To the High Court of Justice

The Petition of Joe Sulky of 1 Moan Street, London

1.   BUSTCO LIMITED, ('the Company'), was incorporated on 30th October 1996 under the Companies Act 1985.

2.   The registered office of the Company is at Suite 1, 1 Poor Street, London.

3.   The nominal capital of the Company is £1000 divided into 1000 shares of £1 each. The amount of the capital paid up or credited as paid up is £2.

4.   The Petitioner is the holder of one share of £1 each. The Petitioner's share devolved on him through the death of a former holder.

5.   The principal objects for which the Company was established are as follows: To carry on business as a general trading company and other objects stated in the memorandum of association of the Company.

6.   The Petitioner and the 2nd Respondent, Ian Flakey, are the sole directors of the Company.

7.   The company is successful and in a winding up there would be a substantial surplus for the shareholders.

8.   As the Petitioner and the 2nd Respondent both hold equal numbers of votes as directors and shareholders under the Articles of Association and there is no provision for a casting vote, the company is placed in an impasse whenever there is a dispute between the Petitioner and the 2nd Respondent.

9.   There is a deadlock between the Petitioner and the 2nd Respondent in the day to day management of the Company and this has delayed and stilted the company's ability to make business decisions and the company's ability to adequately or promptly respond to opportunities or circumstances as they present themselves.

10. The 2nd Respondent has offended suppliers and customers of the Company and hindered the performance of the Company's contractual obligations with them. Specifically but without limitation, the Company's client, Iffy & Sniffy Ltd, were lost due to the 2nd Respondent's behaviour towards the employees of that company. This conduct has prejudiced the Company as it has lost sales and referrals, increased the difficulties in negotiating special rates with suppliers and damaged the goodwill that the Company had hitherto enjoyed.

11. The 2nd Respondent has bullied and insulted the Company's staff and chastised them when they complied with the reasonable directions of the Petitioner. This has prejudiced the Company as it has created difficulties in managing and retaining staff and soured the working relationship with the Company's employees.

12. It has become impossible to conduct the business of the Company satisfactorily under the articles of association.

13. In the circumstances, it is just and equitable that the company should be wound up.

14. The Petitioner consents to a section 127 order in the standard form.

15. The Petitioner therefore prays as follows:

    a. that Bustco Limited may be wound up by the court under the provisions of the Insolvency Act 1986, and/or

    b. that such other order may be made as the court thinks fit.

Note: It is intended to serve this Petition on BUSTCO LIMITED and IAN FLAKEY.

ENDORSEMENT

This Petition having been presented to the Court on [ ] 20[ ] will be heard at the Royal Courts of Justice, Strand, London WC2A 2LL on:

Date [ ] of 20[ ]
Time [ ] am/pm

(or as soon thereafter as the Petition can be heard)

The Solicitor to the Petitioner is:

WIGG & CO
1 LAW STREET
LONDON

CHAPTER 9

PERMISSION TO ACT AS A DIRECTOR OF A COMPANY WITH A PROHIBITED NAME

OBJECTIVE

Subject to three statutory exceptions under the Insolvency Rules, directors and shadow directors are prohibited under section 216 of the Insolvency Act 1986 from reusing any name their former company used in the year leading up to its going into liquidation without the permission of the court. The prohibition lasts 5 years.

Failure to observe the law can carry serious civil and criminal consequences for the offending director.[1]

A prohibited name for these purposes is any name by which the liquidated company was known at any time in the 12 months prior to the liquidation, or any name so similar as to suggest an association with that company.

The three statutory exceptions are:

1. Where a company acquires the whole or substantially the whole, of the business of an insolvent company, under arrangements made by an insolvency practitioner acting as its liquidator,

---

[1]   Section 216 and 217 of the Insolvency Rules 1986.

administrator or administrative receiver, or as supervisor of a voluntary arrangement. Creditors must be notified.[2]

2.   Where an individual affected by section 216 applies for leave of the court to use the prohibited name.[3]

3.   The court's leave is not required where the company, though known by the prohibited name within the meaning of the section has:

   a.   been known by that name for the whole period of 12 months ending with the day before the liquidating company went into liquidation; and

   b.   has not at any time in those 12 months been dormant.[4]

APPLICATION

The application should be made by ordinary application if the company is being compulsorily wound up. The application should be made by originating application if the company went into voluntary liquidation. Three copies of the application need to be filed with the court.

Notice of any such proposed application and a copy of the evidence relied on must be given to:

- the court;
- the Official Receiver;
- the Secretary of State.

The Official Receiver, the Secretary of State and the liquidator do not need to be named as respondents to the application.

COURT FEES

Where the application is made by originating application a court fee of £130 is payable.[5] Where the application is made by ordinary application on notice to other parties, a court fee of £60 is payable.[6] Where the application is made by consent or without notice in existing proceedings a court fee of £30 is payable.[7]

---

2   Rule 4.228 of the Insolvency Rules 1986.

3   Rule 4.229 of the Insolvency Rules 1986. There will be no breach within 7 days of the liquidation. If an application for leave is made there is no breach until 6 weeks and 1 day after the date of liquidation or the day on which the court disposes of the application (whichever is the earliest).

4   Rule 4.230 of the Insolvency Rules 1986.

5   Paragraph 3.5 of Schedule 1 to the Civil Proceedings Fees Order 2008.

6   Paragraph 3.12 of Schedule 1 to the Civil Proceedings Fees Order 2008.

7   Paragraph 3.11 of Schedule 1 to the Civil Proceedings Fees Order 2008.

EVIDENCE

The application should be supported by a witness statement by the company's director. This will need to address:

- who makes the application;
- the deponent's capacity to speak for them;
- the old company's name and business;
- the old company's nominal and paid up share capital;
- details of the circumstances leading to the winding up order being made against the old company;
- how the old company became aware of the winding up order;
- the responsibility of the applicant for the failure of the old company;
- how the goodwill and name was acquired by the old company by the new company (and what price was paid);
- the new company's name and business;
- why the new company operating under a name similar to the old company does not present a risk to the public;
- what the role of the applicant in the new company is proposed to be;
- the attitude of the old company's liquidator/Official Receiver to the application.

And should exhibit:

- the director's/liquidator's report on the old company;
- evidence of the sale of the goodwill or name;
- a letter from the liquidator/the Official Receiver stating that he supports/does not oppose the application;
- written evidence of the new company's assets;
- written evidence of the new company's liabilities.

SERVICE

The address for service on the Secretary of State is Prosecution Section, Room 110, PO Box 203, 21 Bloomsbury Street, London WC1B 3QW.

Where the company is in creditors' voluntary as opposed to compulsory liquidation notice does not need to be sent to the Official Receiver and Secretary of State but should be sent instead to the old company's liquidator.

THE FIRST HEARING

The first hearing is before the registrar or district judge. Advocates are not expected to robe. Normally the court will adjourn the case on the first hearing to give directions for the Official Receiver or liquidator to make a report on the reasons for the failure of the old company and the directors' conduct in respect of this. If they have been ordered to provide a report, the Official Receiver will be entitled to be paid his costs of preparing this and attending on the return date.

KEY STATUTORY PROVISIONS

Sections 216 and 217 of the Insolvency Act 1986

216 Restriction on re-use of company names

(1)   This section applies to a person where a company ('the liquidating company') has gone into insolvent liquidation on or after the appointed day and he was a director or shadow director of the company at any time in the period of 12 months ending with the day before it went into liquidation.

(2)   For the purposes of this section, a name is a prohibited name in relation to such a person if—

    (a)   it is a name by which the liquidating company was known at any time in that period of 12 months, or

    (b)   it is a name which is so similar to a name falling within paragraph (a) as to suggest an association with that company.

(3)   Except with leave of the court or in such circumstances as may be prescribed, a person to whom this section applies shall not at any time in the period of 5 years beginning with the day on which the liquidating company went into liquidation—

    (a)   be a director of any other company that is known by a prohibited name, or

    (b)   in any way, whether directly or indirectly, be concerned or take part in the promotion, formation or management of any such company, or

    (c)   in any way, whether directly or indirectly, be concerned or take part in the carrying on of a business carried on (otherwise than by a company) under a prohibited name.

(4)   If a person acts in contravention of this section, he is liable to imprisonment or a fine, or both.

(5)   In subsection (3) 'the court' means any court having jurisdiction to wind up companies; and on an application for leave under that subsection, the Secretary of State or the official receiver may appear and call the attention of the court to any matters which seem to him to be relevant.

(6)   References in this section, in relation to any time, to a name by which a company is known are to the name of the company at that time or to any name under which the company carries on business at that time.

(7)   For the purposes of this section a company goes into insolvent liquidation if it goes into liquidation at a time when its assets are insufficient for the payment of its debts and other liabilities and the expenses of the winding up.

(8)   In this section 'company' includes a company which may be wound up under Part V of this Act.

217 Personal liability for debts, following contravention of s 216

(1)   A person is personally responsible for all the relevant debts of a company if at any time—

(a)   in contravention of section 216, he is involved in the management of the company, or

(b)   as a person who is involved in the management of the company, he acts or is willing to act on instructions given (without the leave of the court) by a person whom he knows at that time to be in contravention in relation to the company of section 216.

(2)   Where a person is personally responsible under this section for the relevant debts of a company, he is jointly and severally liable in respect of those debts with the company and any other person who, whether under this section or otherwise, is so liable.

(3)   For the purposes of this section the relevant debts of a company are—

(a)   in relation to a person who is personally responsible under paragraph (a) of subsection (1), such debts and other liabilities of the company as are incurred at a time when that person was involved in the management of the company, and

(b)   in relation to a person who is personally responsible under paragraph (b) of that subsection, such debts and other liabilities of the company as are incurred at a time when that person was acting or was willing to act on instructions given as mentioned in that paragraph.

(4)   For the purposes of this section, a person is involved in the management of a company if he is a director of the company or if he is concerned, whether directly or indirectly, or takes part, in the management of the company.

(5)   For the purposes of this section a person who, as a person involved in the management of a company, has at any time acted on instructions given (without the leave of the court) by a person whom he knew at that time to be in contravention in relation to the company of section 216 is presumed, unless the contrary is shown, to have been willing at any time thereafter to act on any instructions given by that person.

(6)   In this section 'company' includes a company which may be wound up under Part V.

Rules 4.226 to 4.230 of the Insolvency Rules 1986

4.226 Preliminary
The Rules in this Chapter—

(a)   relate to the leave required under section 216 (restriction on re-use of name of company in insolvent liquidation) for a person to act as mentioned in section 216(3) in relation to a company with a prohibited name, ...

(b)   prescribe the cases excepted from that provision, that is to say, those in which a person to whom the section applies may so act without that leave [, and

(c)   apply to all windings up to which section 216 applies, whether or not the winding up commenced before the coming into force of the Rules].

4.227 Application for leave under s 216(3)

When considering an application for leave under section 216, the court may call on the liquidator, or any former liquidator, of the liquidating company for a report of the circumstances in which that company became insolvent, and the extent (if any) of the applicant's apparent responsibility for its doing so.

4.228 First excepted case

(1)   This Rule applies where—

  (a)   a person ('the person') was within the period mentioned in section 216(1) a director, or shadow director, of an insolvent company that has gone into insolvent liquidation

  (b)   the person acts in all or any of the ways specified in section 216(3) in connection with, or for the purposes of, the carrying on (or proposed carrying on) of the whole or substantially the whole of the business of the insolvent company where that business (or substantially the whole of it) is (or is to be) acquired from the insolvent company under arrangements—

  (i)   made by its liquidator; or
  (ii)   made before the insolvent company entered into insolvent liquidation by an office-holder acting in relation to it as administrator, administrative receiver or supervisor of a voluntary arrangement under Part 1 of the Act.

(2)   The person, will not be taken to have contravened section 216 if prior to his acting in the circumstances set out in paragraph (1) a notice is, in accordance with the requirements of paragraph (3),—

  (a)   given by the person, to every creditor of the insolvent company whose name and address—

  (i)   is known by him; or
  (ii)   is ascertainable by him on the making of such enquiries as are reasonable in the circumstances; and

  (b)   published in the Gazette.

(3)   The notice referred to in paragraph (2)—

  (a)   may, subject to compliance with sub-paragraph (a), be given and published before the completion of the arrangements referred to in paragraph (1)(b) but must be given and published no later than 28 days after that completion;

  (b)   must state—

  (i)   the name and registered number of the insolvent company;
  (ii)   the name of the person;
  (iii) that it is his intention to act (or, where the insolvent company has not entered insolvent liquidation, to act or continue to act) in all or any of the ways specified in section 216(3) in connection with, or for the purposes of, the carrying on of the whole or substantially the whole of the business of the insolvent company; and

   (iv) the prohibited name or, where the company has not entered insolvent liquidation, the name under which the business is being, or is to be, carried on which would be a prohibited name in respect of the person in the event of the insolvent company entering insolvent liquidation; and

 (c) must in the case of notice given to each creditor of the company be given using Form 4.73.

(4) Notice may in particular be given under this Rule—

 (a) prior to the insolvent company entering insolvent liquidation where the business (or substantially the whole of the business) is, or is to be, acquired by another company under arrangements made by an office-holder acting in relation to the insolvent company as administrator, administrative receiver or supervisor of a voluntary arrangement (whether or not at the time of the giving of the notice the director is a director of that other company); or

 (b) at a time where the person is a director of another company where—

   (i) the other company has acquired, or is to acquire, the whole, or substantially the whole, of the business of the insolvent company under arrangements made by its liquidator; and

   (ii) it is proposed that after the giving of the notice a prohibited name should be adopted by the other company.

4.229 Second excepted case

(1) Where a person to whom section 216 applies as having been a director or shadow director of the liquidating company applies for leave of the court under that section not later than 7 days from the date on which the company went into liquidation, he may, during the period specified in paragraph (2) below, act in any of the ways mentioned in section 216(3), notwithstanding that he has not the leave of the court under that section.

(2) The period referred to in paragraph (1) begins with the day on which the company goes into liquidation and ends either on the day falling six weeks after that date or on the day on which the court disposes of the application for leave under section 216, whichever of those days occurs first.

4.230 Third excepted case

The court's leave under section 216(3) is not required where the company there referred to, though known by a prohibited name within the meaning of the section—

 (a) has been known by that name for the whole of the period of 12 months ending with the day before the liquidating company went into liquidation, and

 (b) has not at any time in those 12 months been dormant within the meaning of section 252(5) of the Companies Act.

9.1 ORDINARY APPLICATION FOR PERMISSION TO ACT AS A DIRECTOR OF A COMPANY WITH A PROHIBITED NAME

Rule 7.2
Ordinary Application

IN THE HIGH COURT OF JUSTICE
CHANCERY DIVISION
COMPANIES COURT

NO: [ ] OF 20[ ]

IN THE MATTER OF BUSTCO LIMITED, REGISTERED NUMBER 011111
AND IN THE MATTER OF THE INSOLVENCY ACT 1986

TAKE NOTICE that IAN FLAKEY intends to apply to the Registrar on:

Date: [ ] 20[ ]
Time: [ ] am/pm
Place: Royal Courts of Justice, Strand, London WC2A 2LL

as a former director of BUSTCO LIMITED for an order that he do have permission to be a director of BUSTCO (BOGNOR REGIS) LIMITED pursuant to section 216(3) of the Insolvency Act 1986.

Signed [ ]
Solicitor for the Applicant
Dated [ ] 20[ ]

The names and addresses of the persons upon whom it is intended to serve this application are:

OFFICIAL RECEIVER

The Applicant's address for service is:

SILK & CO
2 LAW STREET
LONDON

If you do not attend, the Court may make such order as it thinks fit.

9.2 DRAFT ORDER GIVING PERMISSION TO ACT AS A DIRECTOR OF A COMPANY WITH A PROHIBITED NAME

IN THE HIGH COURT OF JUSTICE
CHANCERY DIVISION
COMPANIES COURT

NO: [ ] OF 20[ ]

BEFORE MR REGISTRAR WISE
DATED: [ ] 20[ ]

IN THE MATTER OF BUSTCO LIMITED, REGISTERED NUMBER 011111
AND IN THE MATTER OF THE INSOLVENCY ACT 1986

DRAFT ORDER

UPON the application dated [ ] 20[ ]

AND UPON HEARING Counsel for the Applicant

AND UPON READING a letter from the Official Receiver dated [ ] 20[ ]

IT IS ORDERED:

1. That IAN FLAKEY as a former director of BUSTCO LIMITED do have permission to be a director of BUSTCO (BOGNOR REGIS) LIMITED pursuant to section 216(3) of the Insolvency Act 1986.

2. No order for costs.

9.3 **WITNESS STATEMENT IN SUPPORT OF AN APPLICATION FOR PERMISSION TO ACT AS A DIRECTOR OF A COMPANY WITH A PROHIBITED NAME**

Applicant: I Flakey; 1st; IF1, [ ] OF 20[ ]

IN THE HIGH COURT OF JUSTICE
CHANCERY DIVISION
COMPANIES COURT

NO: [ ] OF 20[ ]

IN THE MATTER OF BUSTCO LIMITED, REGISTERED NUMBER 011111
AND IN THE MATTER OF THE INSOLVENCY ACT 1986

1ST WITNESS STATEMENT OF IAN FLAKEY

I, IAN FLAKEY, of 1, The Washouts, Greenshire, Company Director, STATE AS FOLLOWS:

1. I am the Applicant. I make this witness statement in support of my application for permission pursuant to section 216(3) of the Insolvency Act 1986 to be a director of Bustco (Bognor Regis) Limited ('the new company').

2. The matters deposed to in this witness statement are within my own knowledge except where otherwise indicated, in which case I have explained the source of my information or belief.

3. The old Company, Bustco Limited ('the old company') was incorporated on [ ] July 2000.

4. I was a director from July 2000 until November 2009. This was the first company I had ever been involved in.

5. The old company's principal objects provided for the carrying on of business as a widget makers. I was a personal guarantor of the company's overdraft and provided all the company's start up capital.

6. In November 2009 I discovered that the cleaning lady had been stealing from the company and concealing this by falsifying records to suggest bills had been paid when they had not.

7. I was advised throughout by my accountant, Big & Clever. They advised that the business should be sold to a company they incorporated for me called Bustco (Bognor Regis) Limited in 30th December 2009.

8. The agreement provided for the new company taking on responsibility for £1 million of the old company's debts as its purchase price. Big & Clever made sure that the new company paid the correct price for the assets and an independent valuation was undertaken of these.

9. I am able to refer to a copy of the agreement which has the valuation annexed to it marked 'IF1'. This Honourable Court will note that the invoice shows that the new company bought the 'Bustco' brand and the goodwill associated with that name for £0.5 million. The old company ceased trading on that date and the new company started trading in its place.

10. One month prior to the 12-month trading period envisaged under the Insolvency Rules 1986, on 30th November 2010, Her Majesty's Revenue and Customs obtained a winding up order against the company for £1,000 in unpaid VAT.

11. The new company has proved profitable. I refer to a copy of the new company's accounts to 31st December 2010 which shows it had a turnover of £1 million and made a £50,000 profit in its first year's trading marked 'IF2'.

12. The new company employs three members of staff. It is very important that I am able to be a director in the new company. We are still a very small company and I need to and do take a very hands on role.

13. I am advised that because of the possible effect of section 217 of the Insolvency Act 1986 the correct and prudent course would be for me to apply to be a director the new company.

STATEMENT OF TRUTH

I believe that the facts stated in this Witness Statement are true.

Signed [ ]
Full name [*IAN FLAKEY*]
Dated [ ] 20[ ]

CHAPTER 10

APPLICATION FOR AN ADMINISTRATION ORDER

OBJECTIVE

An administration application may be made to a High Court judge under paragraph 12 of Schedule B1 to the Insolvency Act 1986 by all or any of a director, the company or a creditor of the company. Whilst both the company and the directors would normally be entitled to appoint an administrator using the filing procedure, if a winding-up petition has been presented, they can only appoint an administrator by applying for a court order.

The administration order should be granted if the court is satisfied that the company is or is likely to become unable to pay its debts, and that the administration order is reasonably likely to achieve the purpose of administration.[1] Those purposes are either: (1) the rescue of the company as a going concern; or if the administrator cannot (2) he must achieve a better result for creditors as a whole than would be obtained on winding up; or, if he cannot (3) he should sell the company assets to distribute to the secured creditors, provided he does not harm the interests of the creditors as a whole.

---

[1] *Re AA Mutual International Insurance Ltd* [2005] 2 BCLC 8.

APPLICATION FORM

The application should be in Form 2.1B.[2] The application needs to be in the statutory form. It must contain:

- the name and number of the company to be wound up;
- the name of the applicant;
- the capacity in which the applicant brings the application;
- the date when the company was incorporated and under which Companies Act;
- the address of the registered office;
- the nominal capital of the company;
- the issued paid up capital of the company;
- the principal objects for which the company was established;
- particulars of the debt owed to the petitioner including the amount;
- particulars of the facts which the petitioner relies on to show that the company is insolvent;[3]
- that the applicant believes that the company is insolvent and unable to pay its debts for the reasons stated in his witness statement;
- whether the company is an insurance undertaking, a credit institution; an investment undertaking providing services involving the holding of funds or securities for third parties or a collective investment undertaking;[4]
- whether the EC Regulation applies;
- whether these proceedings will be main proceedings;[5]
- the name of the proposed administrator;
- that the applicant proposes that during the period for which the order is in force, the affairs, business and property of the company be managed by the proposed administrator;
- that the proposed administrator's statement in Form 2.2B is attached to this application;
- the name and address, reference and contact details of the applicant's solicitors for service;
- that the applicant therefore requests that the court make an administration order in relation to the company;
- that the applicant therefore requests that the named proposed administrator be appointed to be the administrator of the company;
- if a winding up petition has been served, the date of the petition was served;
- if a winding up petition been served, that the applicant requests that the court make an order for the dismissal of the winding up petition or that such other order may be made as the court thinks appropriate;
- the signature of the applicant or his solicitor and the capacity of the signatory.

The application notice, together with the consent of the proposed administrator and the witness statement in support needs to be presented at or posted to the Chambers of the Registrar of the Companies Court, Royal Courts of Justice, Thomas More Building, Strand, London or at a Chancery District Registry or a county court with jurisdiction to wind up companies. Before the application notice is presented the central

---

[2]   Rule 2.2(1) of the Insolvency Rules 1986.

[3]   For example that despite being served with a statutory demand, over 3 weeks have now elapsed without the company paying or satisfying the debt or to making any offer to the petitioner to secure or compound the same.

[4]   Article 1(2) of the EC Regulation.

[5]   As defined in Article 3 of the EC Regulation.

index of winding up petitions at TM2.09 of Thomas More Building should be checked. If an existing petition is already current against the company, the applicant should apply that this petition is dismissed as part of the relief sought and the petitioner should be served (see below).

Sufficient copies should be provided to allow the court to seal and date stamp sufficient copies for service (see below).

COURT FEES

The court fee for an administration application is £130.[6]

CONSENT OF THE PROPOSED ADMINISTRATOR

This is Form 2.2B. The proposed administrator needs to sign this confirming his details, the details of any prior relationship he has had with the company, that he is prepared to act as administrator and that he considers that is reasonably likely that at least of the objectives can be achieved. If there is more than one proposed administrator each should sign a separate Form 2.2B and all the forms should be filed and served with the administration application notice

THE WITNESS STATEMENT

An affidavit or witness statement will need to be filed. This will need to address:

- who the deponent is and what his locus is to make the application;
- that the applicant believes that the company is or is likely to become unable to pay its debts as they fall due;[7]
- a statement of the company's financial position including (to the best of the applicant's knowledge and belief) the company's assets and liabilities, including contingent and prospective liabilities;
- what security it is believed that the creditors hold over the company;
- whether any of the security held entitles the holder to appoint and administrator or administrative receiver;
- what other insolvency proceedings have been initiated in relation to the company and, in particular, whether a petition has been presented to wind up the company;
- where more than one person is to be appointed as administrator, which functions are to be undertaken jointly and where any functions are not to be undertaken jointly and which functions are to be exercised by any or all of the administrators;
- whether or not an administrative receiver has been appointed;
- whether the EC Regulations do apply and if so, why?;
- if the EC Regulations do apply whether the proceedings will be main proceedings or territorial proceedings and why?;

---

[6] Paragraph 3.2 of Schedule 1 to the Civil Proceedings Fees Order 2008.

[7] Where the application for an administration order is made by the floating charge holder, he does not need to show the company is insolvent but only that he could appoint an administrator under paragraph 35 of Schedule B1 to the Insolvency Act 1986 and rule 2.4(1) of the Insolvency Rules 1986.

- what the comparative benefits are of the company being put into administration over liquidation (and why?);
- any material that might be germane to the court's decision as to whether or not to appoint an administrator.

Any supporting evidence should be exhibited.

SERVICE ON INTERESTED PARTIES

The application, the witness statement in support and the administrator's consent need to be effected by either the applicant or by someone on his behalf not less than 5 days before the date fixed for the hearing on all the interested parties. An affidavit of service in Form 2.3B needs to be sworn to prove service on any interested parties.

These include:

- the administrative receiver;
- any person petitioning for the winding up of the company;
- the provisional liquidator;
- a Member State liquidator (if appointed in main proceedings in relation to the company);
- the proposed administrator;
- the company;
- any supervisor of a voluntary arrangement under Part I of the Act.

Notice of the application should also be given at the same time to:

- any enforcement officer or other officer who to his knowledge is charged with an execution or other legal process against the company or its property;
- any person whom the applicant is aware of having distrained against the company's property.

Service on the company is by delivering the documents to its registered office. If delivery to a company's registered office is not practicable, service may be effected by delivery to its last known principal place of business in England and Wales. Otherwise, service is by delivering the documents to an address which he has previously notified as his address for service. If he has not notified any such address, service may be effected by delivery to his usual or last known address. Where the person is an authorised deposit-taker or former authorised deposit-taker and he has appointed, or is or may be entitled to appoint, an administrative receiver of the company, or is, or may be, entitled to appoint an administrator of the company he has not notified an address for service, service can be effected on the office where the company maintains a bank account or, where no such office is known to the applicant, the registered office of that person, or, if there is no such office, his usual or last known address. Delivery of documents to any place or address may be made by leaving them there, or sending them by first class post

THE FIRST HEARING

The first hearing is before a High Court judge who is likely to deal with the substantive application without making further directions. Advocates are not expected to robe.

KEY STATUTORY PROVISIONS

Paragraphs 2, 3, 10 to 15 and 37 to 40 of Schedule B1 to the Insolvency Act 1986

2

A person may be appointed as administrator of a company—

    (a)   by administration order of the court under paragraph 10,

    (b)   by the holder of a floating charge under paragraph 14, or

    (c)   by the company or its directors under paragraph 22.

Purpose of administration

3

(1)   The administrator of a company must perform his functions with the objective of—

    (a)   rescuing the company as a going concern, or

    (b)   achieving a better result for the company's creditors as a whole than would be likely if the company were wound up (without first being in administration), or

    (c)   realising property in order to make a distribution to one or more secured or preferential creditors.

(2)   Subject to sub-paragraph (4), the administrator of a company must perform his functions in the interests of the company's creditors as a whole.

(3)   The administrator must perform his functions with the objective specified in sub-paragraph (1)(a) unless he thinks either—

    (a)   that it is not reasonably practicable to achieve that objective, or

    (b)   that the objective specified in sub-paragraph (1)(b) would achieve a better result for the company's creditors as a whole.

(4)   The administrator may perform his functions with the objective specified in sub-paragraph (1)(c) only if—

    (a)   he thinks that it is not reasonably practicable to achieve either of the objectives specified in sub-paragraph (1)(a) and (b), and

    (b)   he does not unnecessarily harm the interests of the creditors of the company as a whole.

Appointment of Administrator by Court
Administration order

10

An administration order is an order appointing a person as the administrator of a company.

Conditions for making order

11

The court may make an administration order in relation to a company only if satisfied—

    (a)   that the company is or is likely to become unable to pay its debts, and

    (b)   that the administration order is reasonably likely to achieve the purpose of administration.

Administration application

12

(1)   An application to the court for an administration order in respect of a company (an 'administration application') may be made only by—

    (a)   the company,

    (b)   the directors of the company,

    (c)   one or more creditors of the company,

    (d)   the designated officer for a magistrates' court in the exercise of the power conferred by section 87A of the Magistrates' Courts Act 1980 (c 43) (fine imposed on company), or

    (e)   a combination of persons listed in paragraphs (a) to (d).

(2)   As soon as is reasonably practicable after the making of an administration application the applicant shall notify—

    (a)   any person who has appointed an administrative receiver of the company,

    (b)   any person who is or may be entitled to appoint an administrative receiver of the company,

    (c)   any person who is or may be entitled to appoint an administrator of the company under paragraph 14, and

    (d)   such other persons as may be prescribed.

(3)   An administration application may not be withdrawn without the permission of the court.

(4)   In sub-paragraph (1) 'creditor' includes a contingent creditor and a prospective creditor.

(5)   Sub-paragraph (1) is without prejudice to section 7(4)(b).

Powers of court

13

(1) On hearing an administration application the court may—

    (a) make the administration order sought;

    (b) dismiss the application;

    (c) adjourn the hearing conditionally or unconditionally;

    (d) make an interim order;

    (e) treat the application as a winding-up petition and make any order which the court could make under section 125;

    (f) make any other order which the court thinks appropriate.

(2) An appointment of an administrator by administration order takes effect—

    (a) at a time appointed by the order, or

    (b) where no time is appointed by the order, when the order is made.

(3) An interim order under sub-paragraph (1)(d) may, in particular—

    (a) restrict the exercise of a power of the directors or the company;

    (b) make provision conferring a discretion on the court or on a person qualified to act as an insolvency practitioner in relation to the company.

(4) This paragraph is subject to paragraph 39.

Appointment of Administrator by Holder of Floating Charge
Power to appoint

14

(1) The holder of a qualifying floating charge in respect of a company's property may appoint an administrator of the company.

(2) For the purposes of sub-paragraph (1) a floating charge qualifies if created by an instrument which—

    (a) states that this paragraph applies to the floating charge,

    (b) purports to empower the holder of the floating charge to appoint an administrator of the company,

(c)   purports to empower the holder of the floating charge to make an appointment which would be the appointment of an administrative receiver within the meaning given by section 29(2), or

(d)   purports to empower the holder of a floating charge in Scotland to appoint a receiver who on appointment would be an administrative receiver.

(3)   For the purposes of sub-paragraph (1) a person is the holder of a qualifying floating charge in respect of a company's property if he holds one or more debentures of the company secured—

(a)   by a qualifying floating charge which relates to the whole or substantially the whole of the company's property,

(b)   by a number of qualifying floating charges which together relate to the whole or substantially the whole of the company's property, or

(c)   by charges and other forms of security which together relate to the whole or substantially the whole of the company's property and at least one of which is a qualifying floating charge.

Restrictions on power to appoint

15

(1)   A person may not appoint an administrator under paragraph 14 unless—

(a)   he has given at least two business days' written notice to the holder of any prior floating charge which satisfies paragraph 14(2), or

(b)   the holder of any prior floating charge which satisfies paragraph 14(2) has consented in writing to the making of the appointment.

(2)   One floating charge is prior to another for the purposes of this paragraph if—

(a)   it was created first, or

(b)   it is to be treated as having priority in accordance with an agreement to which the holder of each floating charge was party.

(3)   Sub-paragraph (2) shall have effect in relation to Scotland as if the following were substituted for paragraph (a)—

'(a) it has priority of ranking in accordance with section 464(4)(b) of the Companies Act 1985 (c 6),'.

Application where company in liquidation

37

(1)   This paragraph applies where the holder of a qualifying floating charge in respect of a company's property could appoint an administrator under paragraph 14 but for paragraph 8(1)(b).

(2)   The holder of the qualifying floating charge may make an administration application.

(3)   If the court makes an administration order on hearing an application made by virtue of sub-paragraph (2)—

    (a)   the court shall discharge the winding-up order,

    (b)   the court shall make provision for such matters as may be prescribed,

    (c)   the court may make other consequential provision,

    (d)   the court shall specify which of the powers under this Schedule are to be exercisable by the administrator, and

    (e)   this Schedule shall have effect with such modifications as the court may specify.

38

(1)   The liquidator of a company may make an administration application.

(2)   If the court makes an administration order on hearing an application made by virtue of sub-paragraph (1)—

    (a)   the court shall discharge any winding-up order in respect of the company,

    (b)   the court shall make provision for such matters as may be prescribed,

    (c)   the court may make other consequential provision,

    (d)   the court shall specify which of the powers under this Schedule are to be exercisable by the administrator, and

    (e)   this Schedule shall have effect with such modifications as the court may specify.

Effect of administrative receivership

39

(1)   Where there is an administrative receiver of a company the court must dismiss an administration application in respect of the company unless—

    (a)   the person by or on behalf of whom the receiver was appointed consents to the making of the administration order,

    (b)   the court thinks that the security by virtue of which the receiver was appointed would be liable to be released or discharged under sections 238 to 240 (transaction at undervalue and preference) if an administration order were made,

(c)   the court thinks that the security by virtue of which the receiver was appointed would be avoided under section 245 (avoidance of floating charge) if an administration order were made, or

(d)   the court thinks that the security by virtue of which the receiver was appointed would be challengeable under section 242 (gratuitous alienations) or 243 (unfair preferences) or under any rule of law in Scotland.

(2)   Sub-paragraph (1) applies whether the administrative receiver is appointed before or after the making of the administration application.

Effect of Administration
Dismissal of pending winding-up petition

40

(1)   A petition for the winding up of a company—

(a)   shall be dismissed on the making of an administration order in respect of the company, and

(b)   shall be suspended while the company is in administration following an appointment under paragraph 14.

(2)   Sub-paragraph (1)(b) does not apply to a petition presented under—

(a)   section 124A (public interest),

(aa) section 124B (SEs), or

(b)   section 367 of the Financial Services and Markets Act 2000 (c 8) (petition by Financial Services Authority).

(3)   Where an administrator becomes aware that a petition was presented under a provision referred to in sub-paragraph (2) before his appointment, he shall apply to the court for directions under paragraph 63.

Rules 2.2 to 2.14 of the Insolvency Rules 1986

2.2 Affidavit in support of administration application

(1)   Where it is proposed to apply to the court for an administration order to be made in relation to a company, the administration application shall be in Form 2.1B and an affidavit complying with Rule 2.4 must be prepared and sworn, with a view to its being filed with the court in support of the application.

(2)   If the administration application is to be made by the company or by the directors, the affidavit shall be made by one of the directors, or the secretary of the company, stating himself to make it on behalf of the company or, as the case may be, on behalf of the directors.

(3) If the application is to be made by creditors, the affidavit shall be made by a person acting under the authority of them all, whether or not himself one of their number. In any case there must be stated in the affidavit the nature of his authority and the means of his knowledge of the matters to which the affidavit relates.

(4) If the application is to be made by the supervisor of a voluntary arrangement under Part I of the Act, it is to be treated as if it were an application by the company.]

2.3 Form of application

(1) If made by the company or by the directors, the application shall state the name of the company and its address for service, which (in the absence of special reasons to the contrary) is that of the company's registered office.

(2) If the application is made by the directors, it shall state that it is so made under paragraph 12(1)(b); but from and after making it is to be treated for all purposes as the application of the company.

(3) If made by a single creditor, the application shall state his name and address for service.

(4) If the application is made by two or more creditors, it shall state that it is so made (naming them); but from and after making it is to be treated for all purposes as the application of only one of them, named in the application as applying on behalf of himself and other creditors. An address for service for that one shall be specified.

(5) There shall be attached to the application a written statement which shall be in Form 2.2B by each of the persons proposed to be administrator stating—

(a) that he consents to accept appointment;

(b) details of any prior professional relationship(s) that he has had with the company to which he is to be appointed as administrator; and

(c) his opinion that it is reasonably likely that the purpose of administration will be achieved.

2.4 Contents of application and affidavit in support

(1) The administration application shall contain a statement of the applicant's belief that the company is, or is likely to become, unable to pay its debts, except where the applicant is the holder of a qualifying floating charge and is making the application in reliance on paragraph 35.

(2) There shall be attached to the application an affidavit in support which shall contain—

(a) a statement of the company's financial position, specifying (to the best of the applicant's knowledge and belief) the company's assets and liabilities, including contingent and prospective liabilities;

(b) details of any security known or believed to be held by creditors of the company, and whether in any case the security is such as to confer power on the holder to appoint an administrative receiver or to appoint an administrator under paragraph 14. If an administrative receiver has been appointed, that fact shall be stated;

(c)   details of any insolvency proceedings in relation to the company including any petition that has been presented for the winding up of the company so far as within the immediate knowledge of the applicant;

(d)   where it is intended to appoint a number of persons as administrators, details of the matters set out in paragraph 100(2) regarding the exercise of the function of the administrators; and

(e)   any other matters which, in the opinion of those intending to make the application for an administration order, will assist the court in deciding whether to make such an order, so far as lying within the knowledge or belief of the applicant.

(3)   Where the application is made by the holder of a qualifying floating charge in reliance on paragraph 35, he shall give sufficient details in the affidavit in support to satisfy the court that he is entitled to appoint an administrator under paragraph 14.

(4)   The affidavit shall state whether, in the opinion of the person making the application, (i) the EC Regulation will apply and (ii) if so, whether the proceedings will be main proceedings or territorial proceedings.

2.5 Filing of application

(1)   The application (and all supporting documents) shall be filed with the court, with a sufficient number of copies for service and use as provided by Rule 2.6.

(2)   Each of the copies filed shall have applied to it the seal of the court and be issued to the applicant; and on each copy there shall be endorsed the date and time of filing.

(3)   The court shall fix a venue for the hearing of the application and this also shall be endorsed on each copy of the application issued under paragraph (2).

(4)   After the application is filed, it is the duty of the applicant to notify the court in writing of the existence of any insolvency proceedings, and any insolvency proceedings under the EC Regulation, in relation to the company, as soon as he becomes aware of them.

2.6 Service of application

(1)   In the following paragraphs of this Rule, references to the application are to a copy of the application issued by the court under Rule 2.5(2) together with the affidavit in support of it and the documents attached to the application.

(2)   Notification for the purposes of paragraph 12(2) shall be by way of service in accordance with Rule 2.8, verified in accordance with Rule 2.9.

(3)   The application shall be served in addition to those persons referred to in paragraph 12(2)—

(a)   if an administrative receiver has been appointed, on him;

(b)   if there is pending a petition for the winding-up of the company, on the petitioner (and also on the provisional liquidator, if any);

(c)   if a member State liquidator has been appointed in main proceedings in relation to the company, on him;

(d)   on the person proposed as administrator;

(e)   on the company, if the application is made by anyone other than the company;

(f)   if a supervisor of a voluntary arrangement under Part I of the Act has been appointed, on him.

2.7 Notice to officers charged with execution of writs or other process, etc
The applicant shall as soon as reasonably practicable after filing the application give notice of its being made to—

(a)   any enforcement officer or other officer who to his knowledge is charged with an execution or other legal process against the company or its property; and

(b)   any person who to his knowledge has distrained against the company or its property.

2.8 Manner in which service to be effected
(1)   Service of the application in accordance with Rule 2.6 shall be effected by the applicant, or his solicitor, or by a person instructed by him or his solicitor, not less than 5 days before the date fixed for the hearing.

(2)   Service shall be effected as follows—

(a)   on the company (subject to paragraph (3) below), by delivering the documents to its registered office;

(b)   on any other person (subject to paragraph (4) below), by delivering the documents to his proper address;

(c)   in either case, in such other manner as the court may direct.

(3)   If delivery to a company's registered office is not practicable, service may be effected by delivery to its last known principal place of business in England and Wales.

(4)   Subject to paragraph (5), for the purposes of paragraph (2)(b) above, a person's proper address is any which he has previously notified as his address for service; but if he has not notified any such address, service may be effected by delivery to his usual or last known address.

(5)   In the case of a person who—

(a)   is an authorised deposit-taker or former authorised deposit-taker;

(b)

      (i)   has appointed, or is or may be entitled to appoint, an administrative receiver of the company, or

      (ii)   is, or may be, entitled to appoint an administrator of the company under paragraph 14; and

(c)   has not notified an address for service,

the proper address is the address of an office of that person where, to the knowledge of the applicant, the company maintains a bank account or, where no such office is known to the applicant, the registered office of that person, or, if there is no such office, his usual or last known address.

(6)   Delivery of documents to any place or address may be made by leaving them there, or sending them by first class post.

2.9 Proof of service

(1)   Service of the application shall be verified by an affidavit of service in Form 2.3B, specifying the date on which, and the manner in which, service was effected.

(2)   The affidavit of service, with a sealed copy of the application exhibited to it, shall be filed with the court as soon as reasonably practicable after service, and in any event not less than 1 day before the hearing of the application.

2.10 Application to appoint specified person as administrator by holder of qualifying floating charge

(1)   Where the holder of a qualifying floating charge applies to the court under paragraph 36(1)(b), he shall produce to the court—

(a)   the written consent of all holders of any prior qualifying floating charge;

(b)   a written statement in the Form 2.2B made by the specified person proposed by him as administrator; and

(c)   sufficient evidence to satisfy the court that he is entitled to appoint an administrator under paragraph 14.

(2)   If an administration order is made appointing the specified person, the costs of the person who made the administration application and the applicant under paragraph 36(1)(b) shall, unless the court otherwise orders, be paid as an expense of the administration.

Chapter 2

2.11 Application where company in liquidation
(1)   Where an administration application is made under paragraph 37 or paragraph 38, the affidavit in support of the administration application shall contain—

(a)   full details of the existing insolvency proceedings, the name and address of the liquidator, the date he was appointed and by whom;

(b)   the reasons why it has subsequently been considered appropriate that an administration application should be made;

(c)   all other matters that would, in the opinion of the applicant, assist the court in considering the need to make provisions in respect of matters arising in connection with the liquidation; and

(d)   the details required in Rules 2.4(2) and (4).

(2)   Where the application is made by the holder of a qualifying floating charge he shall set out sufficient evidence in the affidavit to satisfy the court that he is entitled to appoint an administrator under paragraph 14.

2.12 The hearing
(1)   At the hearing of the administration application, any of the following may appear or be represented—

(a)   the applicant;

(b)   the company;

(c)   one or more of the directors;

(d)   if an administrative receiver has been appointed, that person;

(e)   any person who has presented a petition for the winding-up of the company;

(f)   the person proposed for appointment as administrator;

(g)   if a member State liquidator has been appointed in main proceedings in relation to the company, that person;

(h)   any person that is the holder of a qualifying floating charge;

(j)   any supervisor of a voluntary arrangement under Part I of the Act;

(k)   with the permission of the court, any other person who appears to have an interest justifying his appearance.

(2)   If the court makes an administration order, it shall be in Form 2.4B.

(3)   If the court makes an administration order, the costs of the applicant, and of any person whose costs are allowed by the court, are payable as an expense of the administration.

2.13

Where the court makes an administration order in relation to a company upon an application under paragraph 37 or 38, the court shall include in the order—

(a)   in the case of a liquidator appointed in a voluntary winding-up, his removal from office;

(b)   details concerning the release of the liquidator;

(c)   provision for payment of the expenses of the liquidation;

(d)   provisions regarding any indemnity given to the liquidator;

(e)   provisions regarding the handling or realisation of any of the company's assets in the hands of or under the control of the liquidator;

(f)   such provision as the court thinks fit with respect to matters arising in connection with the liquidation; and

(g)   such other provisions as the court shall think fit.

2.14 Notice of administration order

(1)   If the court makes an administration order, it shall as soon as reasonably practicable send two sealed copies of the order to the person who made the application.

(2)   The applicant shall send a sealed copy of the order as soon as reasonably practicable to the person appointed as administrator.

(3)   If the court makes an order under paragraph 13(1)(d) or any other order under paragraph 13(1)(f), it shall give directions as to the persons to whom, and how, notice of that order is to be given.

10.1 ADMINISTRATION APPLICATION NOTICE

Rule 2.2
Administration application

Name of Company BUSTCO LIMITED	Company number 0123456
In the HIGH COURT OF JUSTICE COMPANIES COURT	*For court use only* Court case number

(a) Insert full name(s)
of applicant(s)

I The application of (a) IAN FLAKEY being

*Delete as applicable

~~*(i) the company, in reliance on paragraph 12(1)(a) of Schedule B1 to the Insolvency Act 1986 ('the Schedule')~~
~~*(ii) the directors, in reliance on paragraph 12(1)(b) of the Schedule~~

Name(s) of all
creditors applying

*(iii) a creditor/a creditor presenting this application on behalf of himself ~~and the following creditors of the company: (b) _____, in reliance on paragraph 12(1)(c) of the Schedule~~

Give details of charge
relied on, date
registered, (if any)
financial limit

~~*(iv) a holder of a qualifying floating charge, in reliance on paragraph 35 of the Schedule:~~
~~(c) _____~~

~~*(v) a holder of a qualifying floating charge, in reliance on paragraph 37 of the Schedule:~~
~~(c) _____~~

~~*(vi) the liquidator of a company, in reliance on paragraph 38 of the Schedule~~

~~*(vii) a [designated officer] for a magistrates' court, in the exercise of the power conferred by section 87A of the Magistrates' Courts Act 1980~~

~~*(viii) the supervisor of a company voluntary arrangement, in reliance on section 7(4)(b) of the Insolvency Act 1986~~

Insert name of
company subject to
application

2 (d) BUSTCO LIMITED
('the company') was incorporated

Insert date of
incorporation

on 30/10/1996 under the Companies Act 1985, and

Insert registered
number

The registered number of the company is 0123456

Insert address of
registered office

3 The registered office of the company is at 1, Poor Street London

Insert amount of
nominal capital and
how it is divided

4 The nominal capital of the company is £ 100 divided into 100 shares of £1 each.

jInsert amount of
capital paid up or
credited as paid up

The amount of the capital paid up or credited as paid up is £2

5 The principal business which is carried on by the company is: Manufacturer of widgets

*Delete as applicable

6 The company *is/is not *an insurance undertaking/credit institution/an investment undertaking providing services involving the holding of funds or securities for third parties/or a collective investment undertaking under Article 1.2 of the EC Regulation

*Delete as applicable
Insert whether main
or territorial
proceedings
(*Delete this
paragraph if
application is in
reliance on paragraph
35 of Schedule B1)

7 For the reasons stated in the *affidavit/witness statement in support of this application it is considered that the EC Regulation *will/will not apply. If it does apply, proceedings will be main proceedings as defined in Article 3 of the EC Regulation.

8 *The applicant(s) believe(s) that the company is or is likely to become unable to pay its debts for the reasons stated in the *affidavit/witness statement in support attached to this application.

Insert full name(s) and
address(es) of
proposed
administrator(s)

9 The applicant(s) propose(s) that during the period for which the order is in force, the affairs, business and property of the company be managed by Mr Grabber of Grabbers LLP
whose statement(s) in Form 2.2B is/are attached to this application.

*Delete as applicable
Insert address for
service – where
applicant is company
or directors this must
be the registered
office of the company
unless special reason
to contrary

10 An affidavit/witness statement in support of this application is attached

11 The *applicant's/applicant's solicitor's address for service is

SILK & CO
1 LAW STREET
LONDON

Insert full name(s) of
proposed
administrator(s)

12 The applicant(s) therefore request(s) as follows:—

(1) that the court make an administration order in relation to BUSTCO LIMITED

(2) that Mr Grabber of Grabbers LLP
be appointed to be the administrator(s) of the said company

(o) Insert details of
any ancillary orders
sought

(3) An order for the dismissal of the winding up petition presented on 6/3/09
or

(4) that such other order may be made as the court thinks appropriate.

*Delete as applicable

Signed

        *Applicant/Applicant's solicitor
(If signing on behalf of firm or company state position or office held)

(Endorsement to be completed by the court]

(p) Insert name and
address of
Court/District
Registry

This application having been presented to the court on _____ will
be heard at (p) _____
_____ on
(Date) _____ at
(Time) _____ hours
(or as soon thereafter as the application can be heard)

The solicitor to the applicant is:—
Name SILK & CO
Address: 1 LAW STREET
LONDON

Telephone No 0207 696 9696

Reference LARRY LAWYER

[Whose agents are:—
Name _____
Address _____
_____
Telephone No _____
Reference _____

10.2   FORM 2.2B – STATEMENT OF PROPOSED ADMINISTRATOR

Rule 2.3
Statement of proposed administrator

Name of Company BUSTCO LIMITED	Company number 013245
In the HIGH COURT OF JUSTICE COMPANIES COURT	*For court use only* Court case number

Insert name and address of proposed administrator	I Mr Grabber of Grabbers LLP hereby certify that I am authorised under the provisions of Part XIII of the Insolvency Act 1986 to act as an insolvency practitioner. IP No: 666 Name of Regulatory Body: INSOLVENCY PRACTITIONERS ASSOCIATION
(b) Insert name of company * Delete as applicable	**2** I consent to act as administrator of BUSTCO LIMITED ('the company') in accordance with the *application/~~notice of appointment~~ of
Insert name of person presenting administration application or making the appointment	IAN FLAKEY
Insert date of application or appointment	Dated 1st APRIL 2008
	3 I am of the opinion that the purpose of administration is reasonably likely to be achieved.
* Delete as applicable	**4** I *~~have~~/have not had any prior professional relationship with the company. (I attach to this Statement a short summary of any prior professional relationship(s) with the company.)

Signed _____

Dated _____]

10.3   FORM 2.3B – AFFIDAVIT OF SERVICE OF ADMINISTRATION APPLICATION

Rule 2.9
Affidavit of service of administration application

Name of Company BUSTCO LIMITED

Company number 012345

In the HIGH COURT OF JUSTICE, CHANCERY DIVISION, COMPANIES COURT

[full name of court]

For court use only
Court case number

(a) Insert full name and address of person making affidavit	I, (a) STEVEN SERVER of THROWIT & RUN PROCESS SERVERS, I SHERLOCK STREET, LONDON
* Delete as applicable	* ~~the applicant~~/acting on behalf of the applicant

STATE ON OATH

I That I did on FRIDAY the Ist day of APRIL 2009, serve the above-named company with a copy of the administration application duly sealed with the seal of the court and its supporting documents by leaving the same at the registered office of the said company at

(b) Insert the address stated in the application to be the company's registered office

I POOR STREET, LONDON

~~**OR** by posting the same on _____ day the~~
~~_____ day of _____ 20 , by ordinary~~
~~post first class mail in an envelope duly pre-paid and properly~~
~~addressed to the said company at its registered office at (b)~~
~~_____~~

_____
_____

(c) Insert name

~~**2** That I did on _____ day the~~
~~_____ day of _____ 20 ,~~
~~serve (c) _____ a person who has appointed or is [or~~
~~may be] entitled to appoint an administrative receiver of the said~~
~~company with a copy of the administration application duly sealed~~
~~with the seal of the court and its supporting documents by leaving~~
~~the same at his proper address at~~

(d) Insert address where served

~~(d) _____~~

~~**OR** by posting the same on _____ day the~~

~~_____ day of_____ 20 , by ordinary post first class mail in an envelope duly pre-paid and properly addressed to the said (c)~~

~~_____~~

~~at (d)_____~~

~~**3** That I did on _____ day the _____ day of_____ 20 , serve (c) _____ the administrative receiver of the said company with a copy of the administration application duly sealed with the seal of the court and its supporting documents by leaving the same at his proper address at (d)~~

~~_____~~

~~**OR** by posting the same on _____ day the _____ day of_____ 20 , by ordinary post first class mail in an envelope duly pre-paid and properly addressed to the said (c)~~

~~_____~~

~~at (d)_____~~

~~**4** That I did on _____ day the _____ day of_____ 20 , serve (c) _____ a holder of a qualifying floating charge being entitled to appoint an administrator of the said company under paragraph 14 of Schedule B1 to the Insolvency Act 1986 with a copy of the administration application duly sealed with the seal of the court and its supporting documents by leaving the same at his proper address at (d)_____~~

~~**OR** by posting the same on _____ day the _____ day of_____ 20 , by ordinary post first class mail in an envelope duly pre-paid and properly addressed to the said (c)~~

~~_____~~

~~at (d)_____~~

5 That I did on Friday the 1st day of APRIL 2009 , serve (c) ANGRY LIMITED who has presented a petition to wind up the said company with a copy of the administration application duly sealed with the seal of the court and its supporting documents by leaving the same at his proper address at (d) 1 UNPAID BILL STREET, LONDON

~~**OR** by posting the same on _____ day the _____ day of_____ 20 , by ordinary post first class mail in an envelope duly pre-paid and properly addressed to the said (c)~~

~~_____~~
~~at (d) _____~~
~~_____~~

~~**6** That I did on _____ day the~~
~~_____ day of _____ 20 , serve (c)~~
~~_____ the provisional liquidator of the said company~~
~~with a copy of the administration application duly sealed with the~~
~~seal of the court and its supporting documents by leaving the same~~
~~at his proper address at~~
~~(d) _____~~
~~**OR** by posting the same on _____ day the~~
~~_____ day of _____ 20 , by ordinary~~
~~post first class mail in an envelope duly pre-paid and properly~~
~~addressed to the said (c)~~
~~_____~~
~~at (d) _____~~
~~_____~~

~~**7** That I did on _____ day the~~
~~_____ day of _____ 20 , serve (c)~~
~~_____ the member State liquidator of the said~~
~~company with a copy of the administration application duly sealed~~
~~with the seal of the court and its supporting documents by leaving~~
~~the same at his proper address at~~
~~(d) _____~~
~~**OR** by posting the same on _____ day the~~
~~_____ day of _____ 20 , by ordinary~~
~~post first class mail in an envelope duly pre-paid and properly~~
~~addressed to the said (c)~~
~~_____~~
~~at (d) _____~~
~~_____~~

8 That I did on FRIDAY the 1st day of APRIL 2008, serve (c) MR
GRABBER OF GRABBER LLP the person proposed to be the
administrator of the said company with a copy of the administration
application duly sealed with the seal of the court and its supporting
documents by leaving the same at his proper address at (d) 1
VULTURE STREET, LONDON
~~**OR** by posting the same on _____ day the~~
~~_____ day of _____ 20 , by ordinary~~
~~post first class mail in an envelope duly pre-paid and properly~~
~~addressed to the said (c)~~
~~_____~~
~~at (d) _____~~
~~_____~~

~~**9** That I did on _____ day the~~
~~_____ day of _____ 20 , serve (c)~~
~~_____ the supervisor of the company voluntary~~
~~arrangement with a copy of the administration application duly~~
~~sealed with the seal of the court and its supporting documents by~~
~~leaving the same at his proper address at (d)~~

_____
_____
_____

~~**OR** by posting the same on _____ day the~~
~~_____ day of _____ 20 , by ordinary~~
~~post first class mail in an envelope duly pre-paid and properly~~
~~addressed to the said (c)~~

_____

~~at (d)~~ _____

_____
_____

A sealed copy of the application and its supporting documents are now produced to me marked 'A'

SWORN by the above named   Signature:
Deponent

This day the _____ 2008   Signature:
BEFORE ME
Name:

_____
Address:

_____
*A Solicitor/Commissioner for
Oaths
(*Delete as applicable)

10.4 WITNESS STATEMENT IN SUPPORT OF AN ADMINISTRATION ORDER AND TO DISMISS A WINDING UP PETITION

Applicant: I Flakey; 1st: IF1: [ ] OF 20[ ]

IN THE HIGH COURT OF JUSTICE
CHANCERY DIVISION
COMPANIES COURT

NO: [ ] OF 20[ ]

IN THE MATTER OF BUSTCO LIMITED
COMPANY NUMBER 0123456
IN THE MATTER OF THE INSOLVENCY ACT 1986

1ST WITNESS STATEMENT OF IAN FLAKEY

I, IAN FLAKEY of Address, director of the above-named company, STATE as follows:

1.   I am a director of Bustco Limited (the 'Company') and also a creditor of the Company. I make this witness statement in support of my application as a director of the Company for the appointment of Mr Grabber of Grabbers LLP as administrator of the Company (the 'Proposed Administrator') and for the dismissal of a winding up petition presented on 1st February 2009 by Angry plc.

2.   Except where I indicate otherwise, the statements in this witness statement are true to the best of my knowledge, information and belief.

3.   There is now produced and shown to me a bundle consisting of true copies of the documents I will refer to in this witness statement marked 'IF1'.

4.   Bustco Limited was incorporated on 30th October 1996 under the Companies Act 1985.

5.   The registered office of the Company is at Suite 1, 1 Poor Street, London.

6.   The nominal capital of the Company is £1000 divided into 1000 shares of £1 each. The amount of the capital paid up or credited as paid up is £2.

7.   The principal objects for which the Company was established are as follows: To carry on business as a general trading company and other objects stated in the memorandum of association of the Company.

8.   The Company's main business was as widget manufacturers. I was one of the company's main directors and its largest shareholder. I loaned the company the sum of £1000 on the basis that the sum would be repayable on demand.

9.   During 2008, given the downturn in the world economy, the demand for widgets fell and we had difficulties with cash flow.

10. Angry plc has filed a winding up petition for unpaid supplies. We simply do not have the money left to pay this sum or the VAT that is now due for payment to Her Majesty's Revenue and Customs. Given the filing of the Winding Up petition and our inability to meet this, I consider that the Company is unable to pay its debts as and when they fall due. It is my opinion that the Company's position has worsened through the deteriorating market conditions and that insufficient income is being generated to meet current overheads.

11. I refer to page [ ] of the exhibit marked 'IF1' which is a true copy of the company's balance sheet, which shows that the company owes £1 million to various creditors and it has assets which appear on the accounts valued at £2,000. This allows a notional value of £1,500 for the goodwill and £500 for the company's widget maker.

12. The Proposed Administrator has certified in his statement filed with the Court that the purpose of the Administration is reasonably likely to be achieved. I have confirmed with him and truly believe that he remains willing and able to take appointment as the Company's administrator. It is my belief that in the circumstances described above it is not reasonably practicable to achieve the rescue of the Company as a going concern in accordance with paragraph 3(1)(a) of Schedule B1 to the Insolvency Act 1986. It is my opinion that the Company cannot continue trading without further working capital.

13. However, I believe that it is possible that an orderly sale of the Company's assets, being the widget maker together with a payment for the company's goodwill, would, in all likelihood, achieve a better result for the Companies creditors as a whole than would be likely if the Company were wound up. On liquidation, the company's goodwill would be valueless as there would no longer any business with which that goodwill could be associated. The widget maker would be unlikely to realise anything because it is rusty and would cost more than its £500 valuation to unbolt it from the floor and remove it.

14. By contrast on an administration, these assets will be sold for £5,000. A notional figure of £3,000 has been offered for the goodwill. I wish to continue the business and would wish to buy the widget maker for sentimental reasons.

15. I refer to page [ ] of the exhibit marked 'IF1' which is a true copy of an estimated comparison statement between Compulsory Liquidation and Administration prepared by Mr Grabber which I believe truly and fairly reflects the comparative positions on liquidation and administration There is no prospect of a recovery in liquidation but (as I will explain) there is a chance for a dividend for unsecured creditors in an administration.

16. There are no secured creditors. There are no creditors who would be entitled to appoint either an administrator or an administrative receiver over the Company.

17. A winding up petition was served on the Company by Angry plc in the sum of £100,000. The petition was served on the Company on 6th March 2009 and will be heard before the High Court on 25 April 2010.

18. The Company's registered office is in the United Kingdom and the Company conducts the administration of its interests within the United Kingdom. To the best of my knowledge and belief therefore, I believe that the EC Regulation will apply to this Application and that these proceedings will be main proceedings as defined in Article 3 of the EC Regulation.

19. For the reasons stated above, I would respectfully request this Court to grant an administration order in the terms sought and dismiss the winding up petition.

STATEMENT OF TRUTH

I believe that the facts stated in this witness statement are true.

Signed [ ]
IAN FLAKEY
Dated [ ] 20[ ]

Applicant: I Flakey: 1st : IFI: [ ] 20[ ]

IN THE HIGH COURT OF JUSTICE
CHANCERY DIVISION
COMPANIES COURT

NO: [ ] of 20[ ]

IN THE MATTER OF BUSTCO LIMITED
COMPANY NUMBER 0123456
IN THE MATTER OF THE INSOLVENCY ACT 1986

EXHIBIT IFI

This is the exhibit marked 'IFI' referred to in the 1st Witness Statement of Ian Flakey

Estimated Comparison Statement

	Notes	Book Value (£)	Administration (£)	Liquidation (£)
Assets				
Tools and Equipment				
Vehicles				
IT Equipment				
Property				
Goodwill				
TOTAL				
Less Statutory fee (@17% after first £2000, up to maximum of £100,000)			Nil	
Secured Creditors (£)				
TOTAL Surplus (Deficiency) after realisation of security available to preferential creditors				
Preferential Creditors (£)				
TOTAL Surplus (Deficiency) available to unsecured				
Unsecured Creditors				
Shareholders loans				
Employee Redundancy and Notice pay				
Bank				
Trade and Expense Creditors				
Deficiency in respect of unsecured creditors				
Estimated dividend (p in £)				

10.5 ADMINISTRATION ORDER (DISMISSING AN EXISTING WINDING UP PETITION)

IN THE HIGH COURT OF JUSTICE
CHANCERY DIVISION
COMPANIES COURT

CASE NO: [ ] OF 20[ ]

IN THE MATTER OF BUSTCO LIMITED
COMPANY NUMBER 0123456
IN THE MATTER OF THE INSOLVENCY ACT 1986

BEFORE THE HONOURABLE MR JUSTICE BEAK
DATED: [ ] 20[ ]

ORDER

UPON THE APPLICATION of IAN FLAKEY of [Address] director of the above-named company ('the Company') presented to the Court on 1st April 2009 in respect of BUSTCO Limited of address

AND UPON HEARING Counsel for the Applicant [and Counsel for Angry plc, the Petitioning Creditor]

AND UPON READING the evidence

AND UPON the Court being satisfied on the evidence before it that the EC Regulation on Insolvency Proceedings (No. 1346/2000) ('the EC Regulation') does apply and that these proceedings are main proceedings as defined in Article 3 of the EC Regulation

IT IS ORDERED that Giles Grabber of Grabbers LLP, of 1 Vulture Street, London be appointed administrator of the Company.

AND IT IS ORDERED that during the period for which this order is in force the affairs, business and property of the Company be managed by the administrator.

AND IT IS ORDERED that the winding up petition of Angry plc number 19 of 2009 presented on 6th March 2009 be dismissed.

AND IT IS FURTHER ORDERED that the costs of the application be paid as an expense of the administration.

This appointment shall take effect from [ ] am/pm on [ ] 20[ ].

Dated [ ] 20[ ]

CHAPTER 11

APPLICATION FOR DIRECTIONS BY AN ADMINISTRATOR

OBJECTIVE

An administrator may apply for directions from the court as to fulfilling his duties,[1] for example as to the appropriate approach to the validity of a charge. The power of the court is limited by the words 'for the purpose of fulfilling his duties'. Thus the court cannot go beyond the purposes for which the order is made.[2]

APPLICATION

The application is made by ordinary application returnable to the district judge or registrar. A copy of the application should be filed at court with one additional copy for each party to be served.[3]

The application should be made on notice to the parties interested in the decision.

---

[1] Paragraph 63 of Schedule B1 to the Insolvency Act 1986.

[2] *Lune Metal Products Ltd* [2007] BCC 217 (the power could not be invoked to allow the court to, say, permit a distribution to creditors).

[3] Rule 7.4(1) of the Insolvency Rules 1986.

COURT FEES

Where the application is made by ordinary application on notice to other parties, a court fee of £60 is payable.[4] Where the application is made without notice in existing proceedings a court fee of £30 is payable.[5]

EVIDENCE

The administrators should file a witness statement in support. This should address:

- that he makes this application as administrator;
- that he seeks the court's directions;
- the question he wants the court to answer;
- why the question needs to be answered;
- the background facts upon which the issue arises;
- the opposing contentions on the question.

The administrator should exhibit:

- evidence of his appointment;
- any documents relevant to the issue;
- any documents relevant to the facts upon which the issue arises.

SERVICE

The usual rule is that, subject to any other express provision, the application must be served at least 14 days before the date fixed for the hearing.[6] However, the court does have power, in cases of urgency, to hear an application immediately with or without notice to the other parties.[7]

Service may be effected by post provided it is addressed to the person it is to be served on and prepaid for either first or second class post.[8] It may be sent to the last known address of the person to be served.[9]

A document sent by first class post is treated as being served on the 2nd business day after posting, unless the contrary is shown.[10] A document sent by second class post is treated as being served on the 4th business day after posting, unless the contrary is shown.[11] The date of posting is presumed to be the date postmarked on the envelope, unless the contrary is shown.[12]

---

[4]　　Paragraph 3.12 of Schedule 1 to the Civil Proceedings Fees Order 2008.

[5]　　Paragraph 3.11 of Schedule 1 to the Civil Proceedings Fees Order 2008.

[6]　　Rule 7.4(5) of the Insolvency Rules 1986.

[7]　　Rule 7.4(6) of the Insolvency Rules 1986.

[8]　　Rule 12.10(1) of the Insolvency Rules 1986.

[9]　　Rule 12.10(1A) of the Insolvency Rules 1986.

[10]　　Rule 12.10(2) of the Insolvency Rules 1986.

[11]　　Rule 12.10(3) of the Insolvency Rules 1986.

[12]　　Rule 12.10(4) of the Insolvency Rules 1986.

Where service of any application or any order of the court is to be made to a person outside England and Wales an application must be made to the registrar for directions as to the manner, timing and proof of service.[13]

The application needs to be supported by a witness statement stating:[14]

- the grounds upon which the application is made;
- in what place the person to be served is either to be found or presumed to be found.

Subject to these provisions, Part 6 of the CPR is deemed to apply under the Insolvency Rules 1986.[15]

THE FIRST HEARING

The first hearing is before the registrar or district judge. Advocates are not expected to robe. The registrar may adjourn the case to the judge or give directions himself.

KEY STATUTORY PROVISIONS

Paragraph 63 of Schedule B1 to the Insolvency Act 1986

63

The administrator of a company may apply to the court for directions in connection with his functions.

---

[13] Rule 12.12(3) of the Insolvency Rules 1986.

[14] Rule 12.12(4) of the Insolvency Rules 1986.

[15] Rule 12.11 of the Insolvency Rules 1986.

11.1 ORDINARY APPLICATION BY THE ADMINISTRATOR FOR DIRECTIONS

Rule 7.2
Ordinary Application

IN THE HIGH COURT OF JUSTICE
CHANCERY DIVISION
COMPANIES COURT

NO: [ ] OF 20[ ]

IN THE MATTER OF BUSTCO LIMITED, REGISTERED NUMBER 011111
AND IN THE MATTER OF THE INSOLVENCY ACT 1986

BETWEEN:-

GILES GRABBER
As Administrator of BUSTCO LIMITED

<u>Applicant</u>

-and-

(1) BRASSIC BANK PLC
(2) IAN FLAKEY

<u>Respondent</u>

TAKE NOTICE that I, Giles Grabber of Grabbers LLP, of 1 Vulture Street, London, as Administrator of BUSTCO LIMITED, intend to apply to the Registrar on:

Date: [ ] 20[ ]
Time: [ ] am/pm
Place: Royal Courts of Justice, Strand, London WC2A 2LL

For directions on the following matters:

1.   Whether and if so to what extent does the debenture and mortgage created on 1st April 2006 by Bustco Limited in favour of the 1st Respondent create a valid and enforceable security over the assets of Bustco Limited?

2.   Such further or other directions as shall to the Court seem fit.

3.   For general liberty to apply.

The grounds upon which I seek the above relief are set out in my witness statement dated 1st April 2009, a true copy of which is served herewith.

Signed [ ]
Solicitor for the Applicant
Dated [ ] 20[ ]

The Applicant's address for service is:

SILK & CO
2 LAW STREET
LONDON

To:
BRASSIC BANK PLC, 1 MONEY STREET, LONDON

If you do not attend, the Court may make such order as it thinks fit.

11.2 WITNESS STATEMENT IN SUPPORT OF AN APPLICATION FOR DIRECTIONS

Applicant: G Grabber: 1st: GG1: [ ] 20[ ]

IN THE HIGH COURT OF JUSTICE
CHANCERY DIVISION
COMPANIES COURT

NO: [ ] OF 20[ ]

IN THE MATTER OF BUSTCO LIMITED, REGISTERED NUMBER 011111
AND IN THE MATTER OF THE INSOLVENCY ACT 1986

BETWEEN:-

GILES GRABBER
As Administrator of BUSTCO LIMITED

Applicant

-and-

(1) BRASSIC BANK PLC
(2) IAN FLAKEY

Respondent

1ST WITNESS STATEMENT OF GILES GRABBER

I, Giles Grabber of Grabbers LLP, of 1 Vulture Street, London, as Administrator of BUSTCO LIMITED, state as follows:

1. I am the Applicant in this application.

2. I make the application in support of my application for directions as to the validity of a mortgage over the freehold property known as and situate at 1 Poor Street, London, registered with Her Majesty's Land Registry under title number 1223345 ('the property') between BUSTCO LIMITED and the Respondent, BRASSIC BANK PLC, given as security over the said property.

3. The matters set out in this witness statement are true and within my own knowledge except where otherwise indicated, in which case I have explained the source of my information or belief.

4. There is now produced and shown to me a bundle consisting of true copies of the documents I will refer to in my witness statements marked 'GG1'.

5. Bustco Limited was incorporated on 30th October 1996 under the Companies Act 1985.

6. The registered office of the Company is at Suite 1, 1 Poor Street, London.

7. The nominal capital of the Company is £1000 divided into 1000 shares of £1 each. The amount of the capital paid up or credited as paid up is £2.

8. The principal objects for which the Company was established are as follows: To carry on business as a general trading company and other objects stated in the memorandum of association of the Company.

9. I was appointed as the administrator of Bustco Limited pursuant to an order of the Court dated 1st April 2008. I refer to page [ ] of 'GG1' which is a true copy of the order appointing me as administrator of Bustco Limited.

10. Bustco Limited appears to have granted Brassic Bank plc a first legal mortgage over their freehold premises, 1 Poor Street, London, which comprises of a warehouse and office building. I refer to page [ ] of 'GG1' which is a true copy of the legal mortgage and to page [ ] of 'GG1' the debenture under which the mortgage was granted.

11. I also refer to page [ ] of 'GG1' which is a true copy of the entries in the land registry affecting the title of the property which shows the legal mortgage.

12. Despite the registration of the mortgage, the director of Bustco Limited, Ian Flakey, disputes that the legal mortgage was validly executed and registered. I also refer to page [ ] of 'GG1' which is a true copy of the correspondence on this issue before my appointment which sets out the detailed legal arguments from the solicitors on both sides.

13. The property at Poor Street is Bustco's principal asset and the issue of whether or not the mortgage is valid will affect the distribution to both Brassic Bank plc and the unsecured creditors.

14. I therefore ask this Honourable Court for directions as to how I should approach the issue of the validity of a mortgage over the freehold property known as and situate at 1 Poor Street, London between BUSTCO LIMITED and the Respondent, BRASSIC BANK PLC, given as security over the said property.

STATEMENT OF TRUTH

I believe that the facts stated in this Witness Statement are true.

Signed [ ]
Full name [*GILES GRABBER*]
Dated [ ] 20[ ]

11.3   DIRECTIONS

IN THE HIGH COURT OF JUSTICE
CHANCERY DIVISION
COMPANIES COURT

NO: [ ] OF 20[ ]

IN THE MATTER OF BUSTCO LIMITED, REGISTERED NUMBER 011111
AND IN THE MATTER OF THE INSOLVENCY ACT 1986

BEFORE MR REGISTRAR WISE
DATED: [ ] 20[ ]

BETWEEN:-

GILES GRABBER
As Administrator of BUSTCO LIMITED

<u>Applicant</u>

-and-

(1) BRASSIC BANK PLC
(2) IAN FLAKEY

<u>Respondent</u>

DRAFT MINUTE OF ORDER

UPON THE APPLICATION of Giles Grabber of Grabbers LLP, Administrator of the above named company, BUSTCO LIMITED ('the Company')

UPON HEARING Counsel for the Applicant and Counsel for Brassic Bank plc, the Respondent

AND UPON READING the evidence noted as being read

IT IS DIRECTED THAT the 1st Respondent's mortgage do take effect and rank as a first legal mortgage over the freehold property known as and situate at 1 Poor Street, London, registered with Her Majesty's Land Registry under title number 1223345 of Bustco Limited.

AND IT IS ORDERED that the 2nd Respondent do pay the 1st Respondent's and the Applicant's costs of and occasioned by the application, such costs to be assessed on a standard basis if not agreed.

AND IT IS ORDERED that the costs of and occasioned by the Applicant (in so far as not recovered from the 2nd Respondent) be paid on an indemnity basis as an expense of the administration.

CHAPTER 12

APPLICATION BY AN ADMINISTRATOR TO SELL PROPERTY SUBJECT TO SECURITY

OBJECTIVE

An administrator[1] may apply to the court for permission to dispose of property subject to security (other than a floating charge) as if it was not subject to that security[2] or goods in the possession of the company under a hire purchase agreement as if the administrator was the owner of the property.[3] A hire purchase agreement, for these purposes, includes a conditional sale agreement, chattel leasing agreement and retention of title agreement.[4]

This however does not affect the priority given to the holder of the security or the owner.[5] The order will usually be made subject to the condition that from the proceeds of sale will be applied to discharge the security or the amount due under the hire purchase agreement: (1) the net proceeds of sale of the property;

---

[1]   Only the administrator may apply: para 71(2)(a) of Schedule B1 to the Insolvency Act 1986.

[2]   Paragraph 71(1) Schedule B1 to the Insolvency Act 1986.

[3]   Paragraph 72(1) Schedule B1 to the Insolvency Act 1986.

[4]   Paragraph 111(1) Schedule B1 to the Insolvency Act 1986.

[5]   Paragraph 71(4) Schedule B1 to the Insolvency Act 1986.

and (2) any additional money required to be added to this to produce the amount determined by the court as the net amount realised upon the sale of the property at market value.[6]

The order is at the discretion of the court and the court will need to be satisfied that disposal of the property would be likely to promote the purpose of the administration of the company.[7]

The leave of the court is not required where the administrator wishes to deal with property subject to a floating charge;[8] disposal does not affect the priority of the floating charge holder.[9]

APPLICATION NOTICE

The application is made by ordinary application. The application should be made on notice to the holder of the security.

COURT FEES

Where the application is made by ordinary application on notice to other parties, a court fee of £60 is payable.[10]

EVIDENCE

The administrators should file a witness statement in support.

This should address:

- that he makes this application as administrator;
- the date of the administration order;
- the purpose of the administration;
- that he seeks the court's permission to sell the property which is subject to security;
- the background facts upon which the issue arises;
- the nature of the asset;
- the value of the asset;
- the nature of the security;
- the value of the debt secured;
- that disposal of the property would be likely to promote the purpose of the administration of the company and why.

---

6   *Stanley J Holmes & Sons Ltd v Davenham Trust plc* [2006] EWCA Civ 1568.
7   Paragraphs 71(2)(b) and 72(b) Schedule B1 to the Insolvency Act 1986.
8   Paragraph 70(1) Schedule B1 to the Insolvency Act 1986.
9   Paragraph 70(2) Schedule B1 to the Insolvency Act 1986.
10   Paragraph 3.12 of Schedule 1 to the Civil Proceedings Fees Order 2008.

The administrator should exhibit:

- evidence of his appointment;
- any documents relevant to the issue of valuation, title, security and the sum secured;
- any documents relevant to the facts upon which the issue arises.

SERVICE

The administrator should immediately upon the court fixing the date for the hearing of the application serve the application and supporting evidence with the date and place of hearing on the holder of the security.[11]

The usual rule is that, subject to any other express provision, the application must be served at least 14 days before the date fixed for the hearing.[12] However, the court does have power, in cases of urgency, to hear an application immediately with or without notice to the other parties.[13]

Service may be effected by post provided it is addressed to the person it is to be served on and prepaid for either first or second class post.[14] It may be sent to the last known address of the person to be served.[15]

A document sent by first class post is treated as being served on the 2nd business day after posting, unless the contrary is shown.[16] A document sent by second class post is treated as being served on the 4th business day after posting, unless the contrary is shown.[17] The date of posting is presumed to be the date postmarked on the envelope, unless the contrary is shown.[18]

Where service of any application or any order of the court is to be made to a person outside England and Wales an application must be made to the registrar for directions as to the manner, timing and proof of service.[19]

The application needs to be supported by a witness statement stating:[20]

- the grounds upon which the application is made;
- in what place the person to be served is either to be found or presumed to be found.

Subject to these provisions, Part 6 of the CPR is deemed to apply under the Insolvency Rules 1986.[21]

---

[11]   Rule 2.66(2) of the Insolvency Rules 1986.
[12]   Rule 7.4(5) of the Insolvency Rules 1986.
[13]   Rule 7.4(6) of the Insolvency Rules 1986.
[14]   Rule 12.10(1) of the Insolvency Rules 1986.
[15]   Rule 12.10(1A) of the Insolvency Rules 1986.
[16]   Rule 12.10(2) of the Insolvency Rules 1986.
[17]   Rule 12.10(3) of the Insolvency Rules 1986.
[18]   Rule 12.10(4) of the Insolvency Rules 1986.
[19]   Rule 12.12(3) of the Insolvency Rules 1986.
[20]   Rule 12.12(4) of the Insolvency Rules 1986.
[21]   Rule 12.11 of the Insolvency Rules 1986.

ORDER

On the order being made, the court will send two sealed copies to the administrator.[22]

The administrator needs to send one copy to the holder of the security or the owner under the agreement.[23]

The administrator needs to send within 14 days[24] the other sealed copy of the order to the registrar of companies with a copy of Form 2.28B.

KEY STATUTORY PROVISIONS

Paragraphs 70 to 73 and 111 of Schedule B1 to the Insolvency Act 1986

Charged property: floating charge

70

(1)   The administrator of a company may dispose of or take action relating to property which is subject to a floating charge as if it were not subject to the charge.

(2)   Where property is disposed of in reliance on sub-paragraph (1) the holder of the floating charge shall have the same priority in respect of acquired property as he had in respect of the property disposed of.

(3)   In sub-paragraph (2) 'acquired property' means property of the company which directly or indirectly represents the property disposed of.

Charged property: non-floating charge

71

(1)   The court may by order enable the administrator of a company to dispose of property which is subject to a security (other than a floating charge) as if it were not subject to the security.

(2)   An order under sub-paragraph (1) may be made only—

(a)   on the application of the administrator, and

(b)   where the court thinks that disposal of the property would be likely to promote the purpose of administration in respect of the company.

(3)   An order under this paragraph is subject to the condition that there be applied towards discharging the sums secured by the security—

(a)   the net proceeds of disposal of the property, and

---

[22]   Rule 2.66(3) of the Insolvency Rules 1986

[23]   Rule 2.66(4) of the Insolvency Rules 1986

[24]   Paragraphs 71(5) and 72(4) of Schedule B1 to the Insolvency Act 1986. It is an offence to fail to comply: paragraphs 71(6) and 72(5) Schedule B1 to the Insolvency Act 1986.

(b)   any additional money required to be added to the net proceeds so as to produce the amount determined by the court as the net amount which would be realised on a sale of the property at market value.

(4)   If an order under this paragraph relates to more than one security, application of money under sub-paragraph (3) shall be in the order of the priorities of the securities.

(5)   An administrator who makes a successful application for an order under this paragraph shall send a copy of the order to the registrar of companies before the end of the period of 14 days starting with the date of the order.

(6)   An administrator commits an offence if he fails to comply with sub-paragraph (5) without reasonable excuse.

Hire-purchase property

72

(1)   The court may by order enable the administrator of a company to dispose of goods which are in the possession of the company under a hire-purchase agreement as if all the rights of the owner under the agreement were vested in the company.

(2)   An order under sub-paragraph (1) may be made only—

(a)   on the application of the administrator, and

(b)   where the court thinks that disposal of the goods would be likely to promote the purpose of administration in respect of the company.

(3)   An order under this paragraph is subject to the condition that there be applied towards discharging the sums payable under the hire-purchase agreement—

(a)   the net proceeds of disposal of the goods, and

(b)   any additional money required to be added to the net proceeds so as to produce the amount determined by the court as the net amount which would be realised on a sale of the goods at market value.

(4)   An administrator who makes a successful application for an order under this paragraph shall send a copy of the order to the registrar of companies before the end of the period of 14 days starting with the date of the order.

(5)   An administrator commits an offence if he fails without reasonable excuse to comply with sub-paragraph (4).

Protection for secured or preferential creditor

73

(1)   An administrator's statement of proposals under paragraph 49 may not include any action which—

(a)   affects the right of a secured creditor of the company to enforce his security,

(b)   would result in a preferential debt of the company being paid otherwise than in priority to its non-preferential debts, or

(c)   would result in one preferential creditor of the company being paid a smaller proportion of his debt than another.

(2)   Sub-paragraph (1) does not apply to—

(a)   action to which the relevant creditor consents,

(b)   a proposal for a voluntary arrangement under Part I of this Act (although this sub-paragraph is without prejudice to section 4(3)), ...

(c)   a proposal for a compromise or arrangement to be sanctioned under Part 26 of the Companies Act 2006 (arrangements and reconstructions), or

(d)   a proposal for a cross-border merger within the meaning of regulation 2 of the Companies (Cross-Border Mergers) Regulations 2007.

(3)   The reference to a statement of proposals in sub-paragraph (1) includes a reference to a statement as revised or modified.

111
(1)   In this Schedule—

'administrative receiver' has the meaning given by section 251,
'administrator' has the meaning given by paragraph 1 and, where the context requires, includes a reference to a former administrator,
...
'correspondence' includes correspondence by telephonic or other electronic means,
'creditors' meeting' has the meaning given by paragraph 50,
'enters administration' has the meaning given by paragraph 1,
'floating charge' means a charge which is a floating charge on its creation,
'in administration' has the meaning given by paragraph 1,
'hire-purchase agreement' includes a conditional sale agreement, a chattel leasing agreement and a retention of title agreement,
'holder of a qualifying floating charge' in respect of a company's property has the meaning given by paragraph 14,
'market value' means the amount which would be realised on a sale of property in the open market by a willing vendor,
'the purpose of administration' means an objective specified in paragraph 3, and
'unable to pay its debts' has the meaning given by section 123.

(1A) In this Schedule, 'company' means—

(a)   a company registered under the Companies Act 2006 in England and Wales or Scotland,

(b)   a company incorporated in an EEA State other than the United Kingdom, or

(c)   a company not incorporated in an EEA State but having its centre of main interests in a member State other than Denmark.

(1B) In sub-paragraph (1A), in relation to a company, 'centre of main interests' has the same meaning as in the EC Regulation and, in the absence of proof to the contrary, is presumed to be the place of its registered office (within the meaning of that Regulation).

(2)   A reference in this Schedule to a thing in writing includes a reference to a thing in electronic form.

(3)   In this Schedule a reference to action includes a reference to inaction

Rules 7.2, 7.4 and 7.8 of the Insolvency Rules 1986

7.2 Interpretation
(1)   In this Chapter, except in so far as the context otherwise requires—

'originating application' means an application to the court which is not an application in pending proceedings before the court; and
'ordinary application' means any other application to the court.

(2)   Every application shall be in the form appropriate to the application concerned.

7.4 Filing and service of application
(1)   The application shall be filed in court, accompanied by one copy and a number of additional copies equal to the number of persons who are to be served with the application.

(2)   Subject as follows in this Rule and the next, or unless the Rule under which the application is brought provides otherwise, or the court otherwise orders, upon the presentation of the documents mentioned in paragraph (1) above, the court shall fix a venue for the application to be heard.

(3)   Unless the court otherwise directs, the applicant shall serve a sealed copy of the application, endorsed with the venue for the hearing, on the respondent named in the application (or on each respondent if more than one).

(4)   The court may give any of the following directions—

(a)   that the application be served upon persons other than those specified by the relevant provision of the Act or Rules;

(b)   that the giving of notice to any person may be dispensed with;

(c)   that notice be given in some way other than that specified in paragraph (3).

(5)   Unless the provision of the Act or Rules under which the application is made provides otherwise, and subject to the next paragraph, the application must be served at least 14 days before the date fixed for the hearing.

(6)   Where the case is one of urgency, the court may (without prejudice to its general power to extend or abridge time limits)—

    (a)   hear the application immediately, either with or without notice to, or the attendance of, other parties, or

    (b)   authorise a shorter period of service than that provided for by paragraph (5);

and any such application may be heard on terms providing for the filing or service of documents, or the carrying out of other formalities, as the court thinks fit.

7.8 Filing and service of affidavits

(1)   Unless the provision of the Act or Rules under which the application is made provides otherwise, or the court otherwise allows—

    (a)   if the applicant intends to rely at the first hearing on affidavit evidence, he shall file the affidavit or affidavits (if more than one) in court and serve a copy or copies on the respondent, not less than 14 days before the date fixed for the hearing, and

    (b)   where a respondent to an application intends to oppose it and to rely for that purpose on affidavit evidence, he shall file the affidavit or affidavits (if more than one) in court and serve a copy or copies on the applicant, not less than 7 days before the date fixed for the hearing.

(2)   Any affidavit may be sworn by the applicant or by the respondent or by some other person possessing direct knowledge of the subject matter of the application.

12.1 ORDINARY APPLICATION BY THE ADMINISTRATOR FOR AN ORDER PERMITTING THE ADMINISTRATOR TO SELL COMPANY'S PROPERTY SUBJECT TO A SECURITY

Rule 7.2
Ordinary Application

IN THE HIGH COURT OF JUSTICE
CHANCERY DIVISION
COMPANIES COURT

NO: [ ] OF 20[ ]

IN THE MATTER OF BUSTCO LIMITED, REGISTERED NUMBER 011111
AND IN THE MATTER OF THE INSOLVENCY ACT 1986

BETWEEN:-

GILES GRABBER
As Administrator of BUSTCO LIMITED

<u>Applicant</u>

-and-

(1) BUSTCO LIMITED
(2) BRASSIC BANK PLC

<u>Respondent</u>

TAKE NOTICE that I, Giles Grabber of Grabbers LLP, of 1 Vulture Street, London, as Administrator of BUSTCO LIMITED, intend to apply to the Judge on:

Date: [ ] 20[ ]
Time: [ ] am/pm
Place: Royal Courts of Justice, Strand, London WC2A 2LL

For an Order in the following terms:

1. That I be authorised to dispose of the freehold property known as and situate at 1 Poor Street, London, registered with Her Majesty's Land Registry under title number 1223345 ['the property'] free of a legal mortgage dated 1st April 2006 between the 1st Respondent, BUSTCO LIMITED, and the 2nd Respondent, BRASSIC BANK PLC, given as security over the said property.

2. That the costs of this application be provided for.

The grounds upon which I seek the above relief are set out in my witness statement dated 1st April 2009, a true copy of which is served herewith.

Signed [ ]
Solicitor for the Applicant
Dated [ ] 20[ ]

The Applicant's address for service is:

SILK & CO
2 LAW STREET
LONDON

To:
BUSTCO, I POOR STREET, LONDON
BRASSIC BANK PLC, I MONEY STREET, LONDON

If you do not attend, the Court may make such order as it thinks fit.

12.2 WITNESS STATEMENT IN SUPPORT OF AN APPLICATION FOR ORDER TO SELL COMPANY'S PROPERTY SUBJECT TO A SECURITY

Applicant: G Grabber: 1st: GG1: [ ] 20[ ]

IN THE HIGH COURT OF JUSTICE
CHANCERY DIVISION
COMPANIES COURT

NO: [ ] OF 20[ ]

IN THE MATTER OF BUSTCO LIMITED, REGISTERED NUMBER 011111
AND IN THE MATTER OF THE INSOLVENCY ACT 1986

BETWEEN:-

GILES GRABBER
As Administrator of BUSTCO LIMITED

<u>Applicant</u>

-and-

(1) BUSTCO LIMITED
(2) BRASSIC BANK PLC

<u>Respondent</u>

_____

1ST WITNESS STATEMENT OF G. GRABBER

_____

I, Giles Grabber of Grabbers LLP, of 1 Vulture Street, London, as Administrator of BUSTCO LIMITED, state as follows:

1. I am the Applicant in this application.

2. I make the application in support of my application that I be authorised to dispose of the freehold property known as and situate at 1 Poor Street, London, registered with Her Majesty's Land Registry under title number 1223345 ('the property') free of a mortgage dated 1st April 2006 between the 1st Respondent, BUSTCO LIMITED, and the 2nd Respondent, BRASSIC BANK PLC, given as security over the said property.

3. The matters set out in this witness statement are true and within my own knowledge except where otherwise indicated, in which case I have explained the source of my information or belief.

4. There is now produced and shown to me a bundle consisting of true copies of the documents I will refer to in my witness statements marked 'GG1'.

5. Bustco Limited was incorporated on 30th October 1996 under the Companies Act 1985.

6. The registered office of the Company is at Suite 1, 1 Poor Street, London.

7. The nominal capital of the Company is £1000 divided into 1000 shares of £1 each. The amount of the capital paid up or credited as paid up is £2.

8. The principal objects for which the Company was established are as follows: To carry on business as a general trading company and other objects stated in the memorandum of association of the Company.

9. I was appointed as the administrator of Bustco Limited pursuant to an order of the Court dated 1st April 2008. I refer to page [ ] of 'GG1' which is a true copy of the order appointing me as administrator of Bustco Limited.

10. Bustco Limited granted Brassic Bank plc a first legal mortgage over their freehold premises, 1 Poor Street, London, which comprises of a warehouse and office building. I refer to page [ ] of 'GG1' which is a true copy of the legal mortgage and to page [ ] of 'GG1' the debenture under which the mortgage was granted.

11. I also refer to page [ ] of 'GG1' which is a true copy of the entries in the land registry affecting the title of the property which shows the legal mortgage.

12. Brassic Bank plc tell me that the sum currently outstanding which is secured by the legal mortgage is £50,001. I also refer to page [ ] of 'GG1' which is a true copy of a letter dated 1st May 2008 confirming that this is the sum presently outstanding under the legal mortgage.

13. Before my appointment a dispute had arisen between Brassic Bank plc and the directors of Bustco Limited dispute the applicability of £5,000 in bank charges raised by Brassic Bank plc. Due to this dispute and without the intervention of this Honourable Court, it is proving impossible to sell the property.

14. I have instructed Sneaky & Creepy, who are commercial estate agents local to the property, to obtain a valuation for the property. I also refer to page [ ] of 'GG1' which is a true copy of their valuation in the sum of £200,000 to 250,000.

15. They tell me that one of their clients, Yakuza plc, is looking for premises in the area and on a speculative basis they have shown them the property. Yakuza plc has indicated that they are prepared to pay an over the market price of £265,000 if we are able to complete quickly. I also refer to page [ ] of 'GG1' which is a true copy of their written offer dated 1 June 2008.

16. In the present difficult market I am anxious that this opportunity is not lost. The sale could discharge the full amount of the monies owed to Brassic Bank plc (including the disputed sums if on my investigation they are indeed found to be due to them).

17.   In the circumstances, I ask that this Honourable Court grant the application as sought.

STATEMENT OF TRUTH

I believe that the facts stated in this Witness Statement are true.

Signed [ ]
Full name [*GILES GRABBER*]
Dated [ ] 20[ ]

12.3 ORDER PERMITTING THE ADMINISTRATOR TO SELL COMPANY'S PROPERTY SUBJECT TO A SECURITY

IN THE HIGH COURT OF JUSTICE
CHANCERY DIVISION
COMPANIES COURT

NO: [ ] OF 20[ ]

IN THE MATTER OF BUSTCO LIMITED, REGISTERED NUMBER 011111
AND IN THE MATTER OF THE INSOLVENCY ACT 1986

BEFORE THE HONOURABLE MR JUSTICE BEAK
DATED: [ ] 20[ ]

BETWEEN:-

GILES GRABBER
As Administrator of BUSTCO LIMITED

Applicant

-and-

(1) BUSTCO LIMITED
(2) BRASSIC BANK PLC

Respondent

_____

DRAFT MINUTE OF ORDER

_____

UPON THE APPLICATION of Giles Grabber of Grabbers LLP, Administrator of the above named company, BUSTCO LIMITED ('the Company')

UPON HEARING Counsel for the Applicant and Counsel for Brassic Bank plc, the 2nd Respondent

AND UPON READING the evidence noted as being read

IT IS ORDERED that the Applicant be and is hereby authorised to dispose of the freehold property known as and situate at 1 Poor Street, London, registered with Her Majesty's Land Registry under title number 1223345 ('the property') on terms no less favourable than those set out in the written offer of Yakuza plc dated 1st June 2008.

AND IT IS ORDERED that upon payment of the purchase price of the said property to the Applicant, the 2nd Respondent do deliver up its legal mortgage over the said property and the entry of the same in the Charges Register affecting the said property be cancelled.

AND IT IS ORDERED that the proceeds of sale of the said property less all reasonable costs and expenses incurred in the sale be paid into a bank account at WEALTHY BANK PLC in the name of the Applicant pending further order of this Honourable Court.

AND IT IS ORDERED that the receipt of the Applicant to the 2nd Respondent shall be good and sufficient discharge for any monies owed by the Company.

AND IT IS ORDERED that the costs of and occasioned by the Applicant and the 2nd Respondent under this application be paid as an expense of the administration.

12.4 NOTICE TO COMPANIES HOUSE OF AN ORDER PERMITTING THE ADMINISTRATOR TO SELL COMPANY'S PROPERTY SUBJECT TO A SECURITY

Notice of order to deal with charged property

2.28B

Name of Company BUSTCO LIMITED
Company number 123456

[full name of court]	In the HIGH COURT OF JUSTICE, CHANCERY DIVISION, COMPANIES COURT Court case number HC 1234
(a) *[Insert full name(s) and address(es) of administrator(s)]*	I/~~We~~ (a) GAVIN GRABBER
* Delete as applicable	administrator(s) of the above company obtained an order for the disposal of *charged property/~~goods in possession of the company under a hire-purchase agreement~~
(b) *[Insert date]*	On (b) 21st JUNE 2008 A copy of the said court order is attached. Signed _____ ~~Joint~~/Administrator(s) Dated _____

Contact Details:
You do not have to give any contact information in the box opposite but if you do, it will help Companies House to contact you if there is a query on the form. The contact information that you give will be visible to searchers of the public record

Tel 0207 000 0000
DX number
666
DX exchange
CHANCERY LANE
Companies House receipt date barcode

When you have completed and signed this form please send it to the Registrar of Companies at:

Companies House, Crown Way, Cardiff, CF14 3UZ
DX 33050 Cardiff

CHAPTER 13

APPLICATION BY A CREDITOR OR MEMBER ALLEGING UNFAIR PREJUDICE BY AN ADMINISTRATOR

OBJECTIVE

A creditor or member may apply to the court to complain that the administrator is either acting or has acted in such a way as to unfairly prejudice his (and others') interests as a member or creditor or proposes to act in such a way.[1] The application may also be made on the basis that the administrator is not undertaking his functions as quickly or as efficiently as reasonably practicable.[2]

The court is given a wide discretion on how to deal with the order. It may grant relief or make any other order it feels appropriate, including making an interim order[3] and may regulate the administrator's functions, require the administrator to do (or not to do) specific acts, require a creditors' meeting to be called or even end the administrator's appointment.[4] The fact that the act was within the administrator's powers or in compliance with a court order allowing the administrator to dispose of company's property subject to a charge or on hire purchase agreement does not prevent the court from reviewing.[5]

---

[1]   Paragraph 75(1) of Schedule B1 to the Insolvency Act 1986.

[2]   Paragraph 75(2) of Schedule B1 to the Insolvency Act 1986.

[3]   Paragraph 75(3) of Schedule B1 to the Insolvency Act 1986.

[4]   Paragraph 75(4) of Schedule B1 to the Insolvency Act 1986.

[5]   Paragraphs 74(5), 71 and 72 of Schedule B1 to the Insolvency Act 1986.

The power however does not allow the court to impede or prevent the implementation of:[6]

- a company voluntary arrangement;
- a compromise or arrangement sanctioned under Part 26 of the Companies Act 2006;
- a cross border merger;[7]
- the administrators proposals approved by a creditor's meeting;[8]
- revisions to the administrators proposals approved by a creditor's meeting.[9]

The court will also not review the reasonable decisions of an administrator to convert an administration into a creditor's voluntary liquidation or reject a proof of debt, even if influenced by a mistake.[10]

APPLICATION NOTICE

The application is made by ordinary application. The application should be made on notice and the administrator should be named as respondent.

The application should set out the particulars of the allegations against the administrator and the relief sought.

COURT FEES

Where the application is made by ordinary application on notice to other parties, a court fee of £60 is payable.[11] Where the application is made by consent a court fee of £30 is payable.[12]

EVIDENCE

The applicant should file a witness statement in support.

This should address:

- the capacity in which the applicant makes this application;
- the date the company was incorporated;
- the registered office of the company;
- the nominal share capital of the company;
- the issued share capital of the company;
- the objects of the company;
- the date of the administration order;
- the purpose of the administration;

---

[6]   Paragraphs 74(6) of Schedule B1 to the Insolvency Act 1986.
[7]   As defined in regulation 2 of the Companies (Cross Border Mergers) Regulations 2007 (SI 2007/2974).
[8]   Paragraph 53 of Schedule B1 to the Insolvency Act 1986.
[9]   Paragraph 54 of Schedule B1 to the Insolvency Act 1986.
[10] *Unidare plc v Cohen* [2006] 2 BCLC 140.
[11] Paragraph 3.12 of Schedule 1 to the Civil Proceedings Fees Order 2008.
[12] Paragraph 3.11 of Schedule 1 to the Civil Proceedings Fees Order 2008.

- the identity of the administrator;
- full particulars of the wrongful or unfair conduct alleged against the administrator;
- how the conduct of the administrator has been unfairly prejudicial to the applicant.

The applicant should exhibit:

- evidence of the applicant's locus;
- evidence of the administrator's appointment;
- evidence of the steps in issue;
- any documents relevant to the issue;
- any documents relevant to the facts upon which the issue arises.

SERVICE

The usual rule is that, subject to any other express provision, the application must be served at least 14 days before the date fixed for the hearing.[13] However, the court does have power, in cases of urgency, to hear an application immediately with or without notice to the other parties.[14]

Service may be effected by post provided it is addressed to the person it is to be served on and prepaid for either first or second class post.[15] It may be sent to the last known address of the person to be served.[16]

A document sent by first class post is treated as being served on the 2nd business day after posting, unless the contrary is shown.[17] A document sent by second class post is treated as being served on the 4th business day after posting, unless the contrary is shown.[18] The date of posting is presumed to be the date postmarked on the envelope, unless the contrary is shown.[19]

Where service of any application or any order of the court is to be made to a person outside England and Wales an application must be made to the registrar for directions as to the manner, timing and proof of service.[20]

The application needs to be supported by a witness statement stating:[21]

- the grounds upon which the application is made;
- in what place the person to be served is either to be found or presumed to be found.

Subject to these provisions, Part 6 of the CPR is deemed to apply under the Insolvency Rules 1986.[22]

---

[13]   Rule 7.4(5) of the Insolvency Rules 1986.

[14]   Rule 7.4(6) of the Insolvency Rules 1986.

[15]   Rule 12.10(1) of the Insolvency Rules 1986.

[16]   Rule 12.10(1A) of the Insolvency Rules 1986.

[17]   Rule 12.10(2) of the Insolvency Rules 1986.

[18]   Rule 12.10(3) of the Insolvency Rules 1986.

[19]   Rule 12.10(4) of the Insolvency Rules 1986.

[20]   Rule 12.12(3) of the Insolvency Rules 1986.

[21]   Rule 12.12(4) of the Insolvency Rules 1986.

THE FIRST HEARING

The first hearing is before the registrar or district judge. Advocates are not expected to robe. Normally the court will adjourn the case on the first hearing and give directions.

ORDER

On the order being made, the court will send a copy to the applicant.

The applicant needs to send one copy to the administrator.

KEY STATUTORY PROVISIONS

Paragraph 74 of Schedule B1 to the Insolvency Act 1986

Challenge to administrator's conduct of company

74

(1)   A creditor or member of a company in administration may apply to the court claiming that—

    (a)   the administrator is acting or has acted so as unfairly to harm the interests of the applicant (whether alone or in common with some or all other members or creditors), or

    (b)   the administrator proposes to act in a way which would unfairly harm the interests of the applicant (whether alone or in common with some or all other members or creditors).

(2)   A creditor or member of a company in administration may apply to the court claiming that the administrator is not performing his functions as quickly or as efficiently as is reasonably practicable.

(3)   The court may—

    (a)   grant relief;

    (b)   dismiss the application;

    (c)   adjourn the hearing conditionally or unconditionally;

    (d)   make an interim order;

    (e)   make any other order it thinks appropriate.

(4)   In particular, an order under this paragraph may—

    (a)   regulate the administrator's exercise of his functions;

---

[22]   Rule 12.11 of the Insolvency Rules 1986.

(b)   require the administrator to do or not do a specified thing;

(c)   require a creditors' meeting to be held for a specified purpose;

(d)   provide for the appointment of an administrator to cease to have effect;

(e)   make consequential provision.

(5)   An order may be made on a claim under sub-paragraph (1) whether or not the action complained of—

(a)   is within the administrator's powers under this Schedule;

(b)   was taken in reliance on an order under paragraph 71 or 72.

(6)   An order may not be made under this paragraph if it would impede or prevent the implementation of—

(a)   a voluntary arrangement approved under Part I,

(b)   a compromise or arrangement sanctioned under art 26 of the Companies Act 2006 (arrangements and reconstructions).

(ba) a cross-border merger within the meaning of regulation 2 of the Companies (Cross-Border Mergers) Regulations 2007, or

(c)   proposals or a revision approved under paragraph 53 or 54 more than 28 days before the day on which the application for the order under this paragraph is made.

13.1   ORDINARY APPLICATION BY A CREDITOR COMPLAINING THAT THE ADMINISTRATOR HAS UNFAIRLY PREJUDICED HIM

Rule 7.2
Ordinary Application

IN THE HIGH COURT OF JUSTICE
CHANCERY DIVISION
COMPANIES COURT

NO: [ ] OF 20[ ]

IN THE MATTER OF BUSTCO LIMITED, REGISTERED NUMBER 011111
AND IN THE MATTER OF THE INSOLVENCY ACT 1986

BETWEEN:-

WILLIAM WHINGER

<u>Applicant</u>

-and-

GILES GRABBER
As Administrator of BUSTCO LIMITED

<u>Respondent</u>

TAKE NOTICE that I, William Whinger of Moan Street, London intend to apply to the Registrar on:

Date: [ ] 20[ ]
Time: [ ] am/pm
Place: Royal Courts of Justice, Strand, London WC2A 2LL

For an Order under paragraph 74 of Schedule B1 to the Insolvency Act 1986 in the following terms:

1.   That Giles Grabber must summon a meeting of the creditors of Bustco Limited (including the Applicant) for the purpose of considering his statement of proposals concerning the administration of Bustco Limited and giving a full and frank account of his actions as administrator and of the conduct of the administration.

2.   That the Respondent pay the Applicant's and Bustco Limited's costs of and occasioned by this application.

The grounds upon which I seek the above relief are set out in my witness statement dated 1st April 2009, a true copy of which is served herewith.

Signed [ ]
Solicitor for the Applicant
Dated [ ] 20[ ]

The Applicant's address for service is:

SILK & CO
2 LAW STREET
LONDON

To:
GILES GRABBER OF GRABBER LLP, 1 VULTURE STREET, LONDON

If you do not attend, the Court may make such order as it thinks fit.

13.2 WITNESS STATEMENT IN SUPPORT OF AN APPLICATION BY A CREDITOR COMPLAINING THAT THE ADMINISTRATOR HAS UNFAIRLY PREJUDICED HIM

Applicant: W Whinger: 1st: WW1: [ ] 20[ ]

IN THE HIGH COURT OF JUSTICE
CHANCERY DIVISION
COMPANIES COURT

NO: [ ] OF 20[ ]

IN THE MATTER OF BUSTCO LIMITED, REGISTERED NUMBER 011111
AND IN THE MATTER OF THE INSOLVENCY ACT 1986

BETWEEN:-

WILLIAM WHINGER

Applicant

-and-

GILES GRABBER
As Administrator of BUSTCO LIMITED

Respondent

_____

1ST WITNESS STATEMENT OF WILLIAM WHINGER

_____

I, William Whinger of Moan Street, London, state as follows:

1.   I am the Applicant in this application. I am a creditor of Bustco Limited.

2.   I make the application in support of my application under paragraph 74 of Schedule B1 to the Insolvency Act 1986 that Giles Grabber be ordered to summon a meeting of the creditors of Bustco Limited (including myself) for the purpose of considering his statement of proposals concerning the administration of Bustco Limited and giving a full and frank account of his actions as administrator and of the conduct of the administration.

3.   The matters set out in this witness statement are true and within my own knowledge except where otherwise indicated, in which case I have explained the source of my information or belief.

4.   There is now produced and shown to me a bundle consisting of true copies of the documents I will refer to in my witness statements marked 'GG1'.

5. I am an unsecured creditor in the sum of £10 in the insolvency of Bustco Limited. I sell stationary and supplied two large boxes of elastic bands to Bustco Limited, the price of which remains due and outstanding. I refer to page [ ] of 'WW1' which is a true copy of my proof of debt with my invoice attached which I sent to Mr Grabber on 1st June 2008.

6. Bustco Limited was incorporated on 30th October 1996 under the Companies Act 1985.

7. The registered office of the Company is at Suite 1, 1 Poor Street, London.

8. The nominal capital of the Company is £1000 divided into 1000 shares of £1 each. The amount of the capital paid up or credited as paid up is £2.

9. The principal objects for which the Company was established are as follows: To carry on business as a general trading company and other objects stated in the memorandum of association of the Company.

10. Mr Grabber was appointed as the administrator of Bustco Limited pursuant to an order of the Court dated 1st April 2008. I refer to page [ ] of 'WW1' which is a true copy of the order appointing him as administrator of Bustco Limited.

11. Mr Grabber is required by paragraph 49 of Schedule B1 to the Insolvency Act 1986 to send notice of his proposals for the administration to all known creditors and to the Registrar of Companies within 56 days of his appointment. No such proposals have been received by me despite the fact that the period of 56 days has now long elapsed.

12. Mr Grabber is required by paragraph 51(2) of Schedule B1 to the Insolvency Act 1986 to hold an initial meeting of all known creditors and to the Registrar of Companies within 70 days of his appointment. No such proposals have been received by me despite the fact that the period of 70 days has now long elapsed.

13. Mr Grabber has failed to comply with his statutory obligations within the requisite time period. I and the other creditors of Bustco Limited are being unfairly prejudiced as we have no information about how the administration is being conducted (if at all).

14. In the circumstances, I ask that this Honourable Court grant the application as sought.

STATEMENT OF TRUTH

I believe that the facts stated in this Witness Statement are true.

Signed [ ]
Full name [*WILLIAM WHINGER*]
Dated [ ] 20[ ]

13.3   ORDER ON AN APPLICATION BY A CREDITOR COMPLAINING THAT THE ADMINISTRATOR HAS UNFAIRLY PREJUDICED HIM

IN THE HIGH COURT OF JUSTICE
CHANCERY DIVISION
COMPANIES COURT

NO: [ ] OF 20[ ]

IN THE MATTER OF BUSTCO LIMITED, REGISTERED NUMBER 011111
AND IN THE MATTER OF THE INSOLVENCY ACT 1986

BEFORE MR REGISTRAR BEAK
DATED: [ ] 20[ ]

BETWEEN:-

WILLIAM WHINGER

Applicant

-and-

GILES GRABBER
As Administrator of BUSTCO LIMITED

Respondent

_____

DRAFT MINUTE OF ORDER

_____

UPON THE APPLICATION of William Whinger, a creditor of the above named company, BUSTCO LIMITED ('the Company') dated [ ] 20[ ].

UPON HEARING Counsel for the Applicant and Counsel for the Respondent

AND UPON READING the evidence noted as being read

IT IS ORDERED that the Respondent must forthwith compile and complete his statement of proposals for the administration of the Company and send the same to the Applicant, all other creditors of the Company and to the Registrar of Companies.

AND IT IS ORDERED that the Respondent must by [ ] 20[ ] summon a meeting of the creditors of the Company (including the Applicant) for the purpose of considering the said statement of proposals concerning the administration of the Company and giving a full and frank account of his actions as administrator and of the conduct of the administration.

AND IT IS ORDERED that the costs of and occasioned by the Applicant and the Company under this application be paid by the Respondent.

CHAPTER 14

APPLICATION BY AN ADMINISTRATOR TO END THE ADMINISTRATION

OBJECTIVE

An administrator may apply to the court for an order that his appointment is to cease to have effect from a specified time.[1]

The administrator is obliged to make this application if:

- he has come to the view that the purpose of the administration cannot be achieved;[2]
- he thinks that the company should never have entered administration;[3]
- a creditors' meeting requires him to make this application;[4]

---

[1] Paragraph 79(1) of Schedule B1 to the Insolvency Act 1986. An administrator is not confined to the mandatory grounds for making an application under this head: *Re TM Kingdom* [2007] BCC 480.

[2] Paragraph 79(2)(a) of Schedule B1 to the Insolvency Act 1986.

[3] Paragraph 79(2)(b) of Schedule B1 to the Insolvency Act 1986.

[4] Paragraph 79(2)(c) of Schedule B1 to the Insolvency Act 1986.

- he was appointed by an order of the court and he thinks that the purposes of the administration have been sufficiently achieved.[5]

APPLICATION

The application is made by ordinary application to the judge. A copy of the application should be filed at court with one additional copy for each party to be served.[6]

Where the administrator also seeks a winding up order, the application should be in the form of a petition.

PROGRESS REPORT

The application notice should have a progress report attached to it, setting out the progress in the administration since the last progress report (if any) or from the date of the company entered administration and a statement indicating what the administrator thinks should be the next steps for the company.[7]

COURT FEES

Where the application is made by ordinary application on notice to other parties, a court fee of £60 is payable.[8]

EVIDENCE

The administrators should file a witness statement in support. This should address:

- that he makes this application as administrator;
- the objects of the administration;
- the reason he seeks the end of his appointment as an administrator;
- what he thinks the next steps should be for the company;[9]
- if the application is made at the request of the creditors meeting, he should indicate whether or not he agrees with the requirement by the creditors;[10]
- if the application is not made at the request of the creditors meeting, he should confirm that he has given notice of his application to the creditors;[11]

---

[5]   Paragraph 79(3) of Schedule B1 to the Insolvency Act 1986. If the administrator was appointed out of court he may choose to either end his appointment by a court application or rely on the alternative procedure under Paragraph 80 of Schedule B1 to the Insolvency Act 1986.

[6]   Rule 7.4(1) of the Insolvency Rules 1986.

[7]   Rule 2.114(1) of the Insolvency Rules 1986.

[8]   Paragraph 3.12 of Schedule 1 to the Civil Proceedings Fees Order 2008.

[9]   Rule 2.114(1) of the Insolvency Rules 1986.

[10]   Rule 2.114(2) of the Insolvency Rules 1986.

[11]   Rule 2.114(3) of the Insolvency Rules 1986.

- if there is an application to wind up, that he has given the creditors' notice whether he intends to seek appointment as liquidator.[12]

The administrator should exhibit:

- evidence of his appointment;
- the progress report (if not separately provided);
- if the application is not made at the request of the creditors meeting, a copy of the notice of his application to the creditors;[13]
- if the application is not made at the request of the creditors meeting, a copies of any responses from the creditors to the notice of his application to the creditors.[14]

NOTICE TO THE CREDITORS

The application should be made on notice to the person who applied for his appointment.

If the administrator combines his application with an application for an order to wind up the company,[15] he must notify the creditors whether he intends to seek appointment as liquidator.[16]

NOTICE TO THE COURT

If the court makes an order to end the administration, the administrator shall send the registrar of companies notice of the court's order in Form 2.33B.

SERVICE

The usual rule is that, subject to any other express provision, the application must be served at least 14 days before the date fixed for the hearing,[17] However, the court does have power, in cases of urgency, to hear an application immediately with or without notice to the other parties.[18]

Service may be effected by post provided it is addressed to the person it is to be served on and prepaid for either first or second class post.[19] It may be sent to the last known address of the person to be served.[20]

---

[12] Rule 2.114(4) of the Insolvency Rules 1986.

[13] Rule 2.114(3) of the Insolvency Rules 1986.

[14] Rule 2.114(3) of the Insolvency Rules 1986.

[15] Section 124 of the Insolvency Act 1986. Whilst no express mention is made of an administrator under section 124 having the power to apply to wind up the company, this does not prevent the application being made because the petition of the administrator is expressed as the petition of the company by its administrator: rule 4.7(7)(a) of the Insolvency Rules 1986.

[16] Rule 2.114(4) of the Insolvency Rules 1986.

[17] Rule 7.4(5) of the Insolvency Rules 1986.

[18] Rule 7.4(6) of the Insolvency Rules 1986.

[19] Rule 12.10(1) of the Insolvency Rules 1986.

[20] Rule 12.10(1A) of the Insolvency Rules 1986.

A document sent by first class post is treated as being served on the 2nd business day after posting, unless the contrary is shown.[21] A document sent by second class post is treated as being served on the 4th business day after posting, unless the contrary is shown.[22] The date of posting is presumed to be the date postmarked on the envelope, unless the contrary is shown.[23]

Where service of any application or any order of the court is to be made to a person outside England and Wales an application must be made to the registrar for directions as to the manner, timing and proof of service.[24]

The application needs to be supported by a witness statement stating:[25]

- the grounds upon which the application is made;
- in what place the person to be served is either to be found or presumed to be found.

Subject to these provisions, Part 6 of the CPR is deemed to apply under the Insolvency Rules 1986.[26]

THE FIRST HEARING

The hearing will be before a High Court judge. The substantive application will be dealt with on the first hearing. Advocates do not robe.

KEY STATUTORY PROVISIONS

Paragraph 79 of Schedule B1 to the Insolvency Act 1986

Court ending administration on application of administrator

79

(1) On the application of the administrator of a company the court may provide for the appointment of an administrator of the company to cease to have effect from a specified time.

(2) The administrator of a company shall make an application under this paragraph if—

(a) he thinks the purpose of administration cannot be achieved in relation to the company,

(b) he thinks the company should not have entered administration, or

(c) a creditors' meeting requires him to make an application under this paragraph.

---

[21]   Rule 12.10(2) of the Insolvency Rules 1986.

[22]   Rule 12.10(3) of the Insolvency Rules 1986.

[23]   Rule 12.10(4) of the Insolvency Rules 1986.

[24]   Rule 12.12(3) of the Insolvency Rules 1986.

[25]   Rule 12.12(4) of the Insolvency Rules 1986.

[26]   Rule 12.11 of the Insolvency Rules 1986.

(3)   The administrator of a company shall make an application under this paragraph if—

(a)   the administration is pursuant to an administration order, and

(b)   the administrator thinks that the purpose of administration has been sufficiently achieved in relation to the company.

(4)   On an application under this paragraph the court may—

(a)   adjourn the hearing conditionally or unconditionally;

(b)   dismiss the application;

(c)   make an interim order;

(d)   make any order it thinks appropriate (whether in addition to, in consequence of or instead of the order applied for).

Rules 2.114, 2.116 and 4.7(7) of the Insolvency Rules 1986

2.114 Application to court by administrator

(1)   An application to court under paragraph 79 for an order ending an administration shall have attached to it a progress report for the period since the last progress report (if any) or the date the company entered administration and a statement indicating what the administrator thinks should be the next steps for the company (if applicable).

(2)   Where the administrator applies to the court because the creditors' meeting has required him to, he shall also attach a statement to the application in which he shall indicate (giving reasons) whether or not he agrees with the creditors' requirement to him to make the application.

(3)   When the administrator applies other than at the request of a creditors' meeting, he shall—

(a)   give notice in writing to the applicant for the administration order under which he was appointed, or the person by whom he was appointed and the creditors of his intention to apply to court at least 7 days before the date that he intends to makes his application; and

(b)   attach to his application to court a statement that he has notified the creditors, and copies of any response from creditors to that notification.

(4)   Where the administrator applies to court under paragraph 79 in conjunction with a petition under section 124 for an order to wind up the company, he shall, in addition to the requirements of paragraph (3), notify the creditors whether he intends to seek appointment as liquidator.

2.116 Notification by administrator of court order

Where the court makes an order to end the administration, the administrator shall notify the registrar of companies in Form 2.33B, attaching a copy of the court order and a copy of his final progress report.

4.7 Presentation and filing of petition

(7)   Where a petition is filed at the instance of a company's administrator the petition shall—

    (a)   be expressed to be the petition of the company by its administrator,

    (b)   state the name of the administrator, [the court case number and the date that the company entered administration], and

    (c)   where applicable, contain an application under paragraph 79 of Schedule B1, requesting that the appointment of the administrator shall cease to have effect.

14.1 ORDINARY APPLICATION BY THE ADMINISTRATOR TO DISCHARGE THE ADMINISTRATION ORDER

Rule 7.2
Ordinary Application

IN THE HIGH COURT OF JUSTICE
CHANCERY DIVISION
COMPANIES COURT

NO: [ ] OF 20[ ]

IN THE MATTER OF BUSTCO LIMITED, REGISTERED NUMBER 011111
AND IN THE MATTER OF THE INSOLVENCY ACT 1986

TAKE NOTICE that I, Giles Grabber of Grabbers LLP, of 1 Vulture Street, London, as Administrator of BUSTCO LIMITED, intend to apply to the Judge on:

Date: [ ] 20[ ]
Time: [ ] am/pm
Place: Royal Courts of Justice, Strand, London WC2A 2LL

For an order in the following terms:

1.   That the administration order be discharged pursuant to paragraph 79(1) of Schedule B1 to the Insolvency Act 1986 on the grounds that the purposes of the administration cannot be achieved in relation to the Company.

2.   That I be released from all liability pursuant to paragraph 79(1) of Schedule B1 to the Insolvency Act 1986.

3.   That my remuneration and expenses incurred in the administration of the Company be fixed by the Court, such expenses to be fixed on a time basis and such expenses to be assessed (where appropriate) on an indemnity basis.

The grounds upon which I seek the above relief are set out in my witness statement dated 1st April 2009, a true copy of which is served herewith.

Signed [ ]
Solicitor for the Applicant
Dated [ ] 20[ ]

The Applicant's address for service is:

SILK & CO
2 LAW STREET
LONDON

It is not intended to serve any person with this application.

14.2   WITNESS STATEMENT IN SUPPORT OF AN APPLICATION BY THE ADMINISTRATOR TO DISCHARGE THE ADMINISTRATION ORDER

Applicant: G Grabber: 1st: GG1: [ ] 20[ ]

IN THE HIGH COURT OF JUSTICE
CHANCERY DIVISION
COMPANIES COURT

NO: [ ] OF 20[ ]

IN THE MATTER OF BUSTCO LIMITED, REGISTERED NUMBER 011111
AND IN THE MATTER OF THE INSOLVENCY ACT 1986

1ST WITNESS STATEMENT OF GILES GRABBER

I, Giles Grabber of Grabbers LLP, of 1 Vulture Street, London, as Administrator of BUSTCO LIMITED, state as follows:

1.   I am the Applicant in this application.

2.   I make the application in support of my application:

    a.   that the administration order be discharged pursuant to paragraph 79(1) of Schedule B1 to the Insolvency Act 1986 on the grounds that the purposes of the administration cannot be achieved in relation to the Company,

    b.   that I be released from all liability pursuant to paragraph 79(1) of Schedule B1 to the Insolvency Act 1986,

    c.   that my remuneration and expenses incurred in the administration of the Company be fixed by the Court, such expenses to be fixed on a time basis and such expenses to be assessed (where appropriate) on an indemnity basis.

3.   The matters set out in this witness statement are true and within my own knowledge except where otherwise indicated, in which case I have explained the source of my information or belief.

4.   There is now produced and shown to me a bundle consisting of true copies of the documents I will refer to in my witness statements marked 'GG1'.

5.   Bustco Limited was incorporated on 30th October 1996 under the Companies Act 1985.

6.   The registered office of the Company is at Suite 1, 1 Poor Street, London.

7.   The nominal capital of the Company is £1000 divided into 1000 shares of £1 each. The amount of the capital paid up or credited as paid up is £2.

8.   The principal objects for which the Company was established are as follows: To carry on business as a general trading company and other objects stated in the memorandum of association of the Company.

9.   I was appointed as the administrator of Bustco Limited pursuant to an order of the Court dated 1st April 2008. I refer to page [ ] of 'GG1' which is a true copy of the order appointing me as administrator of Bustco Limited.

10. When I was appointed it was my belief that in the circumstances described above it is not reasonably practicable to achieve the rescue of the Company as a going concern in accordance with paragraph 3(1)(a) of Schedule B1 to the Insolvency Act 1986. It was my opinion that the Company cannot continue trading without further working capital.

11. However, it was my belief when I was appointed that it is possible that an orderly sale of the Company's assets, being the widget maker together with a payment for the company's goodwill, would, in all likelihood, achieve a better result for the Companies creditors as a whole than would be likely if the Company were wound up. There was an offer from the director, Ian Flakey, to purchase the company's business and assets on a going concern basis. On liquidation the company's goodwill would have been valueless as there would no longer any business with which that goodwill could be associated. The company's widget maker would be unlikely to realise anything because it is rusty and would cost more than its £500 valuation to unbolt it from the floor and remove it.

12. By contrast on an administration, under Mr Flakey's offer these assets were to be sold for £5,000. A notional figure of £3,000 had been offered for the goodwill.

13. Unfortunately, it now transpires that Mr Flakey is a man of straw and never had the resources to honour his offer to purchase the business.

14. I have been unable to find an alternative purchase for the business and assets of the Company.

15. In the circumstances I formed the view that the purposes of the administration can no longer be achieved in relation to the Company.

16. In the circumstances, I am required to apply hat the administration order be discharged pursuant to paragraph 79(1) of Schedule B1 to the Insolvency Act 1986 on the grounds.

17. I also refer to page [ ] of 'GG1' which is a true copy of my progress report in relation to the conduct of the administration to date.

18. I have given notice of my intention to apply to discharge the administration order to Mr Flakey, who originally applied that the Company be placed into administration, and to the creditors of the Company. I refer to page [ ] of 'GG1' which is a true copy of the notice I sent.

19.   I also refer to page [ ] of 'GG1' which is a true copy of the replies I have received in response to the notice of my intention to apply for the discharge of the administration order.

20.   I do not seek appointment as liquidator of the Company.

21.   I therefore ask this Honourable Court to make the order in the terms sought.

STATEMENT OF TRUTH

I believe that the facts stated in this Witness Statement are true.

Signed [ ]
Full name [*GILES GRABBER*]
Dated [ ] 20[ ]

14.3 ORDER DISCHARGING THE ADMINISTRATION ORDER

IN THE HIGH COURT OF JUSTICE
CHANCERY DIVISION
COMPANIES COURT

NO: [ ] OF 20[ ]

IN THE MATTER OF BUSTCO LIMITED, REGISTERED NUMBER 011111
AND IN THE MATTER OF THE INSOLVENCY ACT 1986

BEFORE THE HONOURABLE MR JUSTICE BEAK
DATED: [ ] 20[ ]

DRAFT MINUTE OF ORDER

UPON THE APPLICATION of Giles Grabber of Grabbers LLP, Administrator of the above named company, BUSTCO LIMITED ('the Company')

UPON HEARING Counsel for the Applicant and Counsel for Brassic Bank plc, the Respondent

AND UPON READING the evidence noted as being read

IT IS ORDERED:

1. That the administration order dated 1st April 2008 be discharged pursuant to paragraph 79(1) of Schedule B1 to the Insolvency Act 1986.

2. That the Applicant be released forthwith as administrator of the Company.

3. That the Applicant's remuneration and expenses incurred in the administration of the Company be fixed by the Court, such expenses to be fixed on a time basis and such expenses to be assessed (where appropriate) on an indemnity basis.

14.4   NOTICE TO THE REGISTRAR OF COMPANIES OF THE COURT ORDER DISCHARGING THE ADMINISTRATION ORDER

Rule 2.116
The Insolvency Act 1986

Notice of court order ending administration

                                               2.33B

Name of Company BUSTCO LIMITED
Company number 123456

[full name of court]	In the HIGH COURT OF JUSTICE, CHANCERY DIVISION COMPANIES COURT Court case number 123 OF 2008
(a) *[Insert name(s) and address(es) of administrator(s)]*	I/ We (a) GILES GRABBER OF GRABBERS LLP, OF 1 VULTURE STREET, LONDON
(b) *[Insert name and address of registered office of company]*	having been appointed administrator(s) of (b) BUSTCO LIMITED OF SUITE 1, 1 POOR STREET, LONDON
(c) *[Insert date of appointment]*	on (c) 1st APRIL 2008
(d) *[Insert name of applicant/appointor]*	by (d) IAN FLAKEY
(e) *[Insert date]*	hereby give notice that the court has ordered that the administration shall end on (e) 2ND JULY 2008 and a copy of the court order is attached. I/We attach to this notice a copy of the final progress report. Signed _____ Joint/Administrator(s) Dated 2ND JULY 2008

Contact Details:
You do not have to give any contact information in the box opposite but if you do, it will help to contact you if there is a query on the form. The contact information that you give will be visible to searchers of the public record

Tel 0207 000 0000
DX number
666
DX exchange
CHANCERY LANE
Companies House receipt date barcode

When you have completed and signed this form please send it to the Registrar of Companies at:

Companies House, Crown Way, Cardiff, CF14 3UZ
DX 33050 Cardiff

CHAPTER 15

APPLICATION BY A SECURED CREDITOR TO ENFORCE HIS SECURITY/BRING PROCEEDINGS DURING AN ADMINISTRATION

OBJECTIVE

The conduct of an administration precludes a secured creditor from enforcing his security.[1] There are two exceptions to this rule. Firstly, where he obtains the consent of the administrator[2] and, secondly, where he obtains the consent of the court.[3]

Similar provisions apply to bar during the course of the administration (without either the consent of the administrator or permission of the court) the repossession of the company's goods,[4] the exercise by a landlord of his right of forfeiture or peaceable re-entry[5] or the start or continuation of legal process against the company or its property.[6] Legal process, for this purpose, includes legal proceedings, execution, distress and diligence.[7]

---

[1]   Paragraph 43(2) of Schedule B1 to the Insolvency Act 1986.

[2]   Paragraph 43(2)(a) of Schedule B1 to the Insolvency Act 1986.

[3]   Paragraph 43(2)(b) of Schedule B1 to the Insolvency Act 1986.

[4]   Paragraph 43(3) of Schedule B1 to the Insolvency Act 1986.

[5]   Paragraph 43(4) of Schedule B1 to the Insolvency Act 1986.

[6]   Paragraph 43(5) of Schedule B1 to the Insolvency Act 1986.

[7]   Paragraph 43(5) of Schedule B1 to the Insolvency Act 1986

When considering whether to grant permission, the court will balance the proprietary interests of the secured creditors against the interests of the unsecured creditors.[8]

APPLICATION NOTICE

The application is made by ordinary application to the registrar where there administration was a court appointment. Where the application was made by a paper appointment, the application is made by originating application. The administrator should be named as respondent to the application.

COURT FEES

Where the application is made by ordinary application on notice to other parties, a court fee of £60 is payable.[9]

EVIDENCE

The applicant should serve a witness statement in support.

This should address:

- the capacity in which the deponent makes the application (eg holder of security);
- the nature of the applicant's interest;
- the value of the asset;
- the nature of the security if any;
- the value of the debt owed to the applicant;
- what steps the applicant wishes to take;
- how the applicant's entitlement arises (but for the moratorium) to take the steps he proposes to take;
- the date of the administration order;
- the purpose of the administration;
- that the moratorium created by the administration prevents his taking the proposed steps without the consent of the administrator or the permission of the court;
- whether the administrator's consent has been sought and his response;
- that the applicant seeks permission from the court;
- the nature of the hardship caused to the applicant by being unable to take the proposed steps;
- how taking the proposed steps will affect the likely achievement of the objectives of the administration;
- how taking the proposed steps will affect the interests of the unsecured creditors;
- the nature of the asset.

The applicant should exhibit:

- evidence of the interest that the applicant seeks to enforce;

---

8   *Fashoff (UK) Ltd v Linton* [2008] BCC 542.

9   Paragraph 3.12 of Schedule 1 to the Civil Proceedings Fees Order 2008.

- evidence showing the entitlement to take the proposed steps proposed by the applicant;
- evidence of the level of debt;
- evidence of the value of the asset (if applicable);
- any documents relevant to the issue;
- any documents relevant to the facts upon which the issue arises.

SERVICE

The sealed application showing the return date and supporting evidence needs to be served on the administrator.

The usual rule is that, subject to any other express provision, the application must be served at least 14 days before the date fixed for the hearing,[10] However, the court does have power, in cases of urgency, to hear an application immediately with or without notice to the other parties.[11]

Service may be effected by post provided it is addressed to the person it is to be served on and prepaid for either first or second class post.[12] It may be sent to the last known address of the person to be served.[13]

A document sent by first class post is treated as being served on the 2nd business day after posting, unless the contrary is shown.[14] A document sent by second class post is treated as being served on the 4th business day after posting, unless the contrary is shown.[15] The date of posting is presumed to be the date postmarked on the envelope, unless the contrary is shown.[16]

Where service of any application or any order of the court is to be made to a person outside England and Wales an application must be made to the registrar for directions as to the manner, timing and proof of service.[17]

The application needs to be supported by a witness statement stating:[18]

- the grounds upon which the application is made;
- in what place the person to be served is either to be found or presumed to be found.

Subject to these provisions, Part 6 of the CPR Part 6to apply under the Insolvency Rules 1986.[19]

---

[10] Rule 7.4(5) of the Insolvency Rules 1986.

[11] Rule 7.4(6) of the Insolvency Rules 1986.

[12] Rule 12.10(1) of the Insolvency Rules 1986.

[13] Rule 12.10(1A) of the Insolvency Rules 1986.

[14] Rule 12.10(2) of the Insolvency Rules 1986.

[15] Rule 12.10(3) of the Insolvency Rules 1986.

[16] Rule 12.10(4) of the Insolvency Rules 1986.

[17] Rule 12.12(3) of the Insolvency Rules 1986.

[18] Rule 12.12(4) of the Insolvency Rules 1986.

[19] Rule 12.11 of the Insolvency Rules 1986.

KEY STATUTORY PROVISIONS

Paragraph 43 of Schedule B1 to the Insolvency Act 1986

43

(1)   This paragraph applies to a company in administration.

(2)   No step may be taken to enforce security over the company's property except—

    (a)   with the consent of the administrator, or

    (b)   with the permission of the court.

(3)   No step may be taken to repossess goods in the company's possession under a hire-purchase agreement except—

    (a)   with the consent of the administrator, or

    (b)   with the permission of the court.

(4)   A landlord may not exercise a right of forfeiture by peaceable re-entry in relation to premises let to the company except—

    (a)   with the consent of the administrator, or

    (b)   with the permission of the court.

(5)   In Scotland, a landlord may not exercise a right of irritancy in relation to premises let to the company except—

    (a)   with the consent of the administrator, or

    (b)   with the permission of the court.

(6)   No legal process (including legal proceedings, execution, distress and diligence) may be instituted or continued against the company or property of the company except—

    (a)   with the consent of the administrator, or

    (b)   with the permission of the court.

(6A) An administrative receiver of the company may not be appointed.

(7)   Where the Court gives permission for a transaction under this paragraph it may impose a condition on or a requirement in connection with the transaction.

(8)   In this paragraph 'landlord' includes a person to whom rent is payable.

15.1 APPLICATION FOR LEAVE TO ENFORCE DESPITE THE MORATORIUM UNDER AN ADMINISTRATION

Rule 7.2
Ordinary Application

IN THE HIGH COURT OF JUSTICE
CHANCERY DIVISION
COMPANIES COURT

CASE: [ ] OF 20[ ]

IN THE MATTER OF BUSTCO LIMITED
COMPANY REGISTRATION NUMBER 011111
AND IN THE MATTER OF THE INSOLVENCY ACT 1986

BETWEEN:-

ANGRY PLC

<u>Applicant</u>

-and-

(1) BUSTCO LIMITED
(2) GILES GRABBER
(Administrator of BUSTCO LIMITED)

<u>Respondent</u>

TAKE NOTICE that we, ANGRY PLC, intend to apply to the Registrar on:

Date: [ ] 20[ ]
Time: [ ] am/pm
Place [ ]

For an order in the following terms:

1. For leave from this Honourable Court pursuant to paragraph 43 of Schedule B1 to the Insolvency Act 1986 for ANGRY PLC to exercise its right of peaceable re-entry pursuant to clause 15 of the lease between Angry plc and Bustco Limited dated 1st April 2004.

2. Further and other relief.

3. For an order that the 1st Respondent do pay the Applicant's costs of and occasioned by the application.

Signed [ ]
Solicitor for the Applicant
Dated [ ] 20[ ]

My address for service is:

SMIRK & CO
1 BILE STREET
LONDON

To:
GILES GRABBER, 1 VULTURE STREET, LONDON

If you do not attend, the Court may make such order as it thinks fit.

15.2   WITNESS STATEMENT IN SUPPORT OF AN APPLICATION FOR LEAVE TO ENFORCE DESPITE THE MORATORIUM UNDER THE ADMINISTRATION

Applicant: F Furious: 1st: [ ] 20[ ]

IN THE HIGH COURT OF JUSTICE
CHANCERY DIVISION
COMPANIES COURT

NO: [ ] OF 20[ ]

IN THE MATTER OF BUSTCO LIMITED
COMPANY REGISTRATION NUMBER 011111
AND IN THE MATTER OF THE INSOLVENCY ACT 1986

BETWEEN:-

ANGRY PLC

Applicant

And
(1) BUSTCO LIMITED
(2) GILES GRABBER
(Administrator of BUSTCO LIMITED)

Respondent

1ST WITNESS STATEMENT OF FREDDY FURIOUS

I, FREDDY FURIOUS, of Angry plc, 1 Bile Street, London, Company Director, STATE as follows:

1.   I am a director of the Applicant company. I am duly authorised to make this witness statement on their behalf.

2.   I make this witness statement in support of the Applicant's application for orders granting leave from this Honourable Court pursuant to paragraph 43 of Schedule B1 to the Insolvency Act 1986 for ANGRY PLC to exercise its right of peaceable re-entry pursuant to clause 15 of the lease between Angry plc and Bustco Limited dated 1st April 2004.

3.   The matters stated in this witness statement are true are made from my own knowledge except where otherwise indicated, in which I case I explain the source of my information and belief.

4.   There is now produced and shown to me a bundle marked 'FF1' which contains true copies of the documents I will refer to in support of this application.

5. On 1st April 2004 Angry plc granted Bustco Limited a commercial lease of their factory premises at 1 Poor Street, London for £10,000 per calendar month. I refer to page 1 of 'FF1' which is a true copy of the lease.

6. Under clause 2 of the lease Bustco agreed to pay the rent each month on the first day of each month. The first rental payment would have fallen due on 1st April 2008.

7. Under clause 15 of the lease Angry plc are granted the right to retake possession of the premises in the event that Bustco Limited defaults on any payment of their rent.

8. To date no payments have been made under the lease and Bustco Limited is 12 months in arrears and owes Angry plc £120,000 in unpaid rent.

9. Angry plc has therefore been entitled under the terms of the lease to take peaceable re-entry of the premises since 1st May 2008.

10. On 25th February 2009 I wrote to Bustco Limited stating that I intended to take such steps if they did not pay their arrears by the end of the following month.

11. On 1st March 2009 this Honourable Court made an administration order in respect of the Company.

12. There would be no hardship to the unsecured creditors if the Court were to make the order sought for possession. The lease represents an ongoing liability to the administration of £10,000 per month together even before one considers the ongoing costs of insurance and maintenance. The administrator has shown no intention to trade the business of Bustco Limited from the premises as they are now boarded up.

13. In all the circumstances I ask this Honourable Court to grant the relief sought in this application and grant Angry plc permission to exercise its contractual right to peaceable re-entry of the premises.

STATEMENT OF TRUTH

I believe the facts stated in this witness statement are true.

Signed [ ]
FREDDY FURIOUS
Dated [ ] 20[ ]

15.3 ORDER GRANTING LEAVE TO ENFORCE DESPITE THE MORATORIUM UNDER AN ADMINISTRATION

IN THE HIGH COURT OF JUSTICE
CHANCERY DIVISION
COMPANIES COURT

NO: [ ] OF 20[ ]

IN THE MATTER OF BUSTCO LIMITED
COMPANY REGISTRATION NUMBER 011111
AND IN THE MATTER OF THE INSOLVENCY ACT 1986

BEFORE MR REGISTRAR WISE
DATED: [ ] 20[ ]

BETWEEN:-

ANGRY PLC

Applicant

-and-

(1) BUSTCO LIMITED
(2) GILES GRABBER
(Administrator of BUSTCO LIMITED)

Respondent

DRAFT ORDER

UPON THE APPLICATION of ANGRY PLC, a creditor

AND UPON HEARING Counsel for the Respondents

AND UPON reading the evidence noted as being read

IT IS ORDERED:

1. That ANGRY PLC have leave pursuant to paragraph 49(1) of Schedule B1 to the Insolvency Act 1986 to exercise its right of peaceable re-entry over the premises known as and situate at 1 Poor Street, London pursuant to clause 15 of the lease between Angry plc and Bustco Limited dated 1st April 2004.

2. That the 1st Respondent do pay the Applicant's costs of and occasioned by the application.

CHAPTER 16

APPLICATION FOR LEAVE TO ENFORCE SECURITY OR SEEK POSSESSION DESPITE A MORATORIUM ON A CREDITORS VOLUNTARY ARRANGEMENT

OBJECTIVE

Whilst a creditors voluntary arrangement (CVA) moratorium is in force a company meeting cannot be called or requisitioned, a landlord cannot forfeit the company's lease by peaceable re-entry, security cannot be enforced and goods cannot be repossessed and legal proceedings or process cannot be instituted or proceeded with and execution and distress cannot be levied against the company or its property.

The exception to this rule is where the court gives leave.

APPLICATION

The application is made by ordinary application on notice and should be made to the registrar or district judge.

COURT FEES

Where the application is made by ordinary application on notice to other parties, a court fee of £60 is payable.[1] Where the application is made by consent a court fee of £30 is payable.[2]

EVIDENCE

A witness statement should be prepared in support of the application.

This should address:

- the name and capacity of the deponent to speak for the applicant;
- the nature of the applicant's interest;
- the nature of the security if any;
- the manner or rights of enforcement that the applicant's interest gives him (so far as it is material to the application);
- what steps the applicant wishes to take;
- the amount of money owed to the applicant;
- the value of the asset;
- that a CVA has been entered into and when it was entered into;
- that there is a moratorium is in force;
- that the moratorium created by the CVA prevents his taking the proposed steps without the consent of the administrator or the permission of the court;
- whether the supervisor's consent has been sought and his response;
- that but for the moratorium how the applicant would wish to enforce his interest;
- the consequences for the applicant of his being rendered unable to enforce his interest;
- the consequences for the company and the other creditors of his being allowed to enforce his interest;
- that the applicant seeks permission from the court.

The applicant should exhibit:

- a copy of the arrangement or proposal;
- evidence of the interest that the applicant seeks to enforce;
- evidence showing the entitlement to take the proposed steps proposed by the applicant;
- evidence of the level of debt;
- evidence of the value of the asset (if applicable);
- any documents relevant to the issue;
- any documents relevant to the facts upon which the issue arises.

---

[1]   Paragraph 3.12 of Schedule 1 to the Civil Proceedings Fees Order 2008.
[2]   Paragraph 3.11 of Schedule 1 to the Civil Proceedings Fees Order 2008.

SERVICE

The usual rule is that, subject to any other express provision, the application must be served at least 14 days before the date fixed for the hearing.[3] However, the court does have power, in cases of urgency, to hear an application immediately with or without notice to the other parties.[4]

Service may be effected by post provided it is addressed to the person it is to be served on and prepaid for either first or second class post.[5] It may be sent to the last known address of the person to be served.[6]

A document sent by first class post is treated as being served on the 2nd business day after posting, unless the contrary is shown.[7] A document sent by second class post is treated as being served on the 4th business day after posting, unless the contrary is shown.[8] The date of posting is presumed to be the date postmarked on the envelope, unless the contrary is shown.[9]

Where service of any application or any order of the court is to be made to a person outside England and Wales an application must be made to the registrar for directions as to the manner, timing and proof of service.[10]

The application needs to be supported by a witness statement stating:[11]

- the grounds upon which the application is made;
- in what place the person to be served is either to be found or presumed to be found.

Subject to these provisions, Part 6 of the CPR is deemed to apply under the Insolvency Rules 1986.[12]

Note: if the court grants leave the directors need to send an office copy of the court order to the registrar of companies within 14 days of the order.

---

[3] Rule 7.4(5) of the Insolvency Rules 1986.

[4] Rule 7.4(6) of the Insolvency Rules 1986.

[5] Rule 12.10(1) of the Insolvency Rules 1986.

[6] Rule 12.10(1A) of the Insolvency Rules 1986.

[7] Rule 12.10(2) of the Insolvency Rules 1986.

[8] Rule 12.10(3) of the Insolvency Rules 1986.

[9] Rule 12.10(4) of the Insolvency Rules 1986.

[10] Rule 12.12(3) of the Insolvency Rules 1986.

[11] Rule 12.12(4) of the Insolvency Rules 1986.

[12] Rule 12.11 of the Insolvency Rules 1986.

KEY STATUTORY PROVISIONS

Paragraphs 12 and 20 of Schedule A1 to the Insolvency Act 1986

12

(1)   During the period for which a moratorium is in force for a company—

    (a)   no petition may be presented for the winding up of the company,

    (b)   no meeting of the company may be called or requisitioned except with the consent of the nominee or the leave of the court and subject (where the court gives leave) to such terms as the court may impose,

    (c)   no resolution may be passed or order made for the winding up of the company,

    (d)   no administration application may be made in respect of the company,

    (da) no administrator of the company may be appointed under paragraph 14 or 22 of Schedule B1,

    (e)   no administrative receiver of the company may be appointed,

    (f)   no landlord or other person to whom rent is payable may exercise any right of forfeiture by peaceable re-entry in relation to premises let to the company in respect of a failure by the company to comply with any term or condition of its tenancy of such premises, except with the leave of the court and subject to such terms as the court may impose,

    (g)   no other steps may be taken to enforce any security over the company's property, or to repossess goods in the company's possession under any hire-purchase agreement, except with the leave of the court and subject to such terms as the court may impose, and

    (h)   no other proceedings and no execution or other legal process may be commenced or continued, and no distress may be levied, against the company or its property except with the leave of the court and subject to such terms as the court may impose.

(2)   Where a petition, other than an excepted petition, for the winding up of the company has been presented before the beginning of the moratorium, section 127 shall not apply in relation to any disposition of property, transfer of shares or alteration in status made during the moratorium or at a time mentioned in paragraph 37(5)(a).

(3)   In the application of sub-paragraph (1)(h) to Scotland, the reference to execution being commenced or continued includes a reference to diligence being carried out or continued, and the reference to distress being levied is omitted.

(4)   Paragraph (a) of sub-paragraph (1) does not apply to an excepted petition and, where such a petition has been presented before the beginning of the moratorium or is presented during the moratorium, paragraphs (b) and (c) of that sub-paragraph do not apply in relation to proceedings on the petition.

(5)   For the purposes of this paragraph, 'excepted petition' means a petition under—

    (a)   section 124A or 124B of this Act,

    (b)   section 72 of the Financial Services Act 1986 on the ground mentioned in subsection (1)(b) of that section, or

    (c)   section 92 of the Banking Act 1987 on the ground mentioned in subsection (1)(b) of that section,

    (d)   section 367 of the Financial Services and Markets Act 2000 on the ground mentioned in subsection (3)(b) of that section.

20

(1)   This paragraph applies where—

    (a)   any property of the company is subject to a security, or

    (b)   any goods are in the possession of the company under a hire-purchase agreement.

(2)   If the holder of the security consents, or the court gives leave, the company may dispose of the property as if it were not subject to the security.

(3)   If the owner of the goods consents, or the court gives leave, the company may dispose of the goods as if all rights of the owner under the hire-purchase agreement were vested in the company.

(4)   Where property subject to a security which, as created, was a floating charge is disposed of under sub-paragraph (2), the holder of the security has the same priority in respect of any property of the company directly or indirectly representing the property disposed of as he would have had in respect of the property subject to the security.

(5)   Sub-paragraph (6) applies to the disposal under sub-paragraph (2) or (as the case may be) sub-paragraph (3) of—

    (a)   any property subject to a security other than a security which, as created, was a floating charge, or

    (b)   any goods in the possession of the company under a hire-purchase agreement.

(6)   It shall be a condition of any consent or leave under sub-paragraph (2) or (as the case may be) sub-paragraph (3) that—

    (a)   the net proceeds of the disposal, and

    (b)   where those proceeds are less than such amount as may be agreed, or determined by the court, to be the net amount which would be realised on a sale of the property or goods in the open market by a willing vendor, such sums as may be required to make good the deficiency, shall be applied towards discharging the sums secured by the security or payable under the hire-purchase agreement.

(7)   Where a condition imposed in pursuance of sub-paragraph (6) relates to two or more securities, that condition requires—

(a)   the net proceeds of the disposal, and

(b)   where paragraph (b) of sub-paragraph (6) applies, the sums mentioned in that paragraph,

to be applied towards discharging the sums secured by those securities in the order of their priorities.

(8)   Where the court gives leave for a disposal under sub-paragraph (2) or (3), the directors shall, within 14 days after leave is given, send an office copy of the order giving leave to the registrar of companies.

(9)   If the directors without reasonable excuse fail to comply with sub-paragraph (8), they are liable to a fine.

Rule 1.50 of the Insolvency Rules 1986

1.50 Procedure for admission of creditors' claims for voting purposes
(1)   Subject as follows, at any creditors' meeting the chairman shall ascertain the entitlement of persons wishing to vote and shall admit or reject their claims accordingly.

(2)   The chairman may admit or reject a claim in whole or in part.

(3)   The chairman's decision on any matter under this Rule or under paragraph (3) of Rule 1.49 is subject to appeal to the court by any creditor or member of the company.

(4)   If the chairman is in doubt whether a claim should be admitted or rejected, he shall mark it as objected to and allow votes to be cast in respect of it, subject to such votes being subsequently declared invalid if the objection to the claim is sustained.

(5)   If on an appeal the chairman's decision is reversed or varied, or votes are declared invalid, the court may order another meeting to be summoned, or make such order as it thinks just.

The court's power to make an order under this paragraph is exercisable only if it considers that the circumstances giving rise to the appeal are such as give rise to unfair prejudice or material irregularity.

(6)   An application to the court by way of appeal against the chairman's decision shall not be made after the end of the period of 28 days beginning with the first day on which the report required by paragraph 30(3) of Schedule A1 to the Act has been made to the court.

(7)   The chairman is not personally liable for any costs incurred by any person in respect of an appeal under this Rule

16.1   APPLICATION FOR LEAVE TO ENFORCE DESPITE THE MORATORIUM UNDER THE CREDITORS VOLUNTARY ARRANGEMENT

Rule 7.2
Ordinary Application

IN THE HIGH COURT OF JUSTICE
CHANCERY DIVISION
COMPANIES COURT

NO: [ ] OF 20[ ]

IN THE MATTER OF BUSTCO LIMITED
COMPANY REGISTRATION NUMBER 011111
AND IN THE MATTER OF THE INSOLVENCY ACT 1986

BETWEEN:-

ANGRY PLC

Applicant

-and-

(1) BUSTCO LIMITED
(2) SAMMY SUPERVISOR
(nominee of the voluntary arrangement of BUSTCO LIMITED)

Respondent

TAKE NOTICE that we, ANGRY PLC, intend to apply to the Registrar on:

Date: [ ] 20[ ]
Time: [ ] am/pm
Place: [ ]

For an order in the following terms:

1. For leave from this Honourable Court pursuant to paragraph 12(1) of Schedule A1 to the Insolvency Act 1986 for ANGRY PLC to exercise its right of peaceable re-entry pursuant to clause 15 of the lease between Angry plc and Bustco Limited dated 1st April 2004.

2. Further and other relief.

3. For an order that the 1st Respondent do pay the Applicant's costs of and occasioned by the application.

Signed [ ]
Solicitor for the Applicant
Dated [ ] 20[ ]

My address for service is:

SMIRK & CO
1 BILE STREET
LONDON

To:
SAMMY SUPERVISOR, 1 SLICK STREET, LONDON

If you do not attend, the Court may make such order as it thinks fit.

16.2   WITNESS STATEMENT IN SUPPORT OF AN APPLICATION FOR LEAVE TO ENFORCE DESPITE THE MORATORIUM UNDER THE CREDITORS VOLUNTARY ARRANGEMENT

Applicant: F Furious: 1st: [ ] 20[ ]

IN THE HIGH COURT OF JUSTICE
CHANCERY DIVISION
COMPANIES COURT

NO: [ ] OF 20[ ]

IN THE MATTER OF BUSTCO LIMITED
COMPANY REGISTRATION NUMBER 011111
AND IN THE MATTER OF THE INSOLVENCY ACT 1986

BETWEEN:-

ANGRY PLC

Applicant

-and-

(1) BUSTCO LIMITED
(2) SAMMY SUPERVISOR
(nominee of the voluntary arrangement of BUSTCO LIMITED)

Respondent

1ST WITNESS STATEMENT OF FREDDY FURIOUS

I, FREDDY FURIOUS, of Angry plc, 1 Bile Street, London, Company Director, STATE as follows:

1.   I am a director of the Applicant company. I am duly authorised to make this witness statement on their behalf.

2.   I make this witness statement in support of the Applicant's application for orders granting leave from this Honourable Court pursuant to paragraph 12(1) of Schedule A1 to the Insolvency Act 1986 for ANGRY PLC to exercise its right of peaceable re-entry pursuant to clause 15 of the lease between Angry plc and Bustco Limited dated 1st April 2004.

3.   The matters stated in this witness statement are true are made from my own knowledge except where otherwise indicated, in which I case I explain the source of my information and belief.

4.   There is now produced and shown to me a bundle marked 'FF1' which contains true copies of the documents I will refer to in support of this application.

5.   On 1st April 2004 Angry plc granted Bustco Limited a commercial lease of their factory premises at 1 Poor Street, London for £10,000 per calendar month. I refer to page 1 of 'FF1' which is a true copy of the lease.

6.   Under clause 2 of the lease Bustco agreed to pay the rent each month on the first day of each month. The first rental payment would have fallen due on 1st April 2008.

7.   Under clause 15 of the lease Angry plc are granted the right to retake possession of the premises in the event that Bustco Limited defaults on any payment of their rent.

8.   To date no payments have been made under the lease and Bustco Limited is 12 months in arrears and owes Angry plc £120,000 in unpaid rent.

9.   Angry plc has therefore been entitled under the terms of the lease to take peaceable re-entry of the premises since 1st May 2008.

10. On 25th February 2009 I wrote to Bustco Limited stating that I intended to take such steps if they did not pay their arrears by the end of the following month.

11. On 1st March 2009, Ian Flakey, the director of Bustco Limited, filed the forms at this Honourable Court which were required to obtain a moratorium prior to the approval of a company voluntary arrangement under paragraph 8 of Schedule A1 to the Insolvency Act 1986. I refer to page [ ] of 'FF1' which is a true of the CVA.

12. The proposals under the voluntary arrangement of Bustco Limited make no provision for the ongoing payment of rent in relation to the premises.

13. In all the circumstances I ask this Honourable Court to grant the relief sought in this application and grant Angry plc permission to exercise its contractual right to peaceable re-entry of the premises.

STATEMENT OF TRUTH

I believe the facts stated in this witness statement are true.

Signed [ ]
FREDDY FURIOUS
Dated [ ] 20[ ]

16.3   ORDER GRANTING LEAVE TO ENFORCE DESPITE THE MORATORIUM UNDER THE CREDITORS VOLUNTARY ARRANGEMENT

IN THE HIGH COURT OF JUSTICE
CHANCERY DIVISION
COMPANIES COURT

NO: [ ] OF 20[ ]

IN THE MATTER OF BUSTCO LIMITED
COMPANY REGISTRATION NUMBER 011111
AND IN THE MATTER OF THE INSOLVENCY ACT 1986

BEFORE MR REGISTRAR WISE
DATED: [ ] 20[ ]

BETWEEN:-

ANGRY PLC

Applicant

-and-

(1) BUSTCO LIMITED
(2) SAMMY SUPERVISOR
(nominee of the voluntary arrangement of BUSTCO LIMITED)

Respondent

DRAFT ORDER

UPON THE APPLICATION of ANGRY PLC, a creditor

AND UPON HEARING Counsel for the supervisor and the applicant

AND UPON reading the evidence noted as being read

IT IS ORDERED:

1.   That ANGRY PLC have leave pursuant to paragraph 12(1) of Schedule A1 to the Insolvency Act 1986 to exercise its right of peaceable re-entry over the premises known as and situate at 1 Poor Street, London pursuant to clause 15 of the lease between Angry plc and Bustco Limited dated 1st April 2004.

2.   That the 1st Respondent do pay the Applicant's costs of and occasioned by the application.

CHAPTER 17

APPLICATION TO CHALLENGE DECISIONS MADE BY THE CHAIRMAN ON A MEETING FOR A CREDITORS VOLUNTARY ARRANGEMENT

OBJECTIVE

Creditors and members of the company have a right of appeal to the court against decisions made by the chairman of the company voluntary arrangement meeting.

Issues that could be challenged in this way include decisions like the rejection of a creditor's claim to vote, the value to be put on the voting or even as to the voting itself.

The court has the power to reverse the decision where there has been unfair prejudice or a material irregularity

APPLICATION

The application is made by ordinary application on notice.

The application must be made within 28 days of the decision beginning with the first day upon which the chairman's report was made to the court.

COURT FEES

Where the application is made by ordinary application on notice to other parties, a court fee of £60 is payable.[1] Where the application is made by consent, a court fee of £30 is payable.[2]

SERVICE

The usual rule is that, subject to any other express provision, the application must be served at least 14 days before the date fixed for the hearing.[3] However, the court does have power, in cases of urgency, to hear an application immediately with or without notice to the other parties.[4]

Service may be effected by post provided it is addressed to the person it is to be served on and prepaid for either first or second class post.[5] It may be sent to the last known address of the person to be served.[6]

A document sent by first class post is treated as being served on the 2nd business day after posting, unless the contrary is shown.[7] A document sent by second class post is treated as being served on the 4th business day after posting, unless the contrary is shown.[8] The date of posting is presumed to be the date postmarked on the envelope, unless the contrary is shown.[9]

Where service of any application or any order of the court is to be made to a person outside England and Wales an application must be made to the registrar for directions as to the manner, timing and proof of service.[10]

The application needs to be supported by a witness statement stating:[11]

- the grounds upon which the application is made;
- in what place the person to be served is either to be found or presumed to be found.

Subject to these provisions, Part 6 of the CPR is deemed to apply under the Insolvency Rules 1986.[12]

---

[1]   Paragraph 3.12 of Schedule 1 to the Civil Proceedings Fees Order 2008.
[2]   Paragraph 3.11 of Schedule 1 to the Civil Proceedings Fees Order 2008.
[3]   Rule 7.4(5) of the Insolvency Rules 1986.
[4]   Rule 7.4(6) of the Insolvency Rules 1986.
[5]   Rule 12.10(1) of the Insolvency Rules 1986.
[6]   Rule 12.10(1A) of the Insolvency Rules 1986.
[7]   Rule 12.10(2) of the Insolvency Rules 1986.
[8]   Rule 12.10(3) of the Insolvency Rules 1986.
[9]   Rule 12.10(4) of the Insolvency Rules 1986.
[10]   Rule 12.12(3) of the Insolvency Rules 1986.
[11]   Rule 12.12(4) of the Insolvency Rules 1986.
[12]   Rule 12.11 of the Insolvency Rules 1986.

EVIDENCE

A witness statement should be prepared in support of the application.

This should address:

- the identity of the deponent;
- the stage at which the creditors voluntary arrangement (CVA) has reached;
- what the deponent's interest is in the decision (is he a creditor or member and what value should be given to his vote and why);
- what decision the chairman made;
- when the decision was made;
- why that decision is wrong;
- that there has been unfair prejudice or a material irregularity and why the deponent says this is so.

This should exhibit:

- a copy of the arrangement or proposal;
- proof of the debt relied on;
- any documents evidencing the decision made and its date.

KEY STATUTORY PROVISIONS

Paragraphs 29 to 36 of Schedule A1 to the Insolvency Act 1986

Summoning of meetings

29

(1) Where a moratorium is in force, the nominee shall summon meetings of the company and its creditors for such a time, date (within the period for the time being specified in paragraph 8(3)) and place as he thinks fit.

(2) The persons to be summoned to a creditors' meeting under this paragraph are every creditor of the company of whose claim the nominee is aware.

Conduct of meetings

30

(1) Subject to the provisions of paragraphs 31 to 35, the meetings summoned under paragraph 29 shall be conducted in accordance with the rules.

(2) A meeting so summoned may resolve that it be adjourned (or further adjourned).

(3) After the conclusion of either meeting in accordance with the rules, the chairman of the meeting shall report the result of the meeting to the court, and, immediately after reporting to the court, shall give notice of the result of the meeting to such persons as may be prescribed.

Approval of voluntary arrangement

31

(1)   The meetings summoned under paragraph 29 shall decide whether to approve the proposed voluntary arrangement (with or without modifications).

(2)   The modifications may include one conferring the functions proposed to be conferred on the nominee on another person qualified to act as an insolvency practitioner, or authorised to act as nominee, in relation to the voluntary arrangement.

(3)   The modifications shall not include one by virtue of which the proposal ceases to be a proposal such as is mentioned in section 1.

(4)   A meeting summoned under paragraph 29 shall not approve any proposal or modification which affects the right of a secured creditor of the company to enforce his security, except with the concurrence of the creditor concerned.

(5)   Subject to sub-paragraph (6), a meeting so summoned shall not approve any proposal or modification under which—

   (a)   any preferential debt of the company is to be paid otherwise than in priority to such of its debts as are not preferential debts, or

   (b)   a preferential creditor of the company is to be paid an amount in respect of a preferential debt that bears to that debt a smaller proportion than is borne to another preferential debt by the amount that is to be paid in respect of that other debt.

(6)   The meeting may approve such a proposal or modification with the concurrence of the preferential creditor concerned.

(7)   The directors of the company may, before the beginning of the period of seven days which ends with the meetings (or either of them) summoned under paragraph 29 being held, give notice to the nominee of any modifications of the proposal for which the directors intend to seek the approval of those meetings.

(8)   References in this paragraph to preferential debts and preferential creditors are to be read in accordance with section 386 in Part XII of this Act.

Extension of moratorium

32

(1)   Subject to sub-paragraph (2), a meeting summoned under paragraph 29 which resolves that it be adjourned (or further adjourned) may resolve that the moratorium be extended (or further extended), with or without conditions.

(2)   The moratorium may not be extended (or further extended) to a day later than the end of the period of two months which begins—

    (a)   where both meetings summoned under paragraph 29 are first held on the same day, with that day,

    (b)   in any other case, with the day on which the later of those meetings is first held.

(3)   At any meeting where it is proposed to extend (or further extend) the moratorium, before a decision is taken with respect to that proposal, the nominee shall inform the meeting—

    (a)   of what he has done in order to comply with his duty under paragraph 24 and the cost of his actions for the company, and

    (b)   of what he intends to do to continue to comply with that duty if the moratorium is extended (or further extended) and the expected cost of his actions for the company.

(4)   Where, in accordance with sub-paragraph (3)(b), the nominee informs a meeting of the expected cost of his intended actions, the meeting shall resolve whether or not to approve that expected cost.

(5)   If a decision not to approve the expected cost of the nominee's intended actions has effect under paragraph 36, the moratorium comes to an end.

(6)   A meeting may resolve that a moratorium which has been extended (or further extended) be brought to an end before the end of the period of the extension (or further extension).

(7)   The Secretary of State may by order increase or reduce the period for the time being specified in sub-paragraph (2).

33

(1)   The conditions which may be imposed when a moratorium is extended (or further extended) include a requirement that the nominee be replaced as such by another person qualified to act as an insolvency practitioner, or authorised to act as nominee, in relation to the voluntary arrangement.

(2)   A person may only be appointed as a replacement nominee by virtue of sub-paragraph (1) if he submits to the court a statement indicating his consent to act.

(3)   At any meeting where it is proposed to appoint a replacement nominee as a condition of extending (or further extending) the moratorium—

    (a)   the duty imposed by paragraph 32(3)(b) on the nominee shall instead be imposed on the person proposed as the replacement nominee, and

    (b)   paragraphs 32(4) and (5) and 36(1)(e) apply as if the references to the nominee were to that person.

34

(1) If a decision to extend, or further extend, the moratorium takes effect under paragraph 36, the nominee shall, in accordance with the rules, notify the registrar of companies and the court.

(2) If the moratorium is extended, or further extended, by virtue of an order under paragraph 36(5), the nominee shall, in accordance with the rules, send an office copy of the order to the registrar of companies.

(3) If the nominee without reasonable excuse fails to comply with this paragraph, he is liable to a fine.

Moratorium committee

35

(1) A meeting summoned under paragraph 29 which resolves that the moratorium be extended (or further extended) may, with the consent of the nominee, resolve that a committee be established to exercise the functions conferred on it by the meeting.

(2) The meeting may not so resolve unless it has approved an estimate of the expenses to be incurred by the committee in the exercise of the proposed functions.

(3) Any expenses, not exceeding the amount of the estimate, incurred by the committee in the exercise of its functions shall be reimbursed by the nominee.

(4) The committee shall cease to exist when the moratorium comes to an end.

Effectiveness of decisions

36

(1) Sub-paragraph (2) applies to references to one of the following decisions having effect, that is, a decision, under paragraph 31, 32 or 35, with respect to—

(a) the approval of a proposed voluntary arrangement,

(b) the extension (or further extension) of a moratorium,

(c) the bringing of a moratorium to an end,

(d) the establishment of a committee, or

(e) the approval of the expected cost of a nominee's intended actions.

(2) The decision has effect if, in accordance with the rules—

(a) it has been taken by both meetings summoned under paragraph 29, or

(b) (subject to any order made under sub-paragraph (5)) it has been taken by the creditors' meeting summoned under that paragraph.

(3)   If a decision taken by the creditors' meeting under any of paragraphs 31, 32 or 35 with respect to any of the matters mentioned in sub-paragraph (1) differs from one so taken by the company meeting with respect to that matter, a member of the company may apply to the court.

(4)   An application under sub-paragraph (3) shall not be made after the end of the period of 28 days beginning with—

    (a)   the day on which the decision was taken by the creditors' meeting, or

    (b)   where the decision of the company meeting was taken on a later day, that day.

(5)   On an application under sub-paragraph (3), the court may—

    (a)   order the decision of the company meeting to have effect instead of the decision of the creditors' meeting, or

    (b)   make such other order as it thinks fit.

Rule 1.50 of the Insolvency Rules 1986

1.50 Procedure for admission of creditors' claims for voting purposes]
(1)   Subject as follows, at any creditors' meeting the chairman shall ascertain the entitlement of persons wishing to vote and shall admit or reject their claims accordingly.

(2)   The chairman may admit or reject a claim in whole or in part.

(3)   The chairman's decision on any matter under this Rule or under paragraph (3) of Rule 1.49 is subject to appeal to the court by any creditor or member of the company.

(4)   If the chairman is in doubt whether a claim should be admitted or rejected, he shall mark it as objected to and allow votes to be cast in respect of it, subject to such votes being subsequently declared invalid if the objection to the claim is sustained.

(5)   If on an appeal the chairman's decision is reversed or varied, or votes are declared invalid, the court may order another meeting to be summoned, or make such order as it thinks just.

    The court's power to make an order under this paragraph is exercisable only if it considers that the circumstances giving rise to the appeal are such as give rise to unfair prejudice or material irregularity.

(6)   An application to the court by way of appeal against the chairman's decision shall not be made after the end of the period of 28 days beginning with the first day on which the report required by paragraph 30(3) of Schedule A1 to the Act has been made to the court.

(7)   The chairman is not personally liable for any costs incurred by any person in respect of an appeal under this Rule

17.1 APPLICATION TO CHALLENGE A DECISION BY THE CHAIRMAN ON A MEETING FOR A CREDITORS VOLUNTARY ARRANGEMENT

Rule 7.2
Ordinary Application

IN THE HIGH COURT OF JUSTICE
CHANCERY DIVISION
COMPANIES COURT

NO: [ ] OF 20[ ]

IN THE MATTER OF BUSTCO LIMITED
COMPANY REGISTRATION NUMBER 011111
AND IN THE MATTER OF THE INSOLVENCY ACT 1986

BETWEEN:-

FREDDY FURIOUS

<u>Applicant</u>

-and-

(1) CHARLIE CHAIRMAN
(2) BUSTCO LIMITED

<u>Respondent</u>

TAKE NOTICE that I FREDDY FURIOUS intend to apply to the Registrar on:

Date: [ ] 20[ ]
Time: [ ] am/pm
Place: [ ]

For an order in the following terms:

1.   That the approval of the voluntary arrangement given by the meeting of creditors held on 1st April 2008 in respect of the above named Company be revoked or suspended on such terms as shall to this Honourable Court shall seem just.

2.   Further or alternatively, a direction that Charlie Chairman or such other person as this Honourable Court deems fit do within 14 days convene a further meeting of the creditors of the Company to consider the Applicant's proposals filed herein and that the Applicant be permitted to vote in the full amount of its claim in the sum of £20 and that the expense of convening such further meeting and of this application be an expense of the voluntary arrangement.

3.   Further and other relief.

Signed [ ]
The Applicant
Dated [ ] 20[ ]

My address for service is:

FREDDY FURIOUS
1 BILE STREET
LONDON

To:
CHARLIE CHAIRMAN, 1 CHUMP STREET, LONDON

If you do not attend, the Court may make such order as it thinks fit.

17.2   **WITNESS STATEMENT IN SUPPORT OF AN APPLICATION TO CHALLENGE A DECISION BY THE CHAIRMAN ON A MEETING FOR A CREDITORS VOLUNTARY ARRANGEMENT**

Applicant: F Furious: 1st: FF1: [ ] 20[ ]

IN THE HIGH COURT OF JUSTICE
CHANCERY DIVISION
COMPANIES COURT

NO: [ ] OF 20[ ]

IN THE MATTER OF BUSTCO LIMITED
COMPANY REGISTRATION NUMBER 011111
AND IN THE MATTER OF THE INSOLVENCY ACT 1986

BETWEEN:-

FREDDY FURIOUS

<u>Applicant</u>

-and-

(1) CHARLIE CHAIRMAN
(2) BUSTCO LIMITED

<u>Respondent</u>

1ST WITNESS STATEMENT OF FREDDY FURIOUS

I, FREDDY FURIOUS, of 1 Bile Street, London, Window Cleaner, STATE as follows:

1.   I am the Applicant in this matter. I trade as 'Furious Windows' and I am a creditor of the Bustco Limited.

2.   I make this witness in support of my application for an order:

    a.   that the approval of the voluntary arrangement given by the meeting of creditors held on 1st May 2009 in respect of the above named Company be revoked or suspended on such terms as shall to this Honourable Court shall seem just,

    b.   further or alternatively, a direction that Charlie Chairman or such other person as to this Honourable Court deem fit do within 14 days convene a further meeting of the creditors of the Company to consider the Applicant's proposals filed herein and that the Applicant be permitted to vote in the full amount of its claim in the sum of £20 and that the expense of convening such further meeting and of this application be an expense of the voluntary arrangement.

3. The matters stated in this witness statement are true are made from my own knowledge except where otherwise indicated, in which I case I explain the source of my information and belief.

4. There is now produced and shown to me a bundle consisting of true copies of the documents I will refer to in my witness statement marked 'FF1'.

5. On 1st January 2009 I was asked by Bustco Limited to clean their shop window. I did this for them and we agreed a price for my work at £20. Bustco Limited however did not pay me the £20 or any sum despite my asking for payment.

6. I sent in a proof of debt for the £20 I was owed to the Company. I refer to page [ ] FF1 which is a true copy of my proof of debt.

7. I attended the meeting of creditors of Bustco Limited on 1st May 2009. The chairman of the meeting of creditors, Charlie Chairman, refused to allow the value of my vote to be taken account of for voting purposes on the grounds that he thought the windows weren't left very clean now and he thought Bustco should not have agreed to pay me. I refer to page [ ] of my exhibit marked 'FF1' which is a true copy of the minutes of the meeting.

8. I did in fact clean the shop window and there is no basis for Mr Chairman's rejection of my proof of debt. Indeed I refer this Honourable Court to page [ ] Of my exhibit marked 'FF1' which is a true copy of a birthday card sent to me by Ian Flakey, the director of Bustco on 1st March 2009 which concludes with the words 'PS Thanks for doing such a super job on my company's shop windows. Sorry for the delay in getting you the £20 we owe you'.

9. I would have wished my alternative proposal for the arrangement to be considered. I refer to page [ ] of my exhibit marked 'FF1' which is a true copy of my alternative proposal which I had hoped to be adopted as a variation.

10. However the chairman refused to permit the meeting to consider these matters whether as a variation to the arrangement or at all. He stated that as he had decided not to count the money I said I was owed and he was refusing me the right to either speak or vote at the meeting and he would not permit my proposals to be shown to or considered by the other creditors. I refer to page [ ] of my exhibit marked 'FF1' which is a true copy of the minutes of the meeting.

11. I therefore ask this Honourable Court to make the order in the terms sought.

STATEMENT OF TRUTH

I believe the facts stated in this witness statement are true.

Signed [ ]
FREDDY FURIOUS
Dated [ ] 20[ ]

17.3 ORDER ON AN APPLICATION TO CHALLENGE A DECISION BY THE CHAIRMAN ON A MEETING FOR A CREDITORS VOLUNTARY ARRANGEMENT

IN THE HIGH COURT OF JUSTICE
CHANCERY DIVISION
COMPANIES COURT

NO: [ ] OF 20[ ]

IN THE MATTER OF BUSTCO LIMITED
COMPANY REGISTRATION NUMBER 011111
AND IN THE MATTER OF THE INSOLVENCY ACT 1986

BEFORE MR REGISTRAR WISE
DATED: [ ] 20[ ]

BETWEEN:-

FREDDY FURIOUS

Applicant

-and-

(1) CHARLIE CHAIRMAN
(2) BUSTCO LIMITED

Respondent

DRAFT ORDER

UPON THE APPLICATION of FREDDY FURIOUS, a creditor

AND UPON HEARING Counsel for Charlie Chairman and the Company

AND UPON reading the evidence noted as being read

IT IS ORDERED:

1. That the approval of the voluntary arrangement given by the meeting of creditors held on 1st April 2008 in respect of the above named Company be revoked.

2. That Charlie Chairman do within 14 days convene a further meeting of the creditors of the Company to consider the Applicant's proposals filed herein and that the Applicant be permitted to vote in the full amount of his claim in the sum of £20 and that the expense of convening such further meeting and of this application be an expense of the voluntary arrangement.

CHAPTER 18

APPLICATION TO CHALLENGE AN ACT OR DECISION OF THE SUPERVISOR IN A CREDITORS VOLUNTARY ARRANGEMENT (NO MORATORIUM)

BACKGROUND

The procedure for challenging decisions, acts or omissions of the supervisor is under section 7(3) of the Insolvency Act 1986. The court has unlimited powers to oversee the conduct of the arrangement by the supervisor. The company's creditors or any other person dissatisfied with the act, omission or decision of the supervisor may apply to the court.

APPLICATION NOTICE

The application is made by ordinary application returnable to the registrar.

The application should state:

- which decision is being challenged;
- what decision the court should direct the supervisor to make instead;
- what relief is sought.

The applicant may be:

- any of the company's creditors;
- any person with an interest who is dissatisfied with the decision.

COURT FEES

Where the application is made by ordinary application on notice to other parties, a court fee of £60 is payable.[1] Where the application is made by consent, a court fee of £30 is payable.[2]

EVIDENCE

A witness statement should be prepared in support of the application. A witness statement in support of the application must be filed and served on any respondent not less than 14 days before the hearing.

This should address:

- the identity of the deponent;
- the stage at which the CVA has reached;
- what the deponent's interest is in the decision (is he a creditor or member and what value should be given to is vote and why);
- what decision the supervisor made;
- when the decision was made;
- the date of the meeting and that the applicant has made the application within the applicable 28-day period;
- why that decision is wrong.

This should exhibit:

- a copy of the arrangement or proposal;
- proof of the debt relied on;
- any documents evidencing the decision made and its date.

SERVICE

If the applicant is the supervisor (seeking directions) then the application is without notice unless the company is administration or liquidation. If the company is in administration or liquidation, then the administrator or liquidator should be served and they should be named as respondent. If the applicant is the administrator or liquidator the application can be made without notice, if the applicant is a person entitled to vote at either the creditors' or members' meetings then the supervisor should be served and named as a respondent on the application.

---

[1]   Paragraph 3.12 of Schedule 1 to the Civil Proceedings Fees Order 2008.

[2]   Paragraph 3.11 of Schedule 1 to the Civil Proceedings Fees Order 2008.

The usual rule is that, subject to any other express provision, the application must be served at least 14 days before the date fixed for the hearing.[3] However, the court does have power, in cases of urgency, to hear an application immediately with or without notice to the other parties.[4]

Service may be effected by post provided it is addressed to the person it is to be served on and prepaid for either first or second class post.[5] It may be sent to the last known address of the person to be served.[6]

A document sent by first class post is treated as being served on the 2nd business day after posting, unless the contrary is shown.[7] A document sent by second class post is treated as being served on the 4th business day after posting, unless the contrary is shown.[8] The date of posting is presumed to be the date postmarked on the envelope, unless the contrary is shown.[9]

Where service of any application or any order of the court is to be made to a person outside England and Wales an application must be made to the registrar for directions as to the manner, timing and proof of service.[10]

The application needs to be supported by a witness statement stating:[11]

- the grounds upon which the application is made;
- in what place the person to be served is either to be found or presumed to be found.

Subject to these provisions, Part 6 of the CPR is deemed to apply under the Insolvency Rules 1986.[12]

THE RESPONDENT'S EVIDENCE

Any evidence to be filed by the respondent should be filed not later than 7 days before the hearing.

---

[3] Rule 7.4(5) of the Insolvency Rules 1986.

[4] Rule 7.4(6) of the Insolvency Rules 1986.

[5] Rule 12.10(1) of the Insolvency Rules 1986.

[6] Rule 12.10(1A) of the Insolvency Rules 1986.

[7] Rule 12.10(2) of the Insolvency Rules 1986.

[8] Rule 12.10(3) of the Insolvency Rules 1986.

[9] Rule 12.10(4) of the Insolvency Rules 1986.

[10] Rule 12.12(3) of the Insolvency Rules 1986.

[11] Rule 12.12(4) of the Insolvency Rules 1986.

[12] Rule 12.11 of the Insolvency Rules 1986.

KEY STATUTORY PROVISIONS

Section 7 of the Insolvency Act 1986

7 Implementation of proposal

(1)　This section applies where a voluntary arrangment has effect under section 4A.

(2)　The person who is for the time being carrying out in relation to the voluntary arrangement the functions conferred—

    (a)　on the nominee by virtue of the approval given at one or both of the meetings summoned under section 3,

    (b)　by virtue of section 2(4) or 4(2) on a person other than the nominee,

shall be known as the supervisor of the voluntary arrangement.

(3)　If any of the company's creditors or any other person is dissatisfied by any act, omission or decision of the supervisor, he may apply to the court; and on the application the court may—

    (a)　confirm, reverse or modify any act or decision of the supervisor,

    (b)　give him directions, or

    (c)　make such other order as it thinks fit.

(4)　The supervisor—

    (a)　may apply to the court for directions in relation to any particular matter arising under the voluntary arrangement, and

    (b)　is included among the persons who may apply to the court for the winding up of the company or for an administration order to be made in relation to it.

(5)　The court may, whenever—

    (a)　it is expedient to appoint a person to carry out the functions of the supervisor, and

    (b)　it is inexpedient, difficult or impracticable for an appointment to be made without the assistance of the court,

make an order appointing a person who is qualified to act as an insolvency practitioner [or authorised to act as supervisor, in relation to the voluntary arrangement], either in substitution for the existing supervisor or to fill a vacancy.

(6)　The power conferred by subsection (5) is exercisable so as to increase the number of persons exercising the functions of supervisor or, where there is more than one person exercising those functions, so as to replace one or more of those persons.

18.1   APPLICATION TO CHALLENGE A DECISION BY A SUPERVISOR OF A CREDITORS VOLUNTARY ARRANGEMENT

Rule 7.2
Ordinary Application

IN THE HIGH COURT OF JUSTICE
CHANCERY DIVISION
COMPANIES COURT

NO: [ ] OF 20[ ]

IN THE MATTER OF BUSTCO LIMITED
COMPANY REGISTRATION NUMBER 011111
AND IN THE MATTER OF THE INSOLVENCY ACT 1986

BETWEEN:-

FREDDY FURIOUS

Applicant

-and-

SAMMY SUPERVISOR

Respondent

TAKE NOTICE that I FREDDY FURIOUS intend to apply to the Registrar on

Date: [ ] 20[ ]
Time: [ ] am/pm
Place: [ ]

For an order in the following terms:

1.   That the decision of Sammy Supervisor as supervisor under a the voluntary arrangement dated 1st April 2009 to refuse to accept the Applicant as an unsecured creditor of the above named Company in the sum of £20 be revoked.

2.   Further or alternatively, a direction that Sammy Supervisor do accept the Applicant as an unsecured creditor of the above named Company under the said creditors voluntary arrangement in the sum of £20 and that the Applicant be permitted to vote in the full amount of its claim in the sum of £20.

3.   Such further and other relief as this Honourable Court deems fit do.

4.   That Sammy Supervisor to pay the costs of and occasioned by this application, such costs to be assessed on a summary basis if not agreed.

Signed [ ]
The Applicant
Dated [ ] 20[ ]

My address for service is:

FREDDY FURIOUS
I BILE STREET
LONDON

To:
SAMMY SUPERVISOR, I SLICK STREET, LONDON

If you do not attend, the Court may make such order as it thinks fit.

18.2   WITNESS STATEMENT IN SUPPORT OF AN APPLICATION TO CHALLENGE A DECISION BY A SUPERVISOR OF A CREDITORS VOLUNTARY ARRANGEMENT

Applicant: F Furious: 1st: FF1: [ ] 20[ ]

IN THE HIGH COURT OF JUSTICE
CHANCERY DIVISION
COMPANIES COURT

NO: [ ] OF 20[ ]

IN THE MATTER OF BUSTCO LIMITED
COMPANY REGISTRATION NUMBER 011111
AND IN THE MATTER OF THE INSOLVENCY ACT 1986

BETWEEN:-

FREDDY FURIOUS

Applicant

-and-

SAMMY SUPERVISOR

Respondent

_____

1ST WITNESS STATEMENT OF FREDDY FURIOUS

_____

I, FREDDY FURIOUS, of 1 Bile Street, London, Window Cleaner, STATE as follows:

1.   I am the Applicant in this matter. I trade as 'Furious Windows' and I am a creditor of the Bustco Limited.

2.   I make this witness in support of my application for an order:

   a.   that the decision of Sammy Supervisor as supervisor under a the voluntary arrangement dated 1st April 2009 to refuse to accept the Applicant as an unsecured creditor of the above named Company in the sum of £20 be revoked,

   b.   further or alternatively, a direction that Sammy Supervisor do accept the Applicant as an unsecured creditor of the above named Company under the said creditors voluntary arrangement in the sum of £20 and that the Applicant be permitted to vote in the full amount of its claim in the sum of £20,

    c.   such further and other relief as this Honourable Court deems fit do,

    d.   that Sammy Supervisor to pay the costs of and occasioned by this application, such costs to be assessed on a summary basis if not agreed.

3.   The matters stated in this witness statement are true and are made from my own knowledge except where otherwise indicated, in which I case I explain the source of my information and belief.

4.   There is now produced and shown to me a bundle consisting of true copies of the documents I will refer to in my witness statement marked 'FF1'.

5.   On 1st January 2009 I was asked by Bustco Limited to clean their shop window. I did this for them and we agreed a price for my work at £20. Bustco Limited however did not pay me the £20 or any sum despite my asking for payment.

6.   Bustco Limited entered into a creditor's voluntary arrangement on 1st April 2009 and Sammy Supervisor was appointed the supervisor. I refer to page [ ] of my exhibit marked 'FF1' which is a true copy of the company voluntary arrangement.

7.   I sent in a proof of debt for the £20 I was owed to Mr Supervisor. I refer to page [ ] FF1 which is a true copy of my proof of debt.

8.   On 1st May 2009 Mr Supervisor wrote to me saying that he had decided to reject my proof of debt. He explained that the reason for so doing was because he didn't 'believe a word I said' because 'I had a shifty looking face and came from Cardiff'. I refer to page [ ] of my exhibit marked 'FF1' which is a true copy of Mr Supervisor's letter dated 1st May 2009.

9.   I did in fact clean the shop window and there is no basis for Mr Supervisor's rejection of my proof of debt. Indeed I refer this Honourable Court to page [ ] Of my exhibit marked 'FF1' which is a true copy of a birthday card sent to me by Ian Flakey, the director of Bustco on 1st March 2009 which concludes with the words 'PS Thanks for doing such a super job on my company's shop windows. Sorry for the delay in getting you the £20 we owe you'.

10.   I lodged my application to challenge the supervisor's decision at Court on 27th May 2009.

11.   I therefore ask this Honourable Court to make the order in the terms sought.

STATEMENT OF TRUTH

I believe the facts stated in this witness statement are true.

Signed [ ]
FREDDY FURIOUS
Dated [ ] 20[ ]

18.3   ORDER ON AN APPLICATION TO CHALLENGE A DECISION BY A SUPERVISOR OF A CREDITORS VOLUNTARY ARRANGEMENT

IN THE HIGH COURT OF JUSTICE
CHANCERY DIVISION
COMPANIES COURT

NO: [ ] OF 20[ ]

IN THE MATTER OF BUSTCO LIMITED
COMPANY REGISTRATION NUMBER 011111
AND IN THE MATTER OF THE INSOLVENCY ACT 1986

BEFORE MR REGISTRAR
DATED: [ ] 20[ ]

BETWEEN:-

FREDDY FURIOUS

Applicant

-and-

SAMMY SUPERVISOR

Respondent

DRAFT ORDER

UPON THE APPLICATION of FREDDY FURIOUS, a creditor

AND UPON HEARING Counsel for the supervisor and the Company

AND UPON reading the evidence noted as being read

IT IS ORDERED:

1. That Sammy Supervisor do accept the Applicant as an unsecured creditor of the above named Company under the creditors voluntary arrangement of the above named Company dated 1st April 2009 in the sum of £20 and that the Applicant be permitted to vote in the full amount of its claim in the sum of £20.

2. [*Costs of the application to be provided for*]

CHAPTER 19

APPLICATION BY AN ADMINISTRATIVE RECEIVER FOR AN INDEMNITY BY REASON OF THE INVALIDITY OF HIS APPOINTMENT

OBJECTIVE

An administrator receiver may be appointed out of court and more rarely by court order.

Challenges to the appointment of administrative receivers are becoming more common. The Enterprise Act 2002 significantly curtailed the ability of debenture holders to validly appoint administrative receivers despite the apparent powers under the debenture. Moreover the appointment may also prove to be invalid through the failure to register the charge under the debenture.

Where the appointment is discovered to be invalid (whether by reason of the invalidity of the instrument or otherwise) the administrative receiver may ask the court to require the person who appointed him to indemnify him from liability arising out of the invalidity of his appointment.[1] This is important for the administrator, as if his appointment proves to be invalid, any acts he has undertaken will have been as a trespasser.[2]

---

[1]   Section 34 of the Insolvency Act 1986.

[2]   But see for an unsuccessful claim for unlawful interference with contractual relations: *OBG Ltd v Allan* [2007] 2 WLR 920.

APPLICATION

The application is made by originating application to the registrar. The appointer should be named as respondent.

A copy of the application should be filed at court with one additional copy for each party to be served.[3]

COURT FEES

Where the application is made by originating application a court fee of £130 is payable.[4]

EVIDENCE

The administrative receiver should file a witness statement in support. This should address:

- the identity of the applicant;
- the capacity in which the applicant makes this application;
- the date the company was incorporated;
- the registered office of the company;
- the nominal share capital of the company;
- the issued share capital of the company;
- the objects of the company;
- the date of the debenture and charge;
- that the appointer appointed him as administrative receiver;
- the date of the purported appointment;
- the circumstances of his purported appointment as administrative receiver;
- the reason why the appointment as administrative receiver is invalid;
- the date and circumstances in which the administrative receiver first discovered that his appointment was invalid;
- that he seeks to be indemnified for liabilities arising from the invalidity of his appointment;

The administrative receiver should exhibit:

- evidence of his appointment;
- a copy of the debenture and charge;
- any correspondence relating to the invalidity of the administrative receiver's appointment;
- any correspondence relating to any request by the administrative receiver that the appointer will indemnify him and not object to an order in the terms sought.

SERVICE

The application should served on the appointer.

---

3   Rule 7.4(1) of the Insolvency Rules 1986.

4   Paragraph 3.5 of Schedule 1 to the Civil Proceedings Fees Order 2008.

The usual rule is that, subject to any other express provision, the application must be served at least 14 days before the date fixed for the hearing.[5] However, the court does have power, in cases of urgency, to hear an application immediately with or without notice to the other parties.[6]

Service may be effected by post provided it is addressed to the person it is to be served on and prepaid for either first or second class post.[7] It may be sent to the last known address of the person to be served.[8]

A document sent by first class post is treated as being served on the 2nd business day after posting, unless the contrary is shown.[9] A document sent by second class post is treated as being served on the 4th business day after posting, unless the contrary is shown.[10] The date of posting is presumed to be the date postmarked on the envelope, unless the contrary is shown.[11]

Where service of any application or any order of the court is to be made to a person outside England and Wales an application must be made to the registrar for directions as to the manner, timing and proof of service.[12]

The application needs to be supported by a witness statement stating:[13]

- the grounds upon which the application is made;
- in what place the person to be served is either to be found or presumed to be found.

Subject to these provisions, Part 6 of the CPR is deemed to apply under the Insolvency Rules 1986.[14]

KEY STATUTORY PROVISIONS

Section 34 of the Insolvency Act 1986

34 Liability for invalid appointment

Where the appointment of a person as the receiver or manager of a company's property under powers contained in an instrument is discovered to be invalid (whether by virtue of the invalidity of the instrument or otherwise), the court may order the person by whom or on whose behalf the appointment was made to indemnify the person appointed against any liability which arises solely by reason of the invalidity of the appointment.

---

[5]   Rule 7.4(5) of the Insolvency Rules 1986.

[6]   Rule 7.4(6) of the Insolvency Rules 1986.

[7]   Rule 12.10(1) of the Insolvency Rules 1986.

[8]   Rule 12.10(1A) of the Insolvency Rules 1986.

[9]   Rule 12.10(2) of the Insolvency Rules 1986.

[10]   Rule 12.10(3) of the Insolvency Rules 1986.

[11]   Rule 12.10(4) of the Insolvency Rules 1986.

[12]   Rule 12.12(3) of the Insolvency Rules 1986.

[13]   Rule 12.12(4) of the Insolvency Rules 1986.

[14]   Rule 12.11 of the Insolvency Rules 1986.

19.1 ORIGINATING APPLICATION BY A RECEIVER FOR AN ORDER THAT HIS APPOINTER INDEMNIFY HIM AGAINST LIABILITY BY REASON OF THE INVALIDITY OF HIS APPOINTMENT

Rule 7.2
Originating Application

IN THE HIGH COURT OF JUSTICE
CHANCERY DIVISION
COMPANIES COURT

NO: [ ] OF 20[ ]

IN THE MATTER OF BUSTCO LIMITED
COMPANY REGISTRATION NUMBER 011111
AND IN THE MATTER OF THE INSOLVENCY ACT 1986

BETWEEN:-

RODDY RECEIVER

Applicant

-and-

IAN FLAKEY

Respondent

LET Ian Flakey of Geranium Cottage, London attend before the Registrar on:

Date: [ ] 20[ ]
Time: [ ] am/pm
Place: [ ]

On the hearing of an application by RODDY RECEIVER, the Applicant and Administrative Receiver of Bustco Limited ('the Company') for an order in the following terms:

1. That the Respondent do indemnify the Applicant against all liability arising by virtue of the invalidity of the instrument of appointment dated 1st April 2008 of the Applicant as Administrative Receiver of the Company.

2. That costs be provided for.

The grounds upon which the Applicant claims to be entitled to the order are set out in the witness statement of Roddy Receiver dated 1st May 2009 filed and served herewith.

The names and addresses of the persons upon whom it is intended to serve this application are:

Ian Flakey of Geranium Cottage, London

The Applicant's address for service is:

WIGG & CO
I LAW STREET
LONDON

Signed [ ]
Solicitor for the Applicant
Dated [ ] 20[ ]

If you do not attend, the Court may make such order as it thinks fit.

19.2   WITNESS STATEMENT IN SUPPORT OF AN APPLICATION BY AN ADMINISTRATIVE RECEIVER FOR AN ORDER THAT HIS APPOINTER INDEMNIFY HIM AGAINST LIABILITY BY REASON OF THE INVALIDITY OF HIS APPOINTMENT

Applicant: R Receiver: 1st: RR1: [ ] 20[ ]

IN THE HIGH COURT OF JUSTICE
CHANCERY DIVISION
COMPANIES COURT

NO: [ ] OF 20[ ]

IN THE MATTER OF BUSTCO LIMITED
COMPANY REGISTRATION NUMBER 011111
AND IN THE MATTER OF THE INSOLVENCY ACT 1986

BETWEEN:-

RODDY RECEIVER

<u>Applicant</u>

-and-

IAN FLAKEY

<u>Respondent</u>

FIRST WITNESS STATEMENT OF RODDY RECEIVER

I, RODDY RECEIVER, of 1 Vulture Street, London, Insolvency Practitioner, STATE as follows:

1.   I am the Applicant in this matter and I make this witness statement in support of my application for relief under section 34 of the Insolvency Act 1986.

2.   I am Fellow of the Insolvency Practitioners Association and a licensed Insolvency Practitioner.

3.   The matters stated in this witness statement are true and are made from my own knowledge except where otherwise indicated, in which I case I explain the source of my information and belief.

4.   Bustco Limited was incorporated on 30th October 1996 under the Companies Act 1985.

5.   The registered office of the Company is at Suite 1, 1 Poor Street, London.

6. The nominal capital of the Company is £1000 divided into 1000 shares of £1 each. The amount of the capital paid up or credited as paid up is £2.

7. The principal objects for which the Company was established are as follows: To carry on business as a general trading company and other objects stated in the memorandum of association of the Company.

8. On 1st April 2008 I was appointed as the administrative receiver of Bustco Limited ('the Company') by Ian Flakey pursuant to the terms of a floating charge under a debenture dated 1st April 2007 granted by the Company to Ian Flakey. Ian Flakey is the company's director and major shareholder.

9. There is now produced and shown to me a bundle of documents marked 'RR1'. Page 1 of 'RR1' is a true copy of the debenture.

10. Having commenced my functions, I, in accordance with my usual practice, obtained advice on the validity of my appointment from my solicitors, Wigg & Co. I was advised that the debenture does not benefit from any of the exceptions to the prohibition on appointment of administrative receivers under section 72B to 72GA and Schedule 2A to the Insolvency Act 1986. Page 1 of 'RR1' is a true copy of the advice.

11. As the advice only came one week into my appointment I am concerned that I am liable as a trespasser to the Company and assets in respect of the actions I took in the belief I was an administrative receiver until the discovery of the defect in my appointment.

12. In the premises I ask that the Court orders that the Respondent orders that the Respondent do indemnify me against any liability arising from my defective appointment.

STATEMENT OF TRUTH

I believe the facts stated in this witness statement are true.

Signed [ ]
RODDY RECEIVER
Dated [ ] 20[ ]

**19.3   ORDER THAT HIS APPOINTER INDEMNIFY HIM AGAINST
          LIABILITY BY REASON OF THE INVALIDITY OF HIS
          APPOINTMENT**

IN THE HIGH COURT OF JUSTICE
CHANCERY DIVISION
COMPANIES COURT

NO: [ ] OF 20[ ]

IN THE MATTER OF BUSTCO LIMITED
COMPANY REGISTRATION NUMBER 011111
AND IN THE MATTER OF THE INSOLVENCY ACT 1986

BETWEEN:-

RODDY RECEIVER

<u>Applicant</u>

-and-

IAN FLAKEY

<u>Respondent</u>

DRAFT ORDER

UPON THE APPLICATION of RODDY RECEIVER, the Applicant and purported Administrative Receiver of Bustco Limited ('the Company')

AND UPON HEARING Counsel for the Applicant and for the Respondent

AND UPON reading the evidence noted as being read

IT IS ORDERED:

1.   That the Respondent do indemnify and keep indemnified the Applicant against all damages, costs, liabilities and expenses occasioned by the invalidity of the instrument of appointment dated 1st April 2008 of the Applicant as Administrative Receiver of the Company.

2.   [*Costs of the application to be provided for*]

CHAPTER 20

APPLICATION TO REMOVE AN ADMINISTRATIVE RECEIVER FROM OFFICE

OBJECTIVE

An administrator receiver may only be removed from office by his resignation or by an order of the court.[1] He must vacate office if he ceases to be qualified to act as an insolvency practitioner.[2] The court has no power to appoint a replacement administrative receiver and the replacement must be appointed by the debenture holder.[3]

APPLICATION

The application is made by originating application to the registrar. The administrative receiver should be named as respondent. The applicant will be the debenture holder.

A copy of the application should be filed at court with one additional copy for each party to be served.[4]

---

[1]   Section 45(1) of the Insolvency Act 1986.

[2]   Section 45(2) of the Insolvency Act 1986.

[3]   *Re A & C Supplies Ltd* [1998] BCC 708.

[4]   Rule 7.4(1) of the Insolvency Rules 1986.

COURT FEES

Where the application is made by originating application a court fee of £130 is payable.[5]

EVIDENCE

The applicant should file a witness statement in support. This should address:

- the capacity in which the applicant makes this application (that the applicant is the appointor of administrative receiver);
- the date the company was incorporated;
- the registered office of the company;
- the nominal share capital of the company;
- the issued share capital of the company;
- the objects of the company;
- the date of the debenture and charge;
- the date that the applicant appointed the administrative receiver;
- the circumstances of his purported appointment as administrative receiver;
- the reason why it is said that the appointment of the administrative receiver should cease.

The applicant should exhibit:

- evidence of the appointment;
- a copy of the debenture and charge;
- any documents and correspondence relating to why the administrative receiver's appointment should cease.

SERVICE

The application should served on the administrative receiver.

The usual rule is that, subject to any other express provision, the application must be served at least 14 days before the date fixed for the hearing.[6] However, the court does have power, in cases of urgency, to hear an application immediately with or without notice to the other parties.[7]

Service may be effected by post provided it is addressed to the person it is to be served on and prepaid for either first or second class post.[8] It may be sent to the last known address of the person to be served.[9]

A document sent by first class post is treated as being served on the 2nd business day after posting, unless the contrary is shown.[10] A document sent by second class post is treated as being served on the 4th

---

5   Paragraph 3.5 of Schedule 1 to the Civil Proceedings Fees Order 2008.

6   Rule 7.4(5) of the Insolvency Rules 1986.

7   Rule 7.4(6) of the Insolvency Rules 1986.

8   Rule 12.10(1) of the Insolvency Rules 1986.

9   Rule 12.10(1A) of the Insolvency Rules 1986.

10   Rule 12.10(2) of the Insolvency Rules 1986.

business day after posting, unless the contrary is shown.[11] The date of posting is presumed to be the date postmarked on the envelope, unless the contrary is shown.[12]

Where service of any application or any order of the court is to be made to a person outside England and Wales an application must be made to the registrar for directions as to the manner, timing and proof of service.[13]

The application needs to be supported by a witness statement stating:[14]

- the grounds upon which the application is made;
- in what place the person to be served is either to be found or presumed to be found.

Subject to these provisions, Part 6 of the CPR is deemed to apply under the Insolvency Rules 1986.[15]

NOTICE

Where an administrative receiver vacates office (whether voluntarily or by order of the court) he must give notice to Companies House within 14 days of vacating office.[16]

KEY STATUTORY PROVISIONS

Section 45 of the Insolvency Act 1986

45 Vacation of office
(1) An administrative receiver of a company may at any time be removed from office by order of the court (but not otherwise) and may resign his office by giving notice of his resignation in the prescribed manner to such persons as may be prescribed.

(2) An administrative receiver shall vacate office if he ceases to be qualified to act as an insolvency practitioner in relation to the company.

(3) Where at any time an administrative receiver vacates office—

(a) his remuneration and any expenses properly incurred by him, and

(b) any indemnity to which he is entitled out of the assets of the company,

shall be charged on and paid out of any property of the company which is in his custody or under his control at that time in priority to any security held by the person by or on whose behalf he was appointed.

---

[11] Rule 12.10(3) of the Insolvency Rules 1986.

[12] Rule 12.10(4) of the Insolvency Rules 1986.

[13] Rule 12.12(3) of the Insolvency Rules 1986.

[14] Rule 12.12(4) of the Insolvency Rules 1986.

[15] Rule 12.11 of the Insolvency Rules 1986.

[16] Section 45(4) of the Insolvency Act 1986.

(4)   Where an administrative receiver vacates office otherwise than by death, he shall, within 14 days after his vacation of office, send a notice to that effect to the registrar of companies.

(5)   If an administrative receiver without reasonable excuse fails to comply with subsection (4), he is liable to a fine and, for continued contravention, to a daily default fine.

Rules 3.33 to 3.35 of the Insolvency Rules 1986

3.33 Resignation

(1)   Subject as follows, before resigning his office the administrative receiver shall give at least 7 days' notice of his intention to do so to—

(a)   the person by whom he was appointed, ...

(b)   the company or, if it is then in liquidation, its liquidator, and

(c)   in any case, to the members of the creditors' committee (if any).

(2)   A notice given under this Rule shall specify the date on which the receiver intends his resignation to take effect.

(3)   No notice is necessary if the receiver resigns in consequence of the making of an administration order.

3.34 Receiver deceased

If the administrative receiver dies, the person by whom he was appointed shall, forthwith on his becoming aware of the death, give notice of it to—

(a)   the registrar of companies, ...

(b)   the company or, if it is in liquidation, the liquidator, and

(c)   in any case, to the members of the creditors' committee (if any).

3.35 Vacation of office

(1)   The administrative receiver, on vacating office on completion of the receivership, or in consequence of his ceasing to be qualified as an insolvency practitioner, shall forthwith give notice of his doing so—

(a)   to the company or, if it is in liquidation, the liquidator, and

(b)   ... , to the members of the creditors' committee (if any).

(2)   Where the receiver's office is vacated, the notice to the registrar of companies which is required by section 45(4) may be given by means of an indorsement on the notice required by section 871(2) of the Companies Act (notice for the purposes of the register of charges).

20.1   APPLICATION TO REMOVE AN ADMINISTRATIVE RECEIVER FROM OFFICE

Rule 7.2
Originating Application

IN THE HIGH COURT OF JUSTICE
CHANCERY DIVISION
COMPANIES COURT

NO: [ ] OF 20[ ]

IN THE MATTER OF BUSTCO LIMITED
COMPANY REGISTRATION NUMBER 011111
AND IN THE MATTER OF THE INSOLVENCY ACT 1986

BETWEEN:-

FREDDY FURIOUS

<u>Applicant</u>

-and-

LEONARD LAZY

<u>Respondent</u>

TAKE NOTICE that I, FREDDY FURIOUS, of I Unpaid Bill Street, London, intend to apply to the Registrar on:

Date: [ ] 20[ ]
Time: [ ] am/pm
Place: [ ]

For an order in the following terms:

1.   That LEONARD LAZY be removed from office as administrative receiver of Bustco Ltd pursuant to section 45 of the Insolvency Act 1986.

2.   An order that the Respondent do pay the Applicant's costs of and incidental to this application.

3.   Such further and other order and other relief as this Honourable Court thinks fit.

The grounds upon which I seek the above relief are set out in the 1st witness statement of Freddy Furious dated 1st April 2009, a true copy of which is served herewith.

Signed [ ]
Solicitor for the Applicant.
Dated [ ] 20[ ]

The names and addresses of the persons upon whom it is intended to serve this application are:

Leonard Lazy, 1 Snooze Street, London

The Applicant's address for service is:

SILK & CO
2 LAW STREET
LONDON

If you do not attend, the Court may make such order as it thinks fit.

20.2   WITNESS STATEMENT IN SUPPORT OF AN APPLICATION TO REMOVE AN ADMINISTRATIVE RECEIVER FROM OFFICE

Applicant: F Furious: 1st: FF1: [ ] 20[ ]

IN THE HIGH COURT OF JUSTICE
CHANCERY DIVISION
COMPANIES COURT

NO: [ ] OF 20[ ]

IN THE MATTER OF BUSTCO LIMITED
COMPANY REGISTRATION NUMBER 011111
AND IN THE MATTER OF THE INSOLVENCY ACT 1986

BETWEEN:-

FREDDY FURIOUS

Applicant

-and-

LEONARD LAZY

Respondent

FIRST WITNESS STATEMENT OF FREDDY FURIOUS

I, FREDDY FURIOUS, of 1 Unpaid Bill Street, London, Director, STATE as follows:

1.   I am the Applicant in this matter. I make this witness in support of my application for an order:

    a.   that LEONARD LAZY be removed from office as administrative receiver of Bustco Ltd pursuant to section 45 of the Insolvency Act 1986,

    b.   an order that the Respondent do pay the Applicant's costs of and incidental to this application,

    c.   such further and other order and other relief as this Honourable Court thinks fit.

2.   The matters stated in this witness statement are true are made from my own knowledge except where otherwise indicated, in which I case I explain the source of my information and belief.

3.   There is now produced and shown to me a bundle consisting of true copies of the documents I will refer to in my witness statement marked 'FF1'

4.   Bustco Limited was incorporated on 20th October 1996 under the Companies Act 1985.

5.   The registered office of the Company is at Suite 1, 1 Poor Street, London.

6. The nominal capital of the Company is £1000 divided into 1000 shares of £1 each. The amount of the capital paid up or credited as paid up is £2.

7. The principal objects for which the Company was established are as follows: to carry on business as a general trading company and other objects stated in the memorandum of association of the Company.

8. On 15th July 2008 Bustco Limited granted a debenture to me to secure a loan made by me to Bustco Limited in the sum of £50,0000. I refer to page [ ] of my exhibit marked 'FF1' which is a true copy of the debenture. Under clause 15 the debt became repayable on 1st April 2009. Under clause 23, in the event of any default under the debenture, I have the power to appoint an administrative receiver over Bustco Limited's gold Rolls Royce motor car, registration mark 'BROKE 1'.

9. On 1st April 2009 the £50,000 became due for repayment but Bustco failed to repay the £50,000. Accordingly, as I was entitled to do under the debenture, I appointed Leonard Lazy as administrative receiver over Bustco's Rolls Royce with a view to recovering the money owed to me. I refer to page [ ] of my exhibit marked 'FF1' which is true copy of the certificate of appointment of Leonard Lazy.

10. Although Leonard Lazy has collected the Rolls Royce from Bustco Limited I truly believe that he has taken no steps to sell it, lease it or otherwise advertise it for sale.

11. Instead I truly believe that Leonard Lazy appears to be treating the motorcar as his own. Last month I drove past Leonard Lazy's home and I saw a motorcar I recognised to be the Rolls Royce outside his home.

12. The final straw was yesterday when I saw Leonard Lazy in the Royal Enclosure car park at Ascot Races when I saw him serving a picnic out of the back of a motor car I recognised to be Bustco's Rolls Royce.

13. Seeing Leonard Lazy at Ascot, I asked Leonard Lazy to sell or hire out the Rolls Royce. He simply replied 'Later, man, later. It is just too cool a car'. I refer to page [ ] of my exhibit marked 'FF1' which is a true copy of my attendance note.

14. I then immediately instructed Leonard Lazy to resign as administrator but he refused to do saying 'No way, man. Anyway you can't sack me. I'm now the company's agent'. I refer to page [ ] of my exhibit marked 'FF1' which is a true copy of my attendance note.

15. I therefore ask this Honourable Court to make the order in the terms sought.

STATEMENT OF TRUTH

I believe the facts stated in this witness statement are true.

Signed [ ]
FREDDY FURIOUS
Dated [ ] 20[ ]

20.3 APPLICATION TO REMOVE AN ADMINISTRATIVE RECEIVER FROM OFFICE

IN THE HIGH COURT OF JUSTICE
CHANCERY DIVISION
COMPANIES COURT

NO: [ ] OF 20[ ]

IN THE MATTER OF BUSTCO LIMITED
COMPANY REGISTRATION NUMBER 011111
AND IN THE MATTER OF THE INSOLVENCY ACT 1986

BETWEEN:-

FREDDY FURIOUS

<u>Applicant</u>

-and-

LEONARD LAZY

<u>Respondent</u>

DRAFT ORDER

UPON THE APPLICATION of FREDDY FURIOUS

AND UPON HEARING Counsel for LEONARD LAZY

AND UPON reading the evidence noted as being read

IT IS ORDERED:

1. That LEONARD LAZY be and is removed from office as an administrative receiver of Bustco Ltd from 10th September 2009 in accordance with section 45 of the Insolvency Act 1986.

2. That the Respondent do pay the Applicant's costs of and incidental to this application.

CHAPTER 21

APPLICATION FOR A DECLARATION THAT A TRANSACTION IS INVALIDATED BY VIRTUE OF SECTION 127 OF THE INSOLVENCY ACT 1986

OBJECTIVE

In a winding up by the court, any disposition of the company's property, and any transfer of shares, or alteration in the status of the company's members, made after the commencement of the winding up is, unless the court otherwise orders, void.[1]

Unless the court makes a winding up order on an administration application[2] or a prior resolution has been made for a voluntary winding up,[3] the winding up of a company by the court is deemed to commence at the time of the presentation of the petition for winding up.[4]

---

[1]   Section 127 of the Insolvency Act 1986.

[2]   Where the court makes a winding-up order by virtue of paragraph 13(1)(e) of Schedule B1 to the Insolvency Act 1986 the winding up is deemed to commence on the making of the order: section 129(1A) of the Insolvency Act 1986.

[3]   In circumstances where a resolution for voluntary winding up is passed before the petition for winding up has been heard by the court, winding up commences when the resolution was passed by the company for voluntary winding up: section 129(1) of the Insolvency Act 1986.

[4]   Section 129(2) of the Insolvency Act 1986.

Where a liquidator[5] wishes to challenge such a transfer, the remedy is to seek a declaration and an order to restore the position.

APPLICATION

The application is by ordinary application on notice for a declaration and an order restoring the position to what it would have been had the transaction not been entered into.

The application should be returnable to the registrar in the Companies Court or to the district judge in a Chancery District Registry or county court with insolvency jurisdiction.

The respondent should be the other party to the transaction that the liquidator or administrator is seeking to set aside.

COURT FEES

Where the application is made by ordinary application on notice to other parties, a court fee of £60 is payable.[6] Where the application is made by consent, a court fee of £30 is payable.[7]

SERVICE

The application and the evidence in support will need to be filed at court and served on the respondent as soon as practicable after it is filed and in any event, unless it is necessary to apply ex parte or on short notice, at least 14 days before the date fixed for the hearing.[8]

The usual rule is that, subject to any other express provision, the application must be served at least 14 days before the date fixed for the hearing.[9] However, the court does have power, in cases of urgency, to hear an application immediately with or without notice to the other parties.[10]

Service may be effected by post provided it is addressed to the person it is to be served on and prepaid for either first or second class post.[11] It may be sent to the last known address of the person to be served.[12] A document sent by first class post is treated as being served on the 2nd business day after posting, unless the contrary is shown.[13] A document sent by second class post is treated as being served on the 4th

---

[5]   It would appear that the liquidator cannot assign the right to bring proceedings: *Re Ayala Holdings Ltd (No 2)* [1996] 1 BCLC 467. It is plainly arguable that interested parties have the right to seek relief declaratory relief that a transaction is invalid alongside the liquidator if they can show an interest as the right to seek a declaration is not limited to the liquidator. In such a case the liquidator should be named as a respondent.

[6]   Paragraph 3.12 of Schedule 1 to the Civil Proceedings Fees Order 2008.

[7]   Paragraph 3.11 of Schedule 1 to the Civil Proceedings Fees Order 2008.

[8]   Rule 7.4(5) of the Insolvency Rules 1986.

[9]   Rule 7.4(5) of the Insolvency Rules 1986.

[10]   Rule 7.4(6) of the Insolvency Rules 1986.

[11]   Rule 12.10(1) of the Insolvency Rules 1986.

[12]   Rule 12.10(1A) of the Insolvency Rules 1986.

[13]   Rule 12.10(2) of the Insolvency Rules 1986.

business day after posting, unless the contrary is shown.[14] The date of posting is presumed to be the date postmarked on the envelope, unless the contrary is shown.[15]

Where service of any application or any order of the court is to be made to a person outside England and Wales an application must be made to the registrar for directions as to the manner, timing and proof of service.[16]

The application needs to be supported by a witness statement stating:[17]

- the grounds upon which the application is made;
- in what place the person to be served is either to be found or presumed to be found.

Subject to these provisions, Part 6 of the CPR is deemed to apply under the Insolvency Rules 1986.[18]

EVIDENCE

The application should be supported by a witness statement by the liquidator. This will need to address:

- the order he seeks;
- the date the company was incorporated;
- the date upon which the petition to wind up the company was presented;
- the date upon which the company went into liquidation;
- that he was appointed as liquidator of the company;
- the date upon which he was appointed as liquidator;
- the date of the transaction subject to challenge;
- the particulars of the transaction subject to challenge;
- that no validation order was made which permitted the transaction.[19]

And exhibit:

- evidence of his appointment as liquidator;
- a copy of the petition to wind up the company;
- a copy of the winding up order;
- evidence of the transaction subject to challenge;
- evidence of the date of the transaction.

---

[14] Rule 12.10(3) of the Insolvency Rules 1986.
[15] Rule 12.10(4) of the Insolvency Rules 1986.
[16] Rule 12.12(3) of the Insolvency Rules 1986.
[17] Rule 12.12(4) of the Insolvency Rules 1986.
[18] Rule 12.11 of the Insolvency Rules 1986.
[19] For which see Chapter 6 'Responding to a Petition: Application for a Validation Order'.

THE FIRST HEARING

At the first hearing the registrar or district judge will give directions as to whether points of claim and defence are needed and for the filing of evidence. He may also require the application to be served on other people. He may give directions as to whether witnesses are to attend for cross examination. The first hearing will be unrobed and is likely to be in chambers.

KEY STATUTORY PROVISIONS

Section 127 to 129 of the Insolvency Act 1986

127 Avoidance of property dispositions, etc

(1)   In a winding up by the court, any disposition of the company's property, and any transfer of shares, or alteration in the status of the company's members, made after the commencement of the winding up is, unless the court otherwise orders, void.

(2)   This section has no effect in respect of anything done by an administrator of a company while a winding-up petition is suspended under paragraph 40 of Schedule B1.

128 Avoidance of attachments, etc

(1)   Where a company registered in England and Wales is being wound up by the court, any attachment, sequestration, distress or execution put in force against the estate or effects of the company after the commencement of the winding up is void.

(2)   This section, so far as relates to any estate or effects of the company situated in England and Wales, applies in the case of a company registered in Scotland as it applies in the case of a company registered in England and Wales.

Commencement of winding up

129 Commencement of winding up by the court

(1)   If, before the presentation of a petition for the winding up of a company by the court, a resolution has been passed by the company for voluntary winding up, the winding up of the company is deemed to have commenced at the time of the passing of the resolution; and unless the court, on proof of fraud or mistake, directs otherwise, all proceedings taken in the voluntary winding up are deemed to have been validly taken.

(1A) Where the court makes a winding-up order by virtue of paragraph 13(1)(e) of Schedule B1, the winding up is deemed to commence on the making of the order.

(2)   In any other case, the winding up of a company by the court is deemed to commence at the time of the presentation of the petition for winding up.

21.1   ORDINARY APPLICATION FOR A DECLARATION OF INVALIDITY OF A TRANSFER PURSUANT TO SECTION 127 OF THE INSOLVENCY ACT 1986

Rule 7.2
Ordinary Application

IN THE HIGH COURT OF JUSTICE
CHANCERY DIVISION
COMPANIES COURT

NO: [ ] OF 20[ ]

IN THE MATTER OF BUSTCO LIMITED, REGISTERED NUMBER 011111
AND IN THE MATTER OF THE INSOLVENCY ACT 1986

TAKE NOTICE that I, Giles Grabber of Grabbers LLP, of I Vulture Street, London, as Liquidator of BUSTCO LIMITED, intend to apply to the Registrar on:

Date: [ ] 20[ ]
Time: [ ] am/pm
Place: [ ]

For an order in the following terms:

1.   A declaration that pursuant to section 127(1) of the Insolvency Act 1986 that the bank transfer dated 1st January 2009 of £250,000 from Bustco to Mr Flakey is void.

2.   An order that the Respondent do repay the sum of £250,000.

3.   That there be provision for costs.

The grounds upon which I seek the above relief are set out in the 1st witness statement of Giles Grabber dated 1st April 2009, a true copy of which is served herewith.

Signed [ ]
Solicitor for the Applicant
Dated [ ] 20[ ]

The names and addresses of the persons upon whom it is intended to serve this application are:

Ian Flakey, I Geranium Cottage, London

The Applicant's address for service is:

SILK & CO
2 LAW STREET
LONDON

If you do not attend, the Court may make such order as it thinks fit.

21.2   WITNESS STATEMENT IN SUPPORT OF AN APPLICATION FOR A DECLARATION OF INVALIDITY OF A TRANSFER PURSUANT TO SECTION 127 OF THE INSOLVENCY ACT 1986

Applicant: G Grabber: 1st: GG1: [ ] 20[ ]

IN THE HIGH COURT OF JUSTICE
CHANCERY DIVISION
COMPANIES COURT

NO: [ ] OF 20[ ]

IN THE MATTER OF BUSTCO LIMITED, REGISTERED NUMBER 011111
AND IN THE MATTER OF THE INSOLVENCY ACT 1986

1ST WITNESS STATEMENT OF GILES GRABBER

I, Giles Grabber of Grabbers LLP, of 1 Vulture Street, London, as Liquidator of BUSTCO LIMITED, state as follows:

1.   I am the Applicant in this application. I am the Liquidator of Bustco.

2.   I make the application in support of my application for:

   a.   a declaration that pursuant to section 127(1) of the Insolvency Act 1986 that the bank transfer dated 1st January 2009 of £250,000 from Bustco to Mr Flakey is void,

   b.   an order that the Respondent do repay the sum of £250,000,

   c.   that there be provision for costs.

3.   The matters set out in this witness statement are true and within my own knowledge except where otherwise indicated, in which case I have explained the source of my information or belief.

4.   There is now produced and shown to me a bundle consisting of true copies of the documents I will refer to in my witness statements marked 'GG1'.

5.   Bustco Limited was incorporated on 30th October 1996 under the Companies Act 1985.

6.   The registered office of the Company is at Suite 1, 1 Poor Street, London.

7.   The nominal capital of the Company is £1000 divided into 1000 shares of £1 each. The amount of the capital paid up or credited as paid up is £2.

8.   The principal objects for which the Company was established are as follows: To carry on business as a general trading company and other objects stated in the memorandum of association of the Company.

9.   A petition to wind up Bustco Limited was presented to this Honourable Court on 1st December 2008 by Her Majesty's Revenue and Customs. I refer to page [ ] of 'GG1' which is a true copy of the winding up petition.

10. On 1st January 2009 there was a bank transfer in the sum of £250,000 from Bustco Limited to Mr Flakey. I refer to page [ ] of 'GG1' which is a true copy of the bank statement of Bustco Limited showing the transfer of £250,000 from Bustco Limited to Mr Flakey.

11. A winding up order was made against Bustco on the petition on 1st March 2009. I refer to page [ ] of 'GG1' which is a true copy of the winding up order.

12. I was appointed as the liquidator of Bustco Limited on 1st April 2008.

13. I have written to Mr Flakey inviting him to return the £250,00o and explaining the effect of section 127. In the same letter I gave Mr Flakey notice of my intention to apply for this order to Mr Flakey if he failed to make the payment but to date Mr Flakey has not extended the courtesy of a reply to my letter. I refer to page [ ] of 'GG1' which is a true copy of the letter I sent.

14. I therefore ask this Honourable Court to make the order in the terms sought.

STATEMENT OF TRUTH

I believe that the facts stated in this Witness Statement are true.

Signed [ ]
Full name [*GILES GRABBER*]
Dated [ ] 20[ ]

21.3   DECLARATION OF INVALIDITY UNDER SECTION 127 OF THE INSOLVENCY ACT 1986

IN THE HIGH COURT OF JUSTICE
CHANCERY DIVISION
COMPANIES COURT

NO: [ ] OF 20[ ]

IN THE MATTER OF BUSTCO LIMITED, REGISTERED NUMBER 011111
AND IN THE MATTER OF THE INSOLVENCY ACT 1986

BEFORE MR REGISTRAR WISE
DATED: [ ] 20[ ]

DRAFT MINUTE OF ORDER

UPON THE APPLICATION of Giles Grabber of Grabbers LLP, Administrator of the above named company, BUSTCO LIMITED ('the Company')

UPON HEARING Counsel for the Applicant and Counsel for Ian Flakey, the Respondent

AND UPON READING the evidence noted as being read

IT IS DECLARED THAT:

1.   Pursuant to section 127(1) of the Insolvency Act 1986 that the bank transfer dated 1st January 2009 of £250,000 from the Company to the Respondent is void.

IT IS ORDERED:

2.   That the Respondent do forthwith repay the sum of £250,000 to the Company.

3.   [*Provision for costs*]

CHAPTER 22

APPLICATION TO SET ASIDE A TRANSFER AT AN UNDERVALUE

OBJECTIVE

The court has wide powers on the application of the administrator or the liquidator to rewind transfers of the company's property which have been undertaken at a time when the company is insolvent for no consideration or for significantly less than the value in money or money's worth provided by the company.[1]

To be challenged, the transaction at an undervalue must have occurred at a time in the period of 2 years ending with the onset of insolvency.[2] The onset of insolvency means for these purposes either the presentation of the winding up petition, the filing of the administration notice or application if it concludes with the winding up of the company or the passing of a resolution for the voluntary winding up of the company.[3] This period is only deemed to run whilst the company is unable to pay its debts (or if it is rendered unable to pay its debts by the arrangement); this is presumed where the arrangement is with a connected person.[4]

---

[1]   Section 238 of the Insolvency Act 1986.

[2]   Section 240 of the Insolvency Act 1986.

[3]   Section 129 of the Insolvency Act 1986.

[4]   For the meaning of a connected person see sections 249 and 425 of the Insolvency Act 1986.

APPLICATION

If there have been existing proceedings, the application is by ordinary application in those proceedings on notice for a declaration and an order restoring the position to what it would have been had the transaction not been entered into.

Where there have been no previous proceedings, the application should be made by originating application on notice.

The application should be returnable to the registrar in the Companies Court or to the district judge in a Chancery District Registry or county court with insolvency jurisdiction.

The respondent should be the other party to the transaction that the liquidator or administrator is seeking to set aside.

COURT FEES

Where the application is made by originating application a court fee of £130 is payable.[5] Where the application is made by ordinary application on notice to other parties, a court fee of £60 is payable.[6] Where the application is made by consent or without notice in existing proceedings a court fee of £30 is payable.[7]

EVIDENCE

The application should be supported by a witness statement by the liquidator or administrator. This will need to address:

- the order he seeks;
- the date the company was incorporated;
- the registered office of the company;
- the nominal share capital of the company;
- the issued share capital of the company;
- the objects of the company;
- the date upon which the petition to wind up the company or place it into administration or notice of administration was presented;
- the date upon which the company went into liquidation or administration;
- that he was appointed as liquidator or administrator of the company;
- the date upon which he was appointed as liquidator or administrator;
- the date of the transaction subject to challenge;
- the particulars of the transaction subject to challenge;
- the value of the company's asset transferred under the transaction;
- that the asset was transferred for no consideration or identifying the price it was transferred for and stating that this was significantly less than its value in money or money's worth;

---

[5]   Paragraph 3.5 of Schedule 1 to the Civil Proceedings Fees Order 2008.

[6]   Paragraph 3.12 of Schedule 1 to the Civil Proceedings Fees Order 2008.

[7]   Paragraph 3.11 of Schedule 1 to the Civil Proceedings Fees Order 2008.

- whether the respondent is a connected person and, if so why it is said so;
- that the company was insolvent (or is to be presumed to be insolvent) at the time of the transaction or was rendered insolvent by the transaction;
- the company did not enter into the transaction in good faith and for the purposes of carrying on its business and there would have been no reasonable grounds for believing that the transaction would benefit the company.[8]

And exhibit:

- evidence of his appointment as liquidator or administrator;
- a copy of the petition to wind up the company or place it into administration or notice of administration;
- a copy of the winding up or administration order;
- evidence of the transaction subject to challenge;
- the value of the company's asset transferred under the transaction and of its date and the consideration (if any) paid;
- evidence that the respondent is a connected person (if applicable);
- evidence tending to show the insolvency of the company at the time of the transaction;
- an independent valuation of the property disposed of.

SERVICE

The application and the evidence in support will need to be filed at court and served on the respondent as soon as practicable after it is filed and in any event, unless it is necessary to apply ex parte or on short notice, at least 14 days before the date fixed for the hearing.[9]

The usual rule is that, subject to any other express provision, the application must be served at least 14 days before the date fixed for the hearing.[10] However, the court does have power, in cases of urgency, to hear an application immediately with or without notice to the other parties.[11]

Service may be effected by post provided it is addressed to the person it is to be served on and prepaid for either first or second class post.[12] It may be sent to the last known address of the person to be served.[13]

A document sent by first class post is treated as being served on the 2nd business day after posting, unless the contrary is shown.[14] A document sent by second class post is treated as being served on the 4th

---

[8] Pre-empting the defence under section 238(5) of the Insolvency Act 1986.

[9] Rule 7.4(5) of the Insolvency Rules 1986.

[10] Rule 7.4(5) of the Insolvency Rules 1986.

[11] Rule 7.4(6) of the Insolvency Rules 1986.

[12] Rule 12.10(1) of the Insolvency Rules 1986.

[13] Rule 12.10(1A) of the Insolvency Rules 1986.

[14] Rule 12.10(2) of the Insolvency Rules 1986.

business day after posting, unless the contrary is shown.[15] The date of posting is presumed to be the date postmarked on the envelope, unless the contrary is shown.[16]

Where service of any application or any order of the court is to be made to a person outside England and Wales an application must be made to the registrar for directions as to the manner, timing and proof of service.[17]

The application needs to be supported by a witness statement stating:[18]

- the grounds upon which the application is made;
- in what place the person to be served is either to be found or presumed to be found.

Subject to these provisions, Part 6 of the CPR is deemed to apply under the Insolvency Rules 1986.[19]

THE FIRST HEARING

At the first hearing the registrar or district judge will give directions as to whether points of claim and defence are needed and for the filing of evidence. He may also require the application to be served on other people. He may give directions as to whether witnesses are to attend for cross examination. The first hearing will be unrobed and is likely to be in chambers.

KEY STATUTORY PROVISIONS

Sections 238, 240, 241 and 435 of the Insolvency Act 1986

238 Transactions at an undervalue (England and Wales)
(1)   This section applies in the case of a company where—

(a)   the company enters administration, or

(b)   the company goes into liquidation;

and 'the office-holder' means the administrator or the liquidator, as the case may be.

(2)   Where the company has at a relevant time (defined in section 240) entered into a transaction with any person at an undervalue, the office-holder may apply to the court for an order under this section.

---

[15]   Rule 12.10(3) of the Insolvency Rules 1986.
[16]   Rule 12.10(4) of the Insolvency Rules 1986.
[17]   Rule 12.12(3) of the Insolvency Rules 1986.
[18]   Rule 12.12(4) of the Insolvency Rules 1986.
[19]   Rule 12.11 of the Insolvency Rules 1986.

(3)   Subject as follows, the court shall, on such an application, make such order as it thinks fit for restoring the position to what it would have been if the company had not entered into that transaction.

(4)   For the purposes of this section and section 241, a company enters into a transaction with a person at an undervalue if—

   (a)   the company makes a gift to that person or otherwise enters into a transaction with that person on terms that provide for the company to receive no consideration, or

   (b)   the company enters into a transaction with that person for a consideration the value of which, in money or money's worth, is significantly less than the value, in money or money's worth, of the consideration provided by the company.

(5)   The court shall not make an order under this section in respect of a transaction at an undervalue if it is satisfied—

   (a)   that the company which entered into the transaction did so in good faith and for the purpose of carrying on its business, and

   (b)   that at the time it did so there were reasonable grounds for believing that the transaction would benefit the company.

240 'Relevant time' under ss 238, 239
(1)   Subject to the next subsection, the time at which a company enters into a transaction at an undervalue or gives a preference is a relevant time if the transaction is entered into, or the preference given—

   (a)   in the case of a transaction at an undervalue or of a preference which is given to a person who is connected with the company (otherwise than by reason only of being its employee), at a time in the period of 2 years ending with the onset of insolvency (which expression is defined below),

   (b)   in the case of a preference which is not such a transaction and is not so given, at a time in the period of 6 months ending with the onset of insolvency, ...

   (c)   in either case, at a time between the making of an administration application in respect of the company and the making of an administration order on that application, and

   (d)   in either case, at a time between the filing with the court of a copy of notice of intention to appoint an administrator under paragraph 14 or 22 of Schedule B1 and the making of an appointment under that paragraph.

(2)   Where a company enters into a transaction at an undervalue or gives a preference at a time mentioned in subsection (1)(a) or (b), that time is not a relevant time for the purposes of section 238 or 239 unless the company—

(a) is at that time unable to pay its debts within the meaning of section 123 in Chapter VI of Part IV, or

(b) becomes unable to pay its debts within the meaning of that section in consequence of the transaction or preference;

but the requirements of this subsection are presumed to be satisfied, unless the contrary is shown, in relation to any transaction at an undervalue which is entered into by a company with a person who is connected with the company.

(3) For the purposes of subsection (1), the onset of insolvency is—

(a) in a case where section 238 or 239 applies by reason of an administrator of a company being appointed by administration order, the date on which the administration application is made,

(b) in a case where section 238 or 239 applies by reason of an administrator of a company being appointed under paragraph 14 or 22 of Schedule B1 following filing with the court of a copy of a notice of intention to appoint under that paragraph, the date on which the copy of the notice is filed,

(c) in a case where section 238 or 239 applies by reason of an administrator of a company being appointed otherwise than as mentioned in paragraph (a) or (b), the date on which the appointment takes effect,

(d) in a case where section 238 or 239 applies by reason of a company going into liquidation either following conversion of administration into winding up by virtue of Article 37 of the EC Regulation or at the time when the appointment of an administrator ceases to have effect, the date on which the company entered administration (or, if relevant, the date on which the application for the administration order was made or a copy of the notice of intention to appoint was filed), and

(e) in a case where section 238 or 239 applies by reason of a company going into liquidation at any other time, the date of the commencement of the winding up.

241 Orders under ss 238, 239

(1) Without prejudice to the generality of sections 238(3) and 239(3), an order under either of those sections with respect to a transaction or preference entered into or given by a company may (subject to the next subsection)—

(a) require any property transferred as part of the transaction, or in connection with the giving of the preference, to be vested in the company,

(b) require any property to be so vested if it represents in any person's hands the application either of the proceeds of sale of property so transferred or of money so transferred,

(c) release or discharge (in whole or in part) any security given by the company,

(d) require any person to pay, in respect of benefits received by him from the company, such sums to the office-holder as the court may direct,

(e) provide for any surety or guarantor whose obligations to any person were released or discharged (in whole or in part) under the transaction, or by the giving of the preference, to be under such new or revived obligations to that person as the court thinks appropriate,

(f) provide for security to be provided for the discharge of any obligation imposed by or arising under the order, for such an obligation to be charged on any property and for the security or charge to have the same priority as a security or charge released or discharged (in whole or in part) under the transaction or by the giving of the preference, and

(g) provide for the extent to which any person whose property is vested by the order in the company, or on whom obligations are imposed by the order, is to be able to prove in the winding up of the company for debts or other liabilities which arose from, or were released or discharged (in whole or in part) under or by, the transaction or the giving of the preference.

(2) An order under section 238 or 239 may affect the property of, or impose any obligation on, any person whether or not he is the person with whom the company in question entered into the transaction or (as the case may be) the person to whom the preference was given; but such an order—

(a) shall not prejudice any interest in property which was acquired from a person other than the company and was acquired in good faith and for value or prejudice any interest deriving from such an interest, and

(b) shall not require a person who received a benefit from the transaction or preference [in good faith and for value] to pay a sum to the office-holder, except where that person was a party to the transaction or the payment is to be in respect of a preference given to that person at a time when he was a creditor of the company.

(2A) Where a person has acquired an interest in property from a person other than the company in question, or has received a benefit from the transaction or preference, and at the time of that acquisition or receipt—

(a) he had notice of the relevant surrounding circumstances and of the relevant proceedings, or

(b) he was connected with, or was an associate of, either the company in question or the person with whom that company entered into the transaction or to whom that company gave the preference,

then, unless the contrary is shown, it shall be presumed for the purposes of paragraph (a) or (as the case may be) paragraph (b) of subsection (2) that the interest was acquired or the benefit was received otherwise than in good faith.

(3)   For the purposes of subsection (2A)(a), the relevant surrounding circumstances are (as the case may require)—

    (a)   the fact that the company in question entered into the transaction at an undervalue; or

    (b)   the circumstances which amounted to the giving of the preference by the company in question;

and subsections (3A) to (3C) have effect to determine whether, for those purposes, a person has notice of the relevant proceedings.

(3A) Where section 238 or 239 applies by reason of a company's entering administration, a person has notice of the relevant proceedings if he has notice that—

    (a)   an administration application has been made,

    (b)   an administration order has been made,

    (c)   a copy of a notice of intention to appoint an administrator under paragraph 14 or 22 of Schedule B1 has been filed, or

    (d)   notice of the appointment of an administrator has been filed under paragraph 18 or 29 of that Schedule.

(3B) Where section 238 or 239 applies by reason of a company's going into liquidation at the time when the appointment of an administrator of the company ceases to have effect, a person has notice of the relevant proceedings if he has notice that—

    (a)   an administration application has been made,

    (b)   an administration order has been made,

    (c)   a copy of a notice of intention to appoint an administrator under paragraph 14 or 22 of Schedule B1 has been filed,

    (d)   notice of the appointment of an administrator has been filed under paragraph 18 or 29 of that Schedule, or

    (e)   the company has gone into liquidation.

(3C) In a case where section 238 or 239 applies by reason of the company in question going into liquidation at any other time, a person has notice of the relevant proceedings if he has notice—

    (a)   where the company goes into liquidation on the making of a winding-up order, of the fact that the petition on which the winding-up order is made has been presented or of the fact that the company has gone into liquidation;

(b)   in any other case, of the fact that the company has gone into liquidation.

(4)   The provisions of sections 238 to 241 apply without prejudice to the availability of any other remedy, even in relation to a transaction or preference which the company had no power to enter into or give.

435 Meaning of 'associate'

(1)   For the purposes of this Act any question whether a person is an associate of another person is to be determined in accordance with the following provisions of this section (any provision that a person is an associate of another person being taken to mean that they are associates of each other).

(2)   A person is an associate of an individual if that person is—

(a)   the individual's husband or wife or civil partner,

(b)   a relative of—

(i)   the individual, or

(ii)   the individual's husband or wife or civil partner, or

(c)   the husband or wife or civil partner of a relative of—

(i)   the individual, or

(ii)   the individual's husband or wife or civil partner.

(3)   A person is an associate of any person with whom he is in partnership, and of the husband or wife or civil partner or a relative of any individual with whom he is in partnership; and a Scottish firm is an associate of any person who is a member of the firm.

(4)   A person is an associate of any person whom he employs or by whom he is employed.

(5)   A person in his capacity as trustee of a trust other than—

(a)   a trust arising under any of the second Group of Parts or the Bankruptcy (Scotland) Act 1985, or

(b)   a pension scheme or an employees' share scheme (within the meaning of the Companies Act),

is an associate of another person if the beneficiaries of the trust include, or the terms of the trust confer a power that may be exercised for the benefit of, that other person or an associate of that other person.

(6)   A company is an associate of another company—

(a)   if the same person has control of both, or a person has control of one and persons who are his associates, or he and persons who are his associates, have control of the other, or

(b)   if a group of two or more persons has control of each company, and the groups either consist of the same persons or could be regarded as consisting of the same persons by treating (in one or more cases) a member of either group as replaced by a person of whom he is an associate.

(7)   A company is an associate of another person if that person has control of it or if that person and persons who are his associates together have control of it.

(8)   For the purposes of this section a person is a relative of an individual if he is that individual's brother, sister, uncle, aunt, nephew, niece, lineal ancestor or lineal descendant, treating—

(a)   any relationship of the half blood as a relationship of the whole blood and the stepchild or adopted child of any person as his child, and

(b)   an illegitimate child as the legitimate child of his mother and reputed father;

and references in this section to a husband or wife include a former husband or wife and a reputed husband or wife and references to a civil partner include a former civil partner and a reputed civil partner.

(9)   For the purposes of this section any director or other officer of a company is to be treated as employed by that company.

(10) For the purposes of this section a person is to be taken as having control of a company if—

(a)   the directors of the company or of another company which has control of it (or any of them) are accustomed to act in accordance with his directions or instructions, or

(b)   he is entitled to exercise, or control the exercise of, one third or more of the voting power at any general meeting of the company or of another company which has control of it;

and where two or more persons together satisfy either of the above conditions, they are to be taken as having control of the company.

(11) In this section 'company' includes any body corporate (whether incorporated in Great Britain or elsewhere); and references to directors and other officers of a company and to voting power at any general meeting of a company have effect with any necessary modifications.

22.1 ORDINARY APPLICATION FOR A DECLARATION THAT A PAYMENT IS A TRANSACTION AT AN UNDERVALUE PURSUANT TO SECTION 238 OF THE INSOLVENCY ACT 1986

Rule 7.2
Ordinary Application

IN THE HIGH COURT OF JUSTICE
CHANCERY DIVISION
COMPANIES COURT

NO: [ ] OF 20[ ]

IN THE MATTER OF BUSTCO LIMITED, REGISTERED NUMBER 011111
AND IN THE MATTER OF THE INSOLVENCY ACT 1986

BETWEEN:-

GILES GRABBER

<u>Applicant</u>

-and-

IAN FLAKEY

<u>Respondent</u>

TAKE NOTICE that I, Giles Grabber of Grabbers LLP, of 1 Vulture Street, London, as Liquidator of BUSTCO LIMITED, intend to apply to the Registrar on:

Date: [ ] 20[ ]
Time: [ ] am/pm
Place: Royal Courts of Justice, Strand, London WC2A 2LL

For an order in the following terms:

1. A declaration that the payment of £250,000 by Bustco Limited ('the Company') to the Respondent on or around 1st April 2008 is void against the Applicant as liquidator and that the same constituted a transaction at an undervalue within the meaning of section 238 of the Insolvency Act 1986.

2. An order that the Respondent do pay to the Applicant the sum of £250,000 and/or such other sum as this Honourable Court thinks fit to restore the position to what it would have been if the Company had not entered into the transaction and protecting the interests of the victims of the same.

3. An order that the Respondent do pay the Applicant's costs of and incidental to this application.

4.   Such further and other order and other relief as this Honourable Court thinks fit.

The grounds upon which I seek the above relief are set out in the 1st witness statement of Giles Grabber dated 1st April 2009, a true copy of which is served herewith.

Signed [ ]
Solicitor for the Applicant
Dated [ ] 20[ ]

The names and addresses of the persons upon whom it is intended to serve this application are:

Ian Flakey, 1 Geranium Cottage, London

The Applicant's address for service is:

SILK & CO
2 LAW STREET
LONDON

If you do not attend, the Court may make such order as it thinks fit.

22.2 **WITNESS STATEMENT TO SET ASIDE A TRANSACTION AT AN UNDERVALUE PURSUANT TO SECTION 238 OF THE INSOLVENCY ACT 1986**

Applicant: G Grabber: 1st: GG1: [ ] 20[ ]

IN THE HIGH COURT OF JUSTICE
CHANCERY DIVISION
COMPANIES COURT

NO: [ ] OF 20[ ]

IN THE MATTER OF BUSTCO LIMITED, REGISTERED NUMBER 011111
AND IN THE MATTER OF THE INSOLVENCY ACT 1986

1ST WITNESS STATEMENT OF GILES GRABBER

I, Giles Grabber of Grabbers LLP, of 1 Vulture Street, London, as Liquidator of BUSTCO LIMITED, state as follows:

1.   I am the Applicant in this application. I am the Liquidator of Bustco.

2.   I make the application in support of my application for:

a.   a declaration that the payment of £250,000 by Bustco Limited ('the Company') to the Respondent on or around 1st April 2008 is void against the Applicant as liquidator and that the same constituted a transaction at an undervalue within the meaning of section 238 of the Insolvency Act 1986,

b.   an order that the Respondent do pay to the Applicant the sum of £250,000 and/or such other sum as this Honourable Court thinks fit to restore the position to what it would have been if the Company had not entered into the transaction and protecting the interests of the victims of the same,

c.   an order that the Respondent do pay the Applicant's costs of and incidental to this application,

d.   such further and other order and other relief as this Honourable Court thinks fit

3.   The matters set out in this witness statement are true and within my own knowledge except where otherwise indicated, in which case I have explained the source of my information or belief.

4.   There is now produced and shown to me a bundle of consisting of true copies of the documents I will refer to in my witness statements marked 'GG1'.

5.   Bustco Limited was incorporated on 30th October 1996 under the Companies Act 1985.

6.   A winding up order was made against Bustco on the petition on 1st March 2009. I refer to page [ ] of 'GG1' which is a true copy of the winding up order.

7.   I was appointed as the liquidator of Bustco Limited on 1st April 2009. I refer to page [ ] of 'GG1' which is a true copy of my certificate of appointment.

8.   Bustco Limited's last set of accounts dated 31st December 2008 show that it was balance sheet insolvent as at 31st December 2008 with a deficiency in the sum of £2,000,000. I refer to page [ ] of 'GG1' which is a true copy of the accounts of Bustco Limited. Creditors claims lodged in the liquidation amount to £3,500,000. I refer to page [ ] of 'GG1' which is a true copy of the proofs of debt evidencing the creditors' claims.

9.   Following my appointment I began to investigate the affairs of Bustco Limited. The following matters became apparent.

10. Mr Flakey was at all material times a director of Bustco Limited. He was therefore a connected person for the purposes of the Insolvency Act 1986.

11. On 1st January 2009 there was a bank transfer in the sum of £250,000 from Bustco Limited to Mr Flakey. I refer to page [ ] of 'GG1' which is a true copy of the bank statement of Bustco Limited showing the transfer of £250,000 from Bustco Limited to Mr Flakey. This appears in the accounts as payment for a gobstopper bought from Mr Flakey. I refer to page [ ] of 'GG1' which is a true copy of the accounts of Bustco Limited showing the entry showing the purchase.

12. The true value of the gobstopper (even when not partially sucked) is 5 pence. This is a mere fraction of the £250,000 paid to Mr Flakey for this. I refer to page [ ] of 'GG1' which is a true copy of the price list of Toothy Sweets showing the retail price of their gobstoppers to be 5 pence each.

13. The money paid represented the whole of Bustco Ltd available money in the bank. The company was rendered unable to pay its debts as they fell due and thus insolvent as a result. By making the payment, the monies left in the company were dissipated. This meant that creditors in the winding up can hope for a dividend of no more than 1 penny for each £1 owed to them.

14. On 2nd January 2009 a winding up petition was presented by Her Majesty Revenue & Customs for £1 million in unpaid VAT. I refer to page [ ] of 'GG1' which is a true copy of the petition. The winding up petition had been preceded by a number of letters by HMRC warning that unless they were paid they intended to issue a winding up petition on 2nd January 2009. I refer to page [ ] of 'GG1' which is a true copy of the letters.

15. In the light of the above, the payment to the Respondent was at a significant undervalue to the Company and, given the circumstances and timing of the purchase, it is to be inferred that the payment was made that the payment was not made in good faith or for any purpose connected with carrying on of the Company's business and there can be no grounds for believing the payment was for benefit of the Company.

16. I therefore ask this Honourable Court to make the order in the terms sought.

STATEMENT OF TRUTH

I believe that the facts stated in this Witness Statement are true.

Signed [ ]
Full name [*GILES GRABBER*]
Dated [ ] 20[ ]

22.3   DECLARATION THAT A PAYMENT IS A TRANSACTION AT AN UNDERVALUE PURSUANT TO SECTION 238 OF THE INSOLVENCY ACT 1986

IN THE HIGH COURT OF JUSTICE
CHANCERY DIVISION
COMPANIES COURT

NO: [ ] OF 20[ ]

IN THE MATTER OF BUSTCO LIMITED, REGISTERED NUMBER 011111
AND IN THE MATTER OF THE INSOLVENCY ACT 1986

BEFORE MR REGISTRAR WISE
DATED: [ ] 20[ ]

BETWEEN:-

GILES GRABBER

Applicant

-and-

IAN FLAKEY

Respondent

DRAFT MINUTE OF ORDER

UPON THE APPLICATION of Giles Grabber of Grabbers LLP, Liquidator of the above named company, BUSTCO LIMITED ('the Company')

UPON HEARING Counsel for the Applicant and Counsel for Ian Flakey, the Respondent

AND UPON READING the evidence noted as being read

IT IS DECLARED that the payment of £250,000 by Bustco Limited ('the Company') to the Respondent on or around 1st April 2008 is void against the Applicant as liquidator and that the same constituted a transaction at an undervalue within the meaning of section 238 of the Insolvency Act 1986.

IT IS ORDERED that the Respondent do pay to the Applicant the sum of £250,000.

IT IS ORDERED that the Respondent do pay to the Applicant the costs of and occasioned by the Applicant such costs to be assessed if not agreed.

CHAPTER 23

APPLICATION TO SET ASIDE A PREFERENCE

OBJECTIVE

The court has wide powers on the application of the administrator or the liquidator to restore the position that would have been but for the preference being given to the company's creditors, sureties or guarantors which have been undertaken with a view to improving their position in the event of the company's liquidation.[1]

To be challenged, the preference must have occurred at a time in the time in the period of 2 years ending with the onset of insolvency where the respondent is a connected person or 6 months if the respondent is not.[2] The onset of insolvency means for these purposes either the presentation of the winding up petition, the filing of the administration notice or application or the passing of a resolution to wind up the company.[3] This period is only deemed to run whilst the company is unable to pay its debts (or if it is rendered unable to pay its debts by the arrangement); this is presumed where the arrangement is with a connected person.[4]

---

[1]   Section 239 of the Insolvency Act 1986.

[2]   Section 240 of the Insolvency Act 1986.

[3]   Section 129 of the Insolvency Act 1986.

[4]   For the meaning of a connected person see sections 249 and 425 of the Insolvency Act 1986.

APPLICATION

If there have been existing proceedings, the application is by ordinary application in those proceedings on notice for a declaration and an order restoring the position to what it would have been had the transaction not been entered into.

Where there have been no previous proceedings, the application should be made by originating application on notice.

The application must recite nature of the relief sought and the grounds for bringing the application.[5]

The application should be returnable to the registrar in the Companies Court or to the district judge in a Chancery District Registry or county court with insolvency jurisdiction.

The respondent should be the other party to the transaction that the liquidator or administrator is seeking to set aside.

COURT FEES

Where the application is made by originating application a court fee of £130 is payable.[6] Where the application is made by ordinary application on notice to other parties, a court fee of £60 is payable.[7] Where the application is made by consent or without notice in existing proceedings a court fee of £30 is payable.[8]

EVIDENCE

The application should be supported by a witness statement by the liquidator or administrator. This will need to address:

- the order he seeks;
- that the respondent is a creditor, guarantor or surety of the company;
- particulars of the respondent's loan, indemnity or guarantee;
- the date the company was incorporated;
- the registered office of the company;
- the nominal share capital of the company;
- the issued share capital of the company;
- the objects of the company;
- the date upon which the petition to wind up the company or place it into administration or notice of administration was presented;
- the date upon which the company went into liquidation or administration;
- that he was appointed as liquidator or administrator of the company;
- the date upon which he was appointed as liquidator or administrator;

---

5   Rule 7.3(2) of the Insolvency Rules 1986.
6   Paragraph 3.5 of Schedule 1 to the Civil Proceedings Fees Order 2008.
7   Paragraph 3.12 of Schedule 1 to the Civil Proceedings Fees Order 2008.
8   Paragraph 3.11 of Schedule 1 to the Civil Proceedings Fees Order 2008.

- the date of the transaction subject to challenge;
- the particulars of the arrangement subject to challenge;
- that the arrangement operated to prefer the position of the respondent in the event of the company's insolvent liquidation;
- why it is said that the arrangement operated to prefer the position of the respondent in the event of the company's insolvent liquidation;
- that in entering the arrangement the company had been influenced by a desire to putting the respondent in a better position in the company's insolvent liquidation;
- whether the respondent is a connected person and, if so why;
- that the company was insolvent (or is to be presumed to be insolvent) at the time of the transaction or was rendered insolent by the transaction.

And exhibit:

- evidence of his appointment as liquidator or administrator;
- the respondent's loan, indemnity or guarantee;
- a copy of the petition to wind up the company or place it into administration or notice of administration;
- a copy of the winding up or administration order;
- evidence of the arrangement subject to challenge;
- evidence that the respondent is a connected person (if applicable);
- evidence tending to show the insolvency or financial state of the company at the time of the transaction.

SERVICE

The application and the evidence in support will need to be filed at court and served on the respondent as soon as practicable after it is filed and in any event, unless it is necessary to apply ex parte or on short notice, at least 14 days before the date fixed for the hearing.[9]

The usual rule is that, subject to any other express provision, the application must be served at least 14 days before the date fixed for the hearing.[10] However, the court does have power, in cases of urgency, to hear an application immediately with or without notice to the other parties.[11]

Service may be effected by post provided it is addressed to the person it is to be served on and prepaid for either first or second class post.[12] It may be sent to the last known address of the person to be served.[13]

A document sent by first class post is treated as being served on the 2nd business day after posting, unless the contrary is shown.[14] A document sent by second class post is treated as being served on the 4th

---

[9]   Rule 7.4(5) of the Insolvency Rules 1986.
[10] Rule 7.4(5) of the Insolvency Rules 1986.
[11] Rule 7.4(6) of the Insolvency Rules 1986.
[12] Rule 12.10(1) of the Insolvency Rules 1986.
[13] Rule 12.10(1A) of the Insolvency Rules 1986.
[14] Rule 12.10(2) of the Insolvency Rules 1986.

business day after posting, unless the contrary is shown.[15] The date of posting is presumed to be the date postmarked on the envelope, unless the contrary is shown.[16]

Where service of any application or any order of the court is to be made to a person outside England and Wales an application must be made to the registrar for directions as to the manner, timing and proof of service.[17]

The application needs to be supported by a witness statement stating:[18]

- the grounds upon which the application is made;
- in what place the person to be served is either to be found or presumed to be found.

Subject to these provisions, Part 6 of the CPR is deemed to apply under the Insolvency Rules 1986.[19]

THE FIRST HEARING

At the first hearing the registrar or district judge will give directions as to whether points of claim and defence are needed and for the filing of evidence. He may also require the application to be served on other people. He may give directions as to whether witnesses are to attend for cross examination. The first hearing will be unrobed and is likely to be in chambers.

KEY STATUTORY PROVISIONS

Section 239, 240, 241 and 435 of the Insolvency Act 1986

239 Preferences (England and Wales)
(1)   This section applies as does section 238.

(2)   Where the company has at a relevant time (defined in the next section) given a preference to any person, the office-holder may apply to the court for an order under this section.

(3)   Subject as follows, the court shall, on such an application, make such order as it thinks fit for restoring the position to what it would have been if the company had not given that preference.

(4)   For the purposes of this section and section 241, a company gives a preference to a person if—

(a)   that person is one of the company's creditors or a surety or guarantor for any of the company's debts or other liabilities, and

---

[15]   Rule 12.10(3) of the Insolvency Rules 1986.
[16]   Rule 12.10(4) of the Insolvency Rules 1986.
[17]   Rule 12.12(3) of the Insolvency Rules 1986.
[18]   Rule 12.12(4) of the Insolvency Rules 1986.
[19]   Rule 12.11 of the Insolvency Rules 1986.

(b) the company does anything or suffers anything to be done which (in either case) has the effect of putting that person into a position which, in the event of the company going into insolvent liquidation, will be better than the position he would have been in if that thing had not been done.

(5) The court shall not make an order under this section in respect of a preference given to any person unless the company which gave the preference was influenced in deciding to give it by a desire to produce in relation to that person the effect mentioned in subsection (4)(b).

(6) A company which has given a preference to a person connected with the company (otherwise than by reason only of being its employee) at the time the preference was given is presumed, unless the contrary is shown, to have been influenced in deciding to give it by such a desire as is mentioned in subsection (5).

(7) The fact that something has been done in pursuance of the order of a court does not, without more, prevent the doing or suffering of that thing from constituting the giving of a preference.

240 'Relevant time' under ss 238, 239
(1) Subject to the next subsection, the time at which a company enters into a transaction at an undervalue or gives a preference is a relevant time if the transaction is entered into, or the preference given—

(a) in the case of a transaction at an undervalue or of a preference which is given to a person who is connected with the company (otherwise than by reason only of being its employee), at a time in the period of 2 years ending with the onset of insolvency (which expression is defined below),

(b) in the case of a preference which is not such a transaction and is not so given, at a time in the period of 6 months ending with the onset of insolvency, ...

(c) in either case, at a time between the making of an administration application in respect of the company and the making of an administration order on that application, and

(d) in either case, at a time between the filing with the court of a copy of notice of intention to appoint an administrator under paragraph 14 or 22 of Schedule B1 and the making of an appointment under that paragraph.

(2) Where a company enters into a transaction at an undervalue or gives a preference at a time mentioned in subsection (1)(a) or (b), that time is not a relevant time for the purposes of section 238 or 239 unless the company—

(a) is at that time unable to pay its debts within the meaning of section 123 in Chapter VI of Part IV, or

(b) becomes unable to pay its debts within the meaning of that section in consequence of the transaction or preference;

but the requirements of this subsection are presumed to be satisfied, unless the contrary is shown, in relation to any transaction at an undervalue which is entered into by a company with a person who is connected with the company.

(3)   For the purposes of subsection (1), the onset of insolvency is—

(a)   in a case where section 238 or 239 applies by reason of an administrator of a company being appointed by administration order, the date on which the administration application is made,

(b)   in a case where section 238 or 239 applies by reason of an administrator of a company being appointed under paragraph 14 or 22 of Schedule B1 following filing with the court of a copy of a notice of intention to appoint under that paragraph, the date on which the copy of the notice is filed,

(c)   in a case where section 238 or 239 applies by reason of an administrator of a company being appointed otherwise than as mentioned in paragraph (a) or (b), the date on which the appointment takes effect,

(d)   in a case where section 238 or 239 applies by reason of a company going into liquidation either following conversion of administration into winding up by virtue of Article 37 of the EC Regulation or at the time when the appointment of an administrator ceases to have effect, the date on which the company entered administration (or, if relevant, the date on which the application for the administration order was made or a copy of the notice of intention to appoint was filed), and

(e)   in a case where section 238 or 239 applies by reason of a company going into liquidation at any other time, the date of the commencement of the winding up.

241 Orders under ss 238, 239

(1)   Without prejudice to the generality of sections 238(3) and 239(3), an order under either of those sections with respect to a transaction or preference entered into or given by a company may (subject to the next subsection)—

(a)   require any property transferred as part of the transaction, or in connection with the giving of the preference, to be vested in the company,

(b)   require any property to be so vested if it represents in any person's hands the application either of the proceeds of sale of property so transferred or of money so transferred,

(c)   release or discharge (in whole or in part) any security given by the company,

(d)   require any person to pay, in respect of benefits received by him from the company, such sums to the office-holder as the court may direct,

(e)   provide for any surety or guarantor whose obligations to any person were released or discharged (in whole or in part) under the transaction, or by the giving of the preference, to be under such new or revived obligations to that person as the court thinks appropriate,

(f)   provide for security to be provided for the discharge of any obligation imposed by or arising under the order, for such an obligation to be charged on any property and for the security or charge to have the same priority as a security or charge released or discharged (in whole or in part) under the transaction or by the giving of the preference, and

(g)   provide for the extent to which any person whose property is vested by the order in the company, or on whom obligations are imposed by the order, is to be able to prove in the winding up of the company for debts or other liabilities which arose from, or were released or discharged (in whole or in part) under or by, the transaction or the giving of the preference.

(2)   An order under section 238 or 239 may affect the property of, or impose any obligation on, any person whether or not he is the person with whom the company in question entered into the transaction or (as the case may be) the person to whom the preference was given; but such an order—

(a)   shall not prejudice any interest in property which was acquired from a person other than the company and was acquired in good faith and for value or prejudice any interest deriving from such an interest, and

(b)   shall not require a person who received a benefit from the transaction or preference [in good faith and for value] to pay a sum to the office-holder, except where that person was a party to the transaction or the payment is to be in respect of a preference given to that person at a time when he was a creditor of the company.

(2A) Where a person has acquired an interest in property from a person other than the company in question, or has received a benefit from the transaction or preference, and at the time of that acquisition or receipt—

(a)   he had notice of the relevant surrounding circumstances and of the relevant proceedings, or

(b)   he was connected with, or was an associate of, either the company in question or the person with whom that company entered into the transaction or to whom that company gave the preference,

then, unless the contrary is shown, it shall be presumed for the purposes of paragraph (a) or (as the case may be) paragraph (b) of subsection (2) that the interest was acquired or the benefit was received otherwise than in good faith.

(3)   For the purposes of subsection (2A)(a), the relevant surrounding circumstances are (as the case may require)—

(a) the fact that the company in question entered into the transaction at an undervalue; or

(b) the circumstances which amounted to the giving of the preference by the company in question;

and subsections (3A) to (3C) have effect to determine whether, for those purposes, a person has notice of the relevant proceedings.

(3A) Where section 238 or 239 applies by reason of a company's entering administration, a person has notice of the relevant proceedings if he has notice that—

(a) an administration application has been made,

(b) an administration order has been made,

(c) a copy of a notice of intention to appoint an administrator under paragraph 14 or 22 of Schedule B1 has been filed, or

(d) notice of the appointment of an administrator has been filed under paragraph 18 or 29 of that Schedule.

(3B) Where section 238 or 239 applies by reason of a company's going into liquidation at the time when the appointment of an administrator of the company ceases to have effect, a person has notice of the relevant proceedings if he has notice that—

(a) an administration application has been made,

(b) an administration order has been made,

(c) a copy of a notice of intention to appoint an administrator under paragraph 14 or 22 of Schedule B1 has been filed,

(d) notice of the appointment of an administrator has been filed under paragraph 18 or 29 of that Schedule, or

(e) the company has gone into liquidation.

(3C) In a case where section 238 or 239 applies by reason of the company in question going into liquidation at any other time, a person has notice of the relevant proceedings if he has notice—

(a) where the company goes into liquidation on the making of a winding-up order, of the fact that the petition on which the winding-up order is made has been presented or of the fact that the company has gone into liquidation;

(b) in any other case, of the fact that the company has gone into liquidation.

(4)   The provisions of sections 238 to 241 apply without prejudice to the availability of any other remedy, even in relation to a transaction or preference which the company had no power to enter into or give.

435 Meaning of 'associate'

(1)   For the purposes of this Act any question whether a person is an associate of another person is to be determined in accordance with the following provisions of this section (any provision that a person is an associate of another person being taken to mean that they are associates of each other).

(2)   A person is an associate of an individual if that person is—

    (a)   the individual's husband or wife or civil partner,

    (b)   a relative of—

        (i)   the individual, or

        (ii)   the individual's husband or wife or civil partner, or

    (c)   the husband or wife or civil partner of a relative of—

        (i)   the individual, or

        (ii)   the individual's husband or wife or civil partner.

(3)   A person is an associate of any person with whom he is in partnership, and of the husband or wife or civil partner or a relative of any individual with whom he is in partnership; and a Scottish firm is an associate of any person who is a member of the firm.

(4)   A person is an associate of any person whom he employs or by whom he is employed.

(5)   A person in his capacity as trustee of a trust other than—

    (a)   a trust arising under any of the second Group of Parts or the Bankruptcy (Scotland) Act 1985, or

    (b)   a pension scheme or an employees' share scheme (within the meaning of the Companies Act),

is an associate of another person if the beneficiaries of the trust include, or the terms of the trust confer a power that may be exercised for the benefit of, that other person or an associate of that other person.

(6)   A company is an associate of another company—

(a)   if the same person has control of both, or a person has control of one and persons who are his associates, or he and persons who are his associates, have control of the other, or

(b)   if a group of two or more persons has control of each company, and the groups either consist of the same persons or could be regarded as consisting of the same persons by treating (in one or more cases) a member of either group as replaced by a person of whom he is an associate.

(7)   A company is an associate of another person if that person has control of it or if that person and persons who are his associates together have control of it.

(8)   For the purposes of this section a person is a relative of an individual if he is that individual's brother, sister, uncle, aunt, nephew, niece, lineal ancestor or lineal descendant, treating—

(a)   any relationship of the half blood as a relationship of the whole blood and the stepchild or adopted child of any person as his child, and

(b)   an illegitimate child as the legitimate child of his mother and reputed father;

and references in this section to a husband or wife include a former husband or wife and a reputed husband or wife and references to a civil partner include a former civil partner and a reputed civil partner.

(9)   For the purposes of this section any director or other officer of a company is to be treated as employed by that company.

(10) For the purposes of this section a person is to be taken as having control of a company if—

(a)   the directors of the company or of another company which has control of it (or any of them) are accustomed to act in accordance with his directions or instructions, or

(b)   he is entitled to exercise, or control the exercise of, one third or more of the voting power at any general meeting of the company or of another company which has control of it;

and where two or more persons together satisfy either of the above conditions, they are to be taken as having control of the company.

(11) In this section 'company' includes any body corporate (whether incorporated in Great Britain or elsewhere); and references to directors and other officers of a company and to voting power at any general meeting of a company have effect with any necessary modifications.

23.1 ORDINARY APPLICATION FOR A DECLARATION THAT A PAYMENT IS A PREFERENCE PURSUANT TO SECTION 239 OF THE INSOLVENCY ACT 1986

Rule 7.2
Ordinary Application

IN THE HIGH COURT OF JUSTICE
CHANCERY DIVISION
COMPANIES COURT

NO: [ ] OF 20[ ]

IN THE MATTER OF BUSTCO LIMITED, REGISTERED NUMBER 011111
AND IN THE MATTER OF THE INSOLVENCY ACT 1986

BETWEEN:-

GILES GRABBER

<u>Applicant</u>

-and-

IAN FLAKEY

<u>Respondent</u>

TAKE NOTICE that I, Giles Grabber of Grabbers LLP, of 1 Vulture Street, London, as Liquidator of BUSTCO LIMITED, intend to apply to the Registrar on:

Date: [ ] 20[ ]
Time: [ ] am/pm
Place: Royal Courts of Justice, Strand, London WC2A 2LL

For an order in the following terms:

1. A declaration that the payment of £250,000 by Bustco Limited ('the Company') to the Respondent on or around 1st April 2008 constituted a preference pursuant to section 239 of the Insolvency Act 1986, and /or

2. An order that the Respondent do pay to the Applicant the sum of £250,000 and/or such other sum as this Honourable Court thinks fit to restore the position to what it would have been if the Company had not given the preference pursuant to section 239 of the of the Insolvency Act 1986, and /or

3. An order that the Respondent do pay the Applicant's costs of and incidental to this application.

4.   Such further and other order and other relief as this Honourable Court thinks fit.

The grounds upon which I seek the above relief are set out in the 1st witness statement of Giles Grabber dated 1st April 2009, a true copy of which is served herewith.

Signed [ ]
Solicitor for the Applicant
Dated [ ] 20[ ]

The names and addresses of the persons upon whom it is intended to serve this application are:

Ian Flakey, 1 Geranium Cottage, London

The Applicant's address for service is:

SILK & CO
2 LAW STREET
LONDON

If you do not attend, the Court may make such order as it thinks fit.

23.2   WITNESS STATEMENT TO SET ASIDE A PREFERENCE PURSUANT TO SECTION 239 OF THE INSOLVENCY ACT 1986

Applicant: G Grabber: 1st: GG1: [ ] 20[ ]

IN THE HIGH COURT OF JUSTICE
CHANCERY DIVISION
COMPANIES COURT

NO: [ ] OF 20[ ]

IN THE MATTER OF BUSTCO LIMITED, REGISTERED NUMBER 011111
AND IN THE MATTER OF THE INSOLVENCY ACT 1986

1ST WITNESS STATEMENT OF GILES GRABBER

I, Giles Grabber of Grabbers LLP, of 1 Vulture Street, London, as Liquidator of BUSTCO LIMITED, state as follows:

1.   I am the Applicant in this application. I am the Liquidator of Bustco.

2.   I make the application in support of my application for:

    a.   a declaration that the payment of £250,000 by Bustco Limited ('the Company') to the Respondent on or around 1st April 2008 constituted a preference pursuant to section 239 of the Insolvency Act 1986, and /or

    b.   an order that the Respondent do pay to the Applicant the sum of £250,000 and/or such other sum as this Honourable Court thinks fit to restore the position to what it would have been if the Company had not given the preference pursuant to section 239 of the Insolvency Act 1986, and /or

    c.   an order that the Respondent do pay the Applicant's costs of and incidental to this application,

    d.   such further and other order and other relief as this Honourable Court thinks fit.

3.   The matters set out in this witness statement are true and within my own knowledge except where otherwise indicated, in which case I have explained the source of my information or belief.

4.   There is now produced and shown to me a bundle consisting of true copies of the documents I will refer to in my witness statements marked 'GG1'.

5.   Bustco Limited was incorporated on 30th October 1996 under the Companies Act 1985.

6.   The registered office of the Company is at Suite 1, 1 Poor Street, London.

7.   The nominal capital of the Company is £1000 divided into 1000 shares of £1 each. The amount of the capital paid up or credited as paid up is £2.

8.   The principal objects for which the Company was established are as follows: To carry on business as a general trading company and other objects stated in the memorandum of association of the Company.

9.   A winding up order was made against Bustco on the petition on 1st March 2009. I refer to page [ ] of 'GG1' which is a true copy of the winding up order.

10. I was appointed as the liquidator of Bustco Limited on 1st April 2009. I refer to page [ ] of 'GG1' which is a true copy of my certificate of appointment.

11. Bustco Limited's last set of accounts dated 31st December 2008 show that it was balance sheet insolvent as at 31st December 2008 with a deficiency in the sum of £2,000,000. I refer to page [ ] of 'GG1' which is a true copy of the accounts of Bustco Limited. Creditors' claims lodged in the liquidation amount to £3,500,000. I refer to page [ ] of 'GG1' which is a true copy of the proofs of debt evidencing the creditors' claims.

12. Following my appointment I began to investigate the affairs of Bustco Limited. The following matters became apparent.

13. On 1st January 2009 there was a bank transfer in the sum of £250,000 from Bustco Limited to Mr Flakey. I refer to page [ ] of 'GG1' which is a true copy of the bank statement of Bustco Limited showing the transfer of £250,000 from Bustco Limited to Mr Flakey in repayment of a director's loan made by Mr Flakey. I refer to page [ ] of 'GG1' which is a true copy of the accounts of Bustco Limited showing the directors loan.

14. The payment operated to fully satisfy Bustco's indebtedness to Mr Flakey.

15. The money paid represented the whole of Bustco Ltd available money in the bank. By making the payment, the monies left mean that creditors in the winding up can hope for a dividend of no more than 1 pence for each £ owed them.

16. On 2nd January 2009 a winding up petition was presented by Her Majesty Revenue & Customs for £1 million in unpaid VAT. I refer to page [ ] of 'GG1' which is a true copy of the petition.

17. Due to the proximity of the payments and the onset of insolvency, it is inconceivable that the company was solvent at the date of the payment.

18. Mr Flakey is and was a director of Bustco Limited and was therefore a connected person within the meaning of section 249 of the Insolvency Act 1986.

19. In the light of the above, I am advised that the payment to the Respondent constituted a voidable preference within the meaning of section 239 of the Act in that the payments occurred at a relevant

time within the meaning of section 240(1)(a) of the Act and at the date of payment Bustco was unable to pay its debts within the meaning of section 123 of the Act and/or became so unable as a consequence of the preference.

20. In the circumstances as described above, it may be inferred that the Bustco Limited, in making the payments to Mr Flakey was influenced by a desire to put him into a better position in the event of Bustco Limited going into insolvent liquidation than if the payments had not been made.

21. Further, in any event, Mr Flakey was connected with Bustco Limited at the time the payment was made and thus Bustco Limited is presumed to be influenced in deciding to make it by the desire described above.

22. I therefore ask this Honourable Court to make the order in the terms sought.

STATEMENT OF TRUTH

I believe that the facts stated in this Witness Statement are true.

Signed [ ]
Full name [*GILES GRABBER*]
Dated [ ] 20[ ]

23.3   DECLARATION OF A PREFERENCE PURSUANT TO SECTION 239 OF THE INSOLVENCY ACT 1986

IN THE HIGH COURT OF JUSTICE
CHANCERY DIVISION
COMPANIES COURT

NO: [ ] OF 20[ ]

IN THE MATTER OF BUSTCO LIMITED, REGISTERED NUMBER 011111
AND IN THE MATTER OF THE INSOLVENCY ACT 1986

BEFORE MR REGISTRAR WISE
DATED: [ ] 20[ ]

BETWEEN:-

GILES GRABBER

Applicant

-and-

IAN FLAKEY

Respondent

DRAFT MINUTE OF ORDER

UPON THE APPLICATION of Giles Grabber of Grabbers LLP, Liquidator of the above named company, BUSTCO LIMITED ('the Company')

UPON HEARING Counsel for the Applicant and Counsel for Ian Flakey, the Respondent

AND UPON READING the evidence noted as being read

IT IS DECLARED that the payment of £250,000 by Bustco Limited ('the Company') to the Respondent on or around 1st April 2008 is void against the Applicant as liquidator and that the same constituted a preference within the meaning of section 239 of the Insolvency Act 1986.

IT IS ORDERED that the Respondent do pay to the Applicant the sum of £250,000.

IT IS ORDERED that the Respondent do pay to the Applicant the costs of and occasioned by the Applicant such costs to be assessed if not agreed.

CHAPTER 24

APPLICATION FOR A DECLARATION THAT THE DIRECTOR HAS BEEN ENGAGED IN FRAUDULENT TRADING

OBJECTIVE

The court has the power on the application of the liquidator to make a declaration that a person has been knowingly a party to the carrying on of the business of the company with intent to defraud and may order that they are liable to make a contribution in a sum the court fixes to the company assets.[1]

The application can be made against any person who was a knowing party to the fraudulent trading.[2]

A single instance of fraudulent activity in respect of one creditor suffices to constitute fraudulent trading.[3] Any compensation ordered goes to the general funds in the hands of the liquidator rather than to compensate an individual creditor. This is the case even though the nature of the contribution is

---

[1]   Section 213 of the Insolvency Act 1986.

[2]   *Banque Arabe Internationale d'Investissement SA v Morris* [2002] BCC 407.

[3]   *Morphites v Bernasconi* [2003] BCC 540.

compensatory rather than punitive.[4] The company is only treated as carrying on business up to the time when the winding up petition was presented.[5]

APPLICATION

Only the liquidator has standing to make this application.

If there have been existing proceedings, the application is by ordinary application in those proceedings on notice for a declaration and an order restoring the position.

Where there have been no previous proceedings, the application should be made by originating application on notice.

The application must recite nature of the declaration sought and the grounds for bringing the application.[6]

The application should be returnable to the registrar in the Companies Court or to the district judge in a Chancery District Registry or county court with insolvency jurisdiction.

The respondent should be the person who was a knowing party to the fraudulent trading against whom relief is sought.[7]

COURT FEES

Where the application is made by originating application a court fee of £130 is payable.[8] Where the application is made by ordinary application on notice to other parties, a court fee of £60 is payable.[9] Where the application is made by consent or without notice in existing proceedings a court fee of £30 is payable.[10]

SERVICE

The application will need to be filed at court and served on the respondent as soon as practicable after it is filed and in any event, unless it is necessary to apply ex parte or on short notice, at least 14 days before the date fixed for the hearing.[11]

The usual rule is that, subject to any other express provision, the application must be served at least 14 days before the date fixed for the hearing.[12] However, the court does have power, in cases of urgency, to hear an application immediately with or without notice to the other parties.[13]

---

[4]   *Morphites v Bernasconi* [2003] BCC 540.

[5]   *Carman v Cronos Group SA* [2006] BCC 451.

[6]   Rule 7.3(2) of the Insolvency Rules 1986.

[7]   *Banque Arabe Internationale d'Investissement SA v Morris* [2002] BCC 407.

[8]   Paragraph 3.5 of Schedule 1 to the Civil Proceedings Fees Order 2008.

[9]   Paragraph 3.12 of Schedule 1 to the Civil Proceedings Fees Order 2008.

[10]   Paragraph 3.11 of Schedule 1 to the Civil Proceedings Fees Order 2008.

[11]   Rule 7.4(5) of the Insolvency Rules 1986.

Service may be effected by post provided it is addressed to the person it is to be served on and prepaid for either first or second class post.[14] It may be sent to the last known address of the person to be served.[15]

A document sent by first class post is treated as being served on the 2nd business day after posting, unless the contrary is shown.[16] A document sent by second class post is treated as being served on the 4th business day after posting, unless the contrary is shown.[17] The date of posting is presumed to be the date postmarked on the envelope, unless the contrary is shown.[18]

Where service of any application or any order of the court is to be made to a person outside England and Wales an application must be made to the registrar for directions as to the manner, timing and proof of service.[19]

The application needs to be supported by a witness statement stating:[20]

- the grounds upon which the application is made;
- in what place the person to be served is either to be found or presumed to be found.

Subject to these provisions, Part 6 of the CPR is deemed to apply under the Insolvency Rules 1986.[21]

THE FIRST HEARING

At the first hearing the registrar or district judge will give directions as to whether points of claim and defence are needed and for the filing of evidence. He may also require the application to be served on other people. He may give directions as to whether witnesses are to attend for cross examination. The first hearing will be unrobed and is likely to be in chambers.

EVIDENCE

No evidence needs to be filed before the first hearing. The application will however need in due course to be supported by a witness statement by the liquidator. This will need to address:

- the order he seeks;
- the date the company was incorporated;
- the registered office of the company;
- the nominal share capital of the company;

---

[12]   Rule 7.4(5) of the Insolvency Rules 1986.
[13]   Rule 7.4(6) of the Insolvency Rules 1986.
[14]   Rule 12.10(1) of the Insolvency Rules 1986.
[15]   Rule 12.10(1A) of the Insolvency Rules 1986.
[16]   Rule 12.10(2) of the Insolvency Rules 1986.
[17]   Rule 12.10(3) of the Insolvency Rules 1986.
[18]   Rule 12.10(4) of the Insolvency Rules 1986.
[19]   Rule 12.12(3) of the Insolvency Rules 1986.
[20]   Rule 12.12(4) of the Insolvency Rules 1986.
[21]   Rule 12.11 of the Insolvency Rules 1986.

- the issued share capital of the company;
- the objects of the company;
- the date upon which the petition to wind up the company was presented;
- the date upon which the company went into liquidation;
- that he was appointed as liquidator of the company;
- the date upon which he was appointed as liquidator;
- details of the trading that is being criticised;
- particulars of why the trading was fraudulent;
- that the respondent is a person who was a knowing party to the fraudulent trading;[22]
- particulars of how the respondent was involved;
- particulars of how it is said knowledge can be attributed to the respondent;
- if there is more than one respondent, the role each played in the fraudulent trading;
- that the arrangement operated to cause loss to the company and its creditors;
- particulars of the loss caused to the company or its company by the respondent (or if more than one, attributable to each respondent).

And exhibit:

- evidence of his appointment as liquidator or administrator;
- material showing the fraudulent trading and the respondent's involvement or knowledge of it;
- evidence of the loss caused by the respondent's involvement in the fraudulent trading;
- a copy of the petition to wind up the company;
- a copy of the winding up order.

KEY STATUTORY PROVISIONS

Sections 213 and 215 of the Insolvency Act 1986

213 Fraudulent trading

(1)　If in the course of the winding up of a company it appears that any business of the company has been carried on with intent to defraud creditors of the company or creditors of any other person, or for any fraudulent purpose, the following has effect.

(2)　The court, on the application of the liquidator may declare that any persons who were knowingly parties to the carrying on of the business in the manner above-mentioned are to be liable to make such contributions (if any) to the company's assets as the court thinks proper.

215 Proceedings under ss 213, 214

(1)　On the hearing of an application under section 213 or 214, the liquidator may himself give evidence or call witnesses.

(2)　Where under either section the court makes a declaration, it may give such further directions as it thinks proper for giving effect to the declaration; and in particular, the court may—

---

[22]　*Banque Arabe Internationale d'Investissement SA v Morris* [2002] BCC 407.

(a) provide for the liability of any person under the declaration to be a charge on any debt or obligation due from the company to him, or on any mortgage or charge or any interest in a mortgage or charge on assets of the company held by or vested in him, or any person on his behalf, or any person claiming as assignee from or through the person liable or any person acting on his behalf, and

(b) from time to time make such further order as may be necessary for enforcing any charge imposed under this subsection.

(3) For the purposes of subsection (2), 'assignee'—

(a) includes a person to whom or in whose favour, by the directions of the person made liable, the debt, obligation, mortgage or charge was created, issued or transferred or the interest created, but

(b) does not include an assignee for valuable consideration (not including consideration by way of marriage [or the formation of a civil partnership]) given in good faith and without notice of any of the matters on the ground of which the declaration is made.

(4) Where the court makes a declaration under either section in relation to a person who is a creditor of the company, it may direct that the whole or any part of any debt owed by the company to that person and any interest thereon shall rank in priority after all other debts owed by the company and after any interest on those debts.

(5) Sections 213 and 214 have effect notwithstanding that the person concerned may be criminally liable in respect of matters on the ground of which the declaration under the section is to be made.

24.1   **ORDINARY APPLICATION FOR A DECLARATION THAT A DIRECTOR HAS BEEN ENGAGED IN FRAUDULENT TRADING PURSUANT TO SECTION 216 OF THE INSOLVENCY ACT 1986**

Rule 7.2
Ordinary Application

IN THE HIGH COURT OF JUSTICE
CHANCERY DIVISION
COMPANIES COURT

NO: [ ] OF 20[ ]

IN THE MATTER OF BUSTCO LIMITED, REGISTERED NUMBER 011111
AND IN THE MATTER OF THE INSOLVENCY ACT 1986

BETWEEN:-

GILES GRABBER

<u>Applicant</u>

-and-

IAN FLAKEY

<u>Respondent</u>

TAKE NOTICE that I, Giles Grabber of Grabbers LLP, of 1 Vulture Street, London, as Liquidator of BUSTCO LIMITED, intend to apply to the Registrar on:

Date: [ ] 20[ ]
Time: [ ] am/pm
Place: Royal Courts of Justice, Strand, London WC2A 2LL

For an order in the following terms:

1. A declaration that the Respondent has been knowingly a party to the carrying on of the business of Bustco Limited ('the Company') with intent to defraud creditors of the Company and for other fraudulent purposes and that he is liable to make such contributions to the assets of the Company as this Honourable Court thinks proper pursuant to section 213 of the Insolvency Act 1986, and/or

2. An order that the Respondent do pay to the Applicant the sum found due under paragraph 1, and/or

3. An order that the Respondent do pay the Applicant's costs of and incidental to this application.

4. Such further and other order and other relief as this Honourable Court thinks fit.

The grounds upon which I seek the above relief are set out in the 1st witness statement of Giles Grabber dated 1st April 2009, a true copy of which is served herewith.

Signed [ ]
Solicitor for the Applicant
Dated [ ] 20[ ]

The names and addresses of the persons upon whom it is intended to serve this application are:

Ian Flakey, 1 Geranium Cottage, London

The Applicant's address for service is:

SILK & CO
2 LAW STREET
LONDON

If you do not attend, the Court may make such order as it thinks fit.

24.2 WITNESS STATEMENT FOR A DECLARATION OF FRAUDULENT TRADING PURSUANT TO SECTION 213 OF THE INSOLVENCY ACT 1986

Applicant: G Grabber: 1st: GG1: [ ] 20[ ]

IN THE HIGH COURT OF JUSTICE
CHANCERY DIVISION
COMPANIES COURT

NO: [ ] OF 20[ ]

IN THE MATTER OF BUSTCO LIMITED, REGISTERED NUMBER 011111
AND IN THE MATTER OF THE INSOLVENCY ACT 1986

1ST WITNESS STATEMENT OF GILES GRABBER

I, Giles Grabber of Grabbers LLP, of 1 Vulture Street, London, as Liquidator of BUSTCO LIMITED, state as follows:

1. I am the Applicant in this application. I am the Liquidator of Bustco.

2. I make the application in support of my application for:

   a. a declaration that the Respondent has been knowingly a party to the carrying on of the business of Bustco Limited ('the Company') with intent to defraud creditors of the Company and for other fraudulent purposes and that he is liable to make such contributions to the assets of the Company as this Honourable Court thinks proper pursuant to section 213 of the Insolvency Act 1986, and /or

   b. an order that the Respondent do pay to the Applicant the sum found due under paragraph 1, and /or

   c. an order that the Respondent do pay the Applicant's costs of and incidental to this application,

   d. such further and other order and other relief as this Honourable Court thinks fit.

4. The matters set out in this witness statement are true and within my own knowledge except where otherwise indicated, in which case I have explained the source of my information or belief.

5. There is now produced and shown to me a bundle consisting of true copies of the documents I will refer to in my witness statements marked 'GG1'.

6. Bustco Limited was incorporated on 30th October 1996 under the Companies Act 1985. The share capital of the company is £100 shares divided into 100 ordinary shares of £1 each of which 2 shares have been issued to Mr Flakey. Mr Flakey was the company's sole director at all material times.

7. A winding up order was made against Bustco on the petition on 1st March 2009. I refer to page [ ] of 'GG1' which is a true copy of the winding up order.

8. I was appointed as the liquidator of Bustco Limited on 1st April 2009. I refer to page [ ] of 'GG1' which is a true copy of my certificate of appointment.

9. Following my appointment I began to investigate the affairs of Bustco Limited. The following matters became apparent.

10. Bustco Limited held itself out manufacturers of widgets and continued until the date of its winding up to take orders for the supply of widgets from its customers. Its terms of business required customers to pay for their orders in advance of delivery.

11. In fact, Bustco had on 31st December 2006 sold its widget maker and had, since that date, no means of manufacturing their own widgets and indeed any raw materials for the manufacture of widgets. I can see from the company papers of Bustco Limited that the company further did not pay for, purchase or indeed order any widgets or raw materials from any other suppliers. Nor is there any evidence that Bustco Limited retained any widgets in stock. I refer to page [ ] of 'GG1' which is a true copy of the accounts for 2007 and 2008 signed by Mr Flakey which each show figures of 'nil' under work in progress, payments to suppliers and under stock held.

12. The monies received from the sale of widgets seemed to be wholly deployed in paying Mr Flakey's director's fees. I refer to page [ ] of 'GG1' which is a true copy of the accounts for 2007 and 2008 signed by Mr Flakey. Mr Flakey's wage is shown in the notes to the accounts.

13. In the light of the above, it must have been obvious to Mr Flakey as a director of the Company that the Company had neither the means nor the intention to honour the commitments it was entering into to supply widgets and for which it was taking payment on account from its customers.

14. I therefore ask this Honourable Court to make the order in the terms sought.

STATEMENT OF TRUTH

I believe that the facts stated in this Witness Statement are true.

Signed [ ]
Full name [*GILES GRABBER*]
Dated [ ] 20[ ]

24.3   DECLARATION THAT A DIRECTOR HAS BEEN ENGAGED IN FRAUDULENT TRADING PURSUANT TO SECTION 213 OF THE INSOLVENCY ACT 1986

IN THE HIGH COURT OF JUSTICE
CHANCERY DIVISION
COMPANIES COURT

NO: [ ] OF 20[ ]

IN THE MATTER OF BUSTCO LIMITED, REGISTERED NUMBER 011111
AND IN THE MATTER OF THE INSOLVENCY ACT 1986

BEFORE MR REGISTRAR WISE
DATED: [ ] 20[ ]

BETWEEN:-

GILES GRABBER

<u>Applicant</u>

-and-

IAN FLAKEY

<u>Respondent</u>

DRAFT MINUTE OF ORDER

UPON THE APPLICATION of Giles Grabber of Grabbers LLP, Liquidator of the above named company, BUSTCO LIMITED ('the Company')

UPON HEARING Counsel for the Applicant and Counsel for Ian Flakey, the Respondent

AND UPON READING the evidence noted as being read

IT IS DECLARED that the Respondent, Ian Flakey, as a director the Company was knowingly party to the carrying on of the business of the Company with intent to defraud creditors for the period from 1st April 2008 to liquidation, and is to be personally liable to the extent of £250,000 for its debts and liabilities.

IT IS ORDERED that the Respondent do pay to the Applicant the sum of £250,000 by 4pm 1st June 2009 and such sums shall form part of the general assets of the liquidation of the Company.

IT IS ORDERED that the Respondent do pay to the Applicant the costs of and occasioned by the Applicant such costs to be assessed on the standard basis if not agreed with liberty to the Applicant to indemnify himself in respect thereof out of the assets of the Company.

CHAPTER 25

APPLICATION FOR A DECLARATION THAT THE DIRECTOR HAS BEEN ENGAGED IN WRONGFUL TRADING

OBJECTIVE

The court has the power on the application of the liquidator to make a declaration that a person who is or was a director of the company in liquidation has been carrying on the business of the company as a director at a time when he knew or ought to have concluded that there was no reasonable prospect that the company would avoid going into insolvent liquidation.[1] If the court makes such a declaration, the court can also order that the director is liable to make a contribution in a sum the court fixes to the company assets.[2]

The application can be made against any person who is or was a director the company in liquidation.[3] 'Director' includes a shadow director.[4]

---

[1]   Section 214(1), (2) of the Insolvency Act 1986.

[2]   Section 214(1) of the Insolvency Act 1986.

[3]   Section 214(1) of the Insolvency Act 1986.

[4]   Section 214(7) of the Insolvency Act 1986.

Any compensation ordered goes to the general funds in the hands of the liquidator rather than to compensate an individual creditor. This is the case even though the nature of the contribution is compensatory rather than punitive.[5] The liability of the directors is several rather than joint and several.[6]

The director has a defence if he can show that he took every step with a view to minimizing the potential loss to the company's creditors he ought to have taken with the knowledge that there was no reasonable prospect of the company would avoid going into insolvent liquidation.[7]

The knowledge of the director and the conclusions he ought to have reached is for the purposes of the section are judged against that which might be expected of a reasonably diligent person having both the general knowledge, skill and experience that may reasonably expected of a person carrying out the same functions by that director in relation to the company and the general knowledge, skill and experience that the director has.[8]

APPLICATION

Only the liquidator has standing to make this application.

If there have been existing proceedings, the application is by ordinary application in those proceedings on notice for a declaration and an order restoring the position.

Where there have been no previous proceedings, the application should be made by originating application on notice.

The application must recite nature of the declaration sought and the grounds for bringing the application.[9]

The application should be returnable to the registrar in the Companies Court or to the district judge in a Chancery District Registry or county court with insolvency jurisdiction.

The respondent should be the person against whom relief is sought.[10]

COURT FEES

Where the application is made by originating application a court fee of £130 is payable.[11] Where the application is made by ordinary application on notice to other parties, a court fee of £60 is payable.[12]

---

5   *Morphites v Bernasconi* [2003] BCC 540.

6   *Re Continental Assurance Co of London plc* [2001] BPIR 733.

7   Section 214(3) of the Insolvency Act 1986.

8   Section 214(4) of the Insolvency Act 1986. Thus Know J held he was entitled to assume that the directors knew the companies financial results in the absence of proper accounting records: *Re Produce Marketing Consortium Ltd* (1989) 5 BCC 569.

9   Rule 7.3(2) of the Insolvency Rules 1986.

10   *Banque Arabe Internationale d'Investissement SA v Morris* [2002] BCC 407.

11   Paragraph 3.5 of Schedule 1 to the Civil Proceedings Fees Order 2008.

12   Paragraph 3.12 of Schedule 1 to the Civil Proceedings Fees Order 2008.

Where the application is made by consent or without notice in existing proceedings a court fee of £30 is payable.[13]

SERVICE

The application will need to be filed at court and served on the respondent as soon as practicable after it is filed and in any event, unless it is necessary to apply ex parte or on short notice, at least 14 days before the date fixed for the hearing.[14]

The usual rule is that, subject to any other express provision, the application must be served at least 14 days before the date fixed for the hearing.[15] However, the court does have power, in cases of urgency, to hear an application immediately with or without notice to the other parties.[16]

Service may be effected by post provided it is addressed to the person it is to be served on and prepaid for either first or second class post.[17] It may be sent to the last known address of the person to be served.[18]

A document sent by first class post is treated as being served on the 2nd business day after posting, unless the contrary is shown.[19] A document sent by second class post is treated as being served on the 4th business day after posting, unless the contrary is shown.[20] The date of posting is presumed to be the date postmarked on the envelope, unless the contrary is shown.[21]

Where service of any application or any order of the court is to be made to a person outside England and Wales an application must be made to the registrar for directions as to the manner, timing and proof of service.[22]

The application needs to be supported by a witness statement stating:[23]

- the grounds upon which the application is made;
- in what place the person to be served is either to be found or presumed to be found.

Subject to these provisions, Part 6 of the CPR is deemed to apply under the Insolvency Rules 1986.[24]

---

[13]   Paragraph 3.11 of Schedule 1 to the Civil Proceedings Fees Order 2008.

[14]   Rule 7.4(5) of the Insolvency Rules 1986.

[15]   Rule 7.4(5) of the Insolvency Rules 1986.

[16]   Rule 7.4(6) of the Insolvency Rules 1986.

[17]   Rule 12.10(1) of the Insolvency Rules 1986.

[18]   Rule 12.10(1A) of the Insolvency Rules 1986.

[19]   Rule 12.10(2) of the Insolvency Rules 1986.

[20]   Rule 12.10(3) of the Insolvency Rules 1986.

[21]   Rule 12.10(4) of the Insolvency Rules 1986.

[22]   Rule 12.12(3) of the Insolvency Rules 1986.

[23]   Rule 12.12(4) of the Insolvency Rules 1986.

[24]   Rule 12.11 of the Insolvency Rules 1986.

THE FIRST HEARING

At the first hearing the registrar or district judge will give directions as to whether points of claim are needed and for the filing of evidence. He may also require the application to be served on other people. He may give directions as to whether witnesses are to attend for cross examination. The first hearing is likely to be heard in chambers and the advocates are not expected to robe.

EVIDENCE

No evidence needs to be filed before the first hearing. The application will however need in due course to be supported by a witness statement by the liquidator. This will need to address:

- the order he seeks;
- the date the company was incorporated;
- the registered office of the company;
- the nominal share capital of the company;
- the issued share capital of the company;
- the objects of the company;
- the date upon which the petition to wind up the company was presented;
- the date upon which the company went into liquidation;
- that he was appointed as liquidator of the company;
- the date upon which he was appointed as liquidator;
- the date the company became insolvent;
- that the respondent is or was a director of the company at the time;
- the respondent's role in allowing the company to continue to trade;
- particulars of the matters that the respondent can be said to have known about or ought to have known about;
- the conclusions which might be expected of a reasonably diligent person having both the general knowledge, skill and experience that may reasonably expected of a person carrying out the same functions by that director in relation to the company and the general knowledge, skill and experience that the director has;
- that the respondent was carrying on the business of the company at a time when he knew or ought to have concluded that there was no reasonable prospect of the company would avoid going into insolvent liquidation;
- what steps the director could have taken to minimise the potential loss to the company's creditors;[25]
- if there is more than one respondent, the role each played in the wrongful trading;
- that the arrangement operated to cause loss to the company and its creditors;
- particulars of the loss caused to the company or its company by the respondent (or if more than one, attributable to each respondent).

And exhibit:

- evidence of his appointment as liquidator or administrator;
- the winding up order;

---

[25]   Pre-empting the defence under section 214(3) of the Insolvency Act 1986.

- evidence of the date the company became insolvent;
- material showing the trading at a time when the company was insolvent;
- evidence of the respondent's involvement in and knowledge of the company's wrongful trading;
- any relevant board meetings;
- evidence of the loss caused by the respondent's involvement in the wrongful trading;
- a copy of the petition to wind up the company;
- a copy of the winding up order.

KEY STATUTORY PROVISIONS

Sections 214 and 215 of the Insolvency Act 1986

214 Wrongful trading

(1) Subject to subsection (3) below, if in the course of the winding up of a company it appears that subsection (2) of this section applies in relation to a person who is or has been a director of the company, the court, on the application of the liquidator, may declare that that person is to be liable to make such contribution (if any) to the company's assets as the court thinks proper.

(2) This subsection applies in relation to a person if—

    (a) the company has gone into insolvent liquidation,

    (b) at some time before the commencement of the winding up of the company, that person knew or ought to have concluded that there was no reasonable prospect that the company would avoid going into insolvent liquidation, and

    (c) that person was a director of the company at that time;

but the court shall not make a declaration under this section in any case where the time mentioned in paragraph (b) above was before 28th April 1986.

(3) The court shall not make a declaration under this section with respect to any person if it is satisfied that after the condition specified in subsection (2)(b) was first satisfied in relation to him that person took every step with a view to minimising the potential loss to the company's creditors as (assuming him to have known that there was no reasonable prospect that the company would avoid going into insolvent liquidation) he ought to have taken.

(4) For the purposes of subsections (2) and (3), the facts which a director of a company ought to know or ascertain, the conclusions which he ought to reach and the steps which he ought to take are those which would be known or ascertained, or reached or taken, by a reasonably diligent person having both—

    (a) the general knowledge, skill and experience that may reasonably be expected of a person carrying out the same functions as are carried out by that director in relation to the company, and

    (b) the general knowledge, skill and experience that that director has.

(5)   The reference in subsection (4) to the functions carried out in relation to a company by a director of the company includes any functions which he does not carry out but which have been entrusted to him.

(6)   For the purposes of this section a company goes into insolvent liquidation if it goes into liquidation at a time when its assets are insufficient for the payment of its debts and other liabilities and the expenses of the winding up.

(7)   In this section 'director' includes a shadow director.

(8)   This section is without prejudice to section 213.

215 Proceedings under ss 213, 214

(1)   On the hearing of an application under section 213 or 214, the liquidator may himself give evidence or call witnesses.

(2)   Where under either section the court makes a declaration, it may give such further directions as it thinks proper for giving effect to the declaration; and in particular, the court may—

   (a)   provide for the liability of any person under the declaration to be a charge on any debt or obligation due from the company to him, or on any mortgage or charge or any interest in a mortgage or charge on assets of the company held by or vested in him, or any person on his behalf, or any person claiming as assignee from or through the person liable or any person acting on his behalf, and

   (b)   from time to time make such further order as may be necessary for enforcing any charge imposed under this subsection.

(3)   For the purposes of subsection (2), 'assignee'—

   (a)   includes a person to whom or in whose favour, by the directions of the person made liable, the debt, obligation, mortgage or charge was created, issued or transferred or the interest created, but

   (b)   does not include an assignee for valuable consideration (not including consideration by way of marriage or the formation of a civil partnership) given in good faith and without notice of any of the matters on the ground of which the declaration is made.

(4)   Where the court makes a declaration under either section in relation to a person who is a creditor of the company, it may direct that the whole or any part of any debt owed by the company to that person and any interest thereon shall rank in priority after all other debts owed by the company and after any interest on those debts.

(5)   Sections 213 and 214 have effect notwithstanding that the person concerned may be criminally liable in respect of matters on the ground of which the declaration under the section is to be made.

25.1 **ORDINARY APPLICATION FOR A DECLARATION THAT A DIRECTOR HAS BEEN ENGAGED IN WRONGFUL TRADING PURSUANT TO SECTION 214 OF THE INSOLVENCY ACT 1986**

Rule 7.2
Ordinary Application

IN THE HIGH COURT OF JUSTICE
CHANCERY DIVISION
COMPANIES COURT

NO: [ ] OF 20[ ]

IN THE MATTER OF BUSTCO LIMITED, REGISTERED NUMBER 011111
AND IN THE MATTER OF THE INSOLVENCY ACT 1986

BETWEEN:-

GILES GRABBER

Applicant

-and-

IAN FLAKEY

Respondent

TAKE NOTICE that I, Giles Grabber of Grabbers LLP, of 1 Vulture Street, London, as Liquidator of BUSTCO LIMITED, intend to apply to the Registrar on:

Date: [ ] 20[ ]
Time: [ ] am/pm
Place: Royal Courts of Justice, Strand, London WC2A 2LL

For an order in the following terms:

1. A declaration that the Respondent knew or ought to have concluded that there was no reason able prospect that Bustco Limited ('the Company') would avoid going into insolvent liquidation no later than 1st April 2007.

2. A declaration that the Respondent is liable to make a contribution of £250,000 to the assets of the Company or of such sum as this Honourable Court thinks proper pursuant to section 214 of the Insolvency Act 1986, and /or

3. An order that the Respondent do pay to the Applicant the sum found due under paragraph 2.

4. An order that the Respondent do pay the Applicant's costs of and incidental to this application.

5.　　All further and other accounts, inquiries, orders and directions as this Honourable Court thinks fit.

The grounds upon which I seek the above relief are set out in the 1st witness statement of Giles Grabber dated 1st April 2009, a true copy of which is served herewith.

Signed [ ]
Solicitor for the Applicant
Dated [ ] 20[ ]

The names and addresses of the persons upon whom it is intended to serve this application are:

Ian Flakey, 1 Geranium Cottage, London

The Applicant's address for service is:

SILK & CO
2 LAW STREET
LONDON

If you do not attend, the Court may make such order as it thinks fit.

25.2 WITNESS STATEMENT FOR A DECLARATION OF WRONGFUL TRADING PURSUANT TO SECTION 214 OF THE INSOLVENCY ACT 1986

Applicant: G Grabber: 1st: GG1: [ ] 20[ ]

IN THE HIGH COURT OF JUSTICE
CHANCERY DIVISION
COMPANIES COURT

NO: [ ] OF 20[ ]

IN THE MATTER OF BUSTCO LIMITED, REGISTERED NUMBER 011111
AND IN THE MATTER OF THE INSOLVENCY ACT 1986

1ST WITNESS STATEMENT OF GILES GRABBER

I, Giles Grabber of Grabbers LLP, of 1 Vulture Street, London, as Liquidator of BUSTCO LIMITED, state as follows:

1.   I am the Applicant in this application. I am the Liquidator of Bustco.

2.   I make the application in support of my application for:

   a.   a declaration that the Respondent knew or ought to have concluded that there was no reasonable prospect that Bustco Limited ('the Company') would avoid going into insolvent liquidation no later than 1st April 2007,

   b.   a declaration that the Respondent is liable to make a contribution of £250,000 to the assets of the Company or of such sum as this Honourable Court thinks proper pursuant to section 214 of the Insolvency Act 1986, and /or

   c.   an order that the Respondent do pay to the Applicant the sum found due,

   d.   an order that the Respondent do pay the Applicant's costs of and incidental to this application,

   e.   all further and other accounts, inquiries, orders and directions as this Honourable Court thinks fit.

3.   The matters set out in this witness statement are true and within my own knowledge except where otherwise indicated, in which case I have explained the source of my information or belief.

4.   There is now produced and shown to me a bundle consisting of true copies of the documents I will refer to in my witness statements marked 'GG1'.

5.   Bustco Limited was incorporated on 30th October 1996 under the Companies Act 1985. The share capital of the company is £100 shares divided into 100 ordinary shares of £1 each of which 2 shares have been issued to Mr Flakey. Mr Flakey was the company's sole director at all material times.

6.   A winding up order was made against Bustco on 1st March 2009. I refer to page [ ] of 'GG1' which is a true copy of the winding up order.

7.   I was appointed as the liquidator of Bustco Limited on 1st April 2009. I refer to page [ ] of 'GG1' which is a true copy of my certificate of appointment.

8.   Following my appointment I began to investigate the affairs of Bustco Limited. The following matters became apparent.

9.   Bustco Limited's last set of accounts dated 31st December 2007 show that it was balance sheet insolvent as at 31st December 2007 with a deficiency in the sum of £2,000,000. These are signed off by Mr Flakey as the company's director. I refer to page [ ] of 'GG1' which is a true copy of the accounts of Bustco Limited. Creditors claims lodged in the liquidation amount to £3,500,000. I refer to page [ ] of 'GG1' which is a true copy of the proofs of debt evidencing the creditors' claims. It is apparent from the accountant's note to the accounts that the price per widget sold exceeded its cost of manufacture.

10.   Notwithstanding that Bustco Limited was balance sheet insolvent and making a net loss on its trading of £25,000 per week or a 5 pence loss on each widget sold, Bustco Limited continued to place orders for raw materials from its suppliers. These suppliers represent the greater part of the creditors in the liquidation.

11.   I have been able to identify 23 suppliers and trade creditors who have either issued proceedings or sent a letter before action against Bustco Limited for unpaid trade debts totaling £250,000 during the 24 months following 31st December 2006. Where court proceedings were issued, Bustco Limited has not defended them. I refer to page [ ] of 'GG1' which is a true copy of the court documents, pleadings and letters before action I have located so far.

12.   On 2nd January 2009 a winding up petition was presented by Her Majesty Revenue & Customs for £1 million in unpaid VAT. I refer to page [ ] of 'GG1' which is a true copy of the petition. The winding up petition had been preceded by a number of letters by HMRC warning that unless they were paid they intended to issue a winding up petition on 2nd January 2009. I refer to page [ ] of 'GG1' which is a true copy of the letters.

13.   In the light of the above, it must have been obvious in the period from 31st December 2006 alternatively 31st December 2007 that it must have been obvious to Mr Flakey that there was no reasonable prospect that Bustco Limited would avoid going into insolvent liquidation.

14.   I therefore ask this Honourable Court to make the order in the terms sought.

STATEMENT OF TRUTH

I believe that the facts stated in this Witness Statement are true.

Signed [ ]
Full name [*GILES GRABBER*]
Dated [ ] 20[ ]

25.3   DECLARATION THAT A DIRECTOR HAS BEEN ENGAGED IN WRONGFUL TRADING PURSUANT TO SECTION 214 OF THE INSOLVENCY ACT 1986

IN THE HIGH COURT OF JUSTICE
CHANCERY DIVISION
COMPANIES COURT

NO: [ ] OF 20[ ]

IN THE MATTER OF BUSTCO LIMITED, REGISTERED NUMBER 011111
AND IN THE MATTER OF THE INSOLVENCY ACT 1986

BEFORE MR REGISTRAR WISE
DATED: [ ] 20[ ]

BETWEEN:-

GILES GRABBER

<u>Applicant</u>

-and-

IAN FLAKEY

<u>Respondent</u>

DRAFT MINUTE OF ORDER

UPON THE APPLICATION of Giles Grabber of Grabbers LLP, Liquidator of the above named company, BUSTCO LIMITED ('the Company')

UPON HEARING Counsel for the Applicant and Counsel for Ian Flakey, the Respondent

AND UPON READING the evidence noted as being read

IT IS DECLARED that the Respondent, Ian Flakey, knew or ought to have concluded that there was no reasonable prospect that Bustco Limited ('the Company') would avoid going into insolvent liquidation no later than 1st April 2007.

AND IT IS DECLARED that the Respondent is liable to make contributions of £250,000 to the assets of the Company or of such sum as this Honourable Court thinks proper pursuant to section 214 of the Insolvency Act 1986.

AND IT IS ORDERED that the Respondent do pay to the Applicant £250,000 by 4pm on 21st August 2009.

AND IT IS ORDERED that the Respondent do pay the Applicant's costs of and incidental to this application, such costs to be subject to a detailed assessment if not agreed.

CHAPTER 26

APPLICATION TO SET ASIDE A TRANSACTION DEFRAUDING CREDITORS

OBJECTIVE

The court has wide powers to rewind transfers of the company's property which have been undertaken at a time when the company is insolvent for no consideration or for significantly less than the value in money or money's worth provided by the company where the transaction has been entered into for the purpose of either putting assets beyond the reach of a person who is making or may make a claim against the company or otherwise prejudicing such a person's interests in such a claim.[1] This does not need to be the sole or main purpose of the transfer but should be shown to be a real and substantial purpose behind the transaction.[2]

Transaction is flexibly interpreted and covers arrangements spanning from formal contracts to informal understandings.[3] Fraud does not need to be shown. Nor does the company need to be insolvent at the time of the transaction.

---

[1]   Section 423 of the Insolvency Act 1986.

[2]   *Hashmi v IRC* [2002] EWCA Civ 981.

[3]   *Feakins v DEFRA* [2006] BPIR 895.

APPLICATION

If there have been existing proceedings, the application is by ordinary application in those proceedings on notice for a declaration and an order restoring the position to what it would have been had the transaction not been entered into.

The application must recite nature of the declaration sought and the grounds for bringing the application.[4]

Where there have been no previous proceedings, the application should be made by originating application on notice.

The application should be returnable to the registrar in the Companies Court or to the district judge in a Chancery District Registry or county court with insolvency jurisdiction.

The applicant can be the Official Receiver, the liquidator or administrator of the company or a victim of the company. If the company is in administration or liquidation a victim will need the permission of the court to make this application. Victim is flexibly interpreted.[5] A creditor can be a victim for these purposes.[6] Her Majesty's Revenue and Customs can be a victim for these purposes where the purpose of the transaction was to mislead them as to the tax liability.[7]

The respondent should be the person who made the transfer and any other party to the transaction that the applicant is seeking to set aside.

COURT FEES

Where the application is made by originating application a court fee of £130 is payable.[8] Where the application is made by ordinary application on notice to other parties, a court fee of £60 is payable.[9] Where the application is made by consent or without notice in existing proceedings a court fee of £30 is payable.[10]

EVIDENCE

The application should be supported by a witness statement by the liquidator or administrator. This will need to address:

- the capacity in which the deponent makes this application (eg victim, liquidator, etc);
- the order he seeks;
- the date the company was incorporated;
- the registered office of the company;

---

[4] Rule 7.3(2) of the Insolvency Rules 1986.

[5] *Hill v Spread Trustee Co Ltd* [2006] BPIR 789.

[6] *Re Ayala Holdings Ltd* [1993] BCLC 256.

[7] *Hill v Spread Trustee Co Ltd* [2006] BPIR 789.

[8] Paragraph 3.5 of Schedule 1 to the Civil Proceedings Fees Order 2008.

[9] Paragraph 3.12 of Schedule 1 to the Civil Proceedings Fees Order 2008.

[10] Paragraph 3.11 of Schedule 1 to the Civil Proceedings Fees Order 2008.

- the nominal share capital of the company;
- the issued share capital of the company;
- the objects of the company;
- the date upon which the petition to wind up the company or place it into administration or notice of administration was presented (if applicable);
- the date upon which the company went into liquidation or administration (if applicable);
- the date of the transaction subject to challenge;
- the particulars of the transaction subject to challenge;
- the value of the company's asset transferred under the transaction;
- that the asset was transferred for no consideration or identifying the price it was hearing transferred for and stating that this was significantly less than its value in money or money's worth;
- why it is said that the transaction has been entered into for the purpose of either putting assets beyond the reach of a person who is making or may make a claim against the company or otherwise prejudicing such a person's interests in such a claim;
- (in so far that there is an application to set aside the transaction) that the proposed order will not prejudice any interest in property that was acquired in good faith, for value and without notice of the relevant circumstances;[11]
- (in so far that there is an application to set aside the transaction) that the proposed order will not require a person and who has received a benefit from the transaction in good faith, for value and without notice of the relevant circumstances to pay any sum unless he was not a party to the transaction.[12]

And exhibit:

- (as applicable) evidence of his appointment as liquidator or administrator or of the basis upon which the applicant asserts he was a victim of the transaction;
- (as applicable) a copy of the winding up or administration order;
- evidence of the transaction subject to challenge;
- evidence of the company's ownership of the asset transferred;
- evidence of the transaction under which the company's asset was transferred and of its date and the consideration (if any) paid;
- an independent valuation of the property disposed of.

THE FIRST HEARING

At the first hearing the registrar or district judge will give directions as to whether points of claim are needed and for the filing of evidence. He may also require the application to be served on other people. He may give directions as to whether witnesses are to attend for cross examination. The first hearing is likely to be heard in chambers and the advocates are not expected to robe.

---

[11]   Pre-empting the possible defence under section 425(2) of the Insolvency Act 1986.

[12]   Pre-empting the possible defence under section 425(2) of the Insolvency Act 1986.

SERVICE

The application and the evidence in support will need to be filed at court and served on the respondent as soon as practicable after it is filed and in any event, unless it is necessary to apply ex parte or on short notice, at least 14 days before the date fixed for the hearing.[13]

The usual rule is that, subject to any other express provision, the application must be served at least 14 days before the date fixed for the hearing.[14] However, the court does have power, in cases of urgency, to hear an application immediately with or without notice to the other parties.[15]

Service may be effected by post provided it is addressed to the person it is to be served on and prepaid for either first or second class post.[16] It may be sent to the last known address of the person to be served.[17]

A document sent by first class post is treated as being served on the 2nd business day after posting, unless the contrary is shown.[18] A document sent by second class post is treated as being served on the 4th business day after posting, unless the contrary is shown.[19] The date of posting is presumed to be the date postmarked on the envelope, unless the contrary is shown.[20]

Where service of any application or any order of the court is to be made to a person outside England and Wales an application must be made to the registrar for directions as to the manner, timing and proof of service.[21]

The application needs to be supported by a witness statement stating:[22]

- the grounds upon which the application is made;
- in what place the person to be served is either to be found or presumed to be found.

Subject to these provisions, Part 6 of the CPR is deemed to apply under the Insolvency Rules 1986.[23]

---

[13]   Rule 7.4(5) of the Insolvency Rules 1986.

[14]   Rule 7.4(5) of the Insolvency Rules 1986.

[15]   Rule 7.4(6) of the Insolvency Rules 1986.

[16]   Rule 12.10(1) of the Insolvency Rules 1986.

[17]   Rule 12.10(1A) of the Insolvency Rules 1986.

[18]   Rule 12.10(2) of the Insolvency Rules 1986.

[19]   Rule 12.10(3) of the Insolvency Rules 1986.

[20]   Rule 12.10(4) of the Insolvency Rules 1986.

[21]   Rule 12.12(3) of the Insolvency Rules 1986.

[22]   Rule 12.12(4) of the Insolvency Rules 1986.

[23]   Rule 12.11 of the Insolvency Rules 1986.

KEY STATUTORY PROVISIONS

Sections 423 to 425 of the Insolvency Act 1986

423 Transactions defrauding creditors

(1)   This section relates to transactions entered into at an undervalue; and a person enters into such a transaction with another person if—

(a)   he makes a gift to the other person or he otherwise enters into a transaction with the other on terms that provide for him to receive no consideration;

(b)   he enters into a transaction with the other in consideration of marriage [or the formation of a civil partnership]; or

(c)   he enters into a transaction with the other for a consideration the value of which, in money or money's worth, is significantly less than the value, in money or money's worth, of the consideration provided by himself.

(2)   Where a person has entered into such a transaction, the court may, if satisfied under the next subsection, make such order as it thinks fit for—

(a)   restoring the position to what it would have been if the transaction had not been entered into, and

(b)   protecting the interests of persons who are victims of the transaction.

(3)   In the case of a person entering into such a transaction, an order shall only be made if the court is satisfied that it was entered into by him for the purpose—

(a)   of putting assets beyond the reach of a person who is making, or may at some time make, a claim against him, or

(b)   of otherwise prejudicing the interests of such a person in relation to the claim which he is making or may make.

(4)   In this section 'the court' means the High Court or—

(a)   if the person entering into the transaction is an individual, any other court which would have jurisdiction in relation to a bankruptcy petition relating to him;

(b)   if that person is a body capable of being wound up under Part IV or V of this Act, any other court having jurisdiction to wind it up.

(5)   In relation to a transaction at an undervalue, references here and below to a victim of the transaction are to a person who is, or is capable of being, prejudiced by it; and in the following two sections the person entering into the transaction is referred to as 'the debtor'.

424 Those who may apply for an order under s 423

(1)   An application for an order under section 423 shall not be made in relation to a transaction except—

    (a)   in a case where the debtor has been adjudged bankrupt or is a body corporate which is being wound up or [is in administration], by the official receiver, by the trustee of the bankrupt's estate or the liquidator or administrator of the body corporate or (with the leave of the court) by a victim of the transaction;

    (b)   in a case where a victim of the transaction is bound by a voluntary arrangement approved under Part I or Part VIII of this Act, by the supervisor of the voluntary arrangement or by any person who (whether or not so bound) is such a victim; or

    (c)   in any other case, by a victim of the transaction.

(2)   An application made under any of the paragraphs of subsection (1) is to be treated as made on behalf of every victim of the transaction.

425 Provision which may be made by order under s 423

(1)   Without prejudice to the generality of section 423, an order made under that section with respect to a transaction may (subject as follows)—

    (a)   require any property transferred as part of the transaction to be vested in any person, either absolutely or for the benefit of all the persons on whose behalf the application for the order is treated as made;

    (b)   require any property to be so vested if it represents, in any person's hands, the application either of the proceeds of sale of property so transferred or of money so transferred;

    (c)   release or discharge (in whole or in part) any security given by the debtor;

    (d)   require any person to pay to any other person in respect of benefits received from the debtor such sums as the court may direct;

    (e)   provide for any surety or guarantor whose obligations to any person were released or discharged (in whole or in part) under the transaction to be under such new or revived obligations as the court thinks appropriate;

    (f)   provide for security to be provided for the discharge of any obligation imposed by or arising under the order, for such an obligation to be charged on any property and for such security or charge to have the same priority as a security or charge released or discharged (in whole or in part) under the transaction.

(2)   An order under section 423 may affect the property of, or impose any obligation on, any person whether or not he is the person with whom the debtor entered into the transaction; but such an order—

(a) shall not prejudice any interest in property which was acquired from a person other than the debtor and was acquired in good faith, for value and without notice of the relevant circumstances, or prejudice any interest deriving from such an interest, and

(b) shall not require a person who received a benefit from the transaction in good faith, for value and without notice of the relevant circumstances to pay any sum unless he was a party to the transaction.

(3) For the purposes of this section the relevant circumstances in relation to a transaction are the circumstances by virtue of which an order under section 423 may be made in respect of the transaction.

(4) In this section 'security' means any mortgage, charge, lien or other security.

26.1   **ORDINARY APPLICATION FOR A DECLARATION THAT A PAYMENT IS A TRANSACTION DEFRAUDING CREDITORS PURSUANT TO SECTION 423 OF THE INSOLVENCY ACT 1986**

Rule 7.2
Ordinary Application

IN THE HIGH COURT OF JUSTICE
CHANCERY DIVISION
COMPANIES COURT

NO: [ ] OF 20[ ]

IN THE MATTER OF BUSTCO LIMITED, REGISTERED NUMBER 011111
AND IN THE MATTER OF THE INSOLVENCY ACT 1986

BETWEEN:-

GILES GRABBER

<u>Applicant</u>

-and-

IAN FLAKEY

<u>Respondent</u>

TAKE NOTICE that I, Giles Grabber of Grabbers LLP, of 1 Vulture Street, London, as Liquidator of BUSTCO LIMITED, intend to apply to the Registrar on:

Date: [ ] 20[ ]
Time: [ ] am/pm
Place: Royal Courts of Justice, Strand, London WC2A 2LL

For an order in the following terms:

1.   A declaration that the payment of £250,000 by Bustco Limited ('the Company') to the Respondent on or around 1st April 2008 is void against the Applicant as liquidator and that the same:

     a.   constituted a transaction at an undervalue within the meaning of section 423 of the Insolvency Act 1986,

     b.   was entered into for the purpose of either putting assets beyond the reach of the Company's creditors or otherwise prejudicing the interests of the company's creditors in relation to the claims which they were or might make.

2.   An order that the Respondent do pay to the Applicant the sum of £250,000 and/or such other sum as this Honourable Court thinks fit to restore the position to what it would have been if the Company had not entered into the transaction and protecting the interests of the victims of the same.

3.   An order that the Respondent do pay the Applicant's costs of and incidental to this application.

4.   Such further and other order and other relief as this Honourable Court thinks fit.

The grounds upon which I seek the above relief are set out in the 1st witness statement of Giles Grabber dated 1st April 2009, a true copy of which is served herewith.

Signed [ ]
Solicitor for the Applicant
Dated [ ] 20[ ]

The names and addresses of the persons upon whom it is intended to serve this application are:

Ian Flakey, 1 Geranium Cottage, London

The Applicant's address for service is:

SILK & CO
2 LAW STREET
LONDON

If you do not attend, the Court may make such order as it thinks fit.

26.2 WITNESS STATEMENT TO SET ASIDE A FRAUDULENT TRANSACTION PURSUANT TO SECTION 423 OF THE INSOLVENCY ACT 1986

Applicant: G Grabber: 1st: GG1: [ ] 20[ ]

IN THE HIGH COURT OF JUSTICE
CHANCERY DIVISION
COMPANIES COURT

NO: [ ] OF 20[ ]

IN THE MATTER OF BUSTCO LIMITED, REGISTERED NUMBER 011111
AND IN THE MATTER OF THE INSOLVENCY ACT 1986

1ST WITNESS STATEMENT OF GILES GRABBER

I, Giles Grabber of Grabbers LLP, of 1 Vulture Street, London, as Liquidator of BUSTCO LIMITED, state as follows:

1. I am the Applicant in this application. I am the Liquidator of Bustco.

2. I make the application in support of my application for:

    a. a declaration that the payment of £250,000 by Bustco Limited ('the Company') to the Respondent on or around 1st April 2008 is void against the Applicant as liquidator and that the same:

        i. constituted a transaction at an undervalue within the meaning of section 423 of the Insolvency Act 1986,

        ii. was entered into for the purpose of either putting assets beyond the reach of the Company's creditors or otherwise prejudicing the interests of the company's creditors in relation to the claims which they were or might make,

    b. an order that the Respondent do pay to the Applicant the sum of £250,000 and/or such other sum as this Honourable Court thinks fit to restore the position to what it would have been if the Company had not entered into the transaction and protecting the interests of the victims of the same,

    c. an order that the Respondent do pay the Applicant's costs of and incidental to this application,

    d. such further and other order and other relief as this Honourable Court thinks fit.

3.   The matters set out in this witness statement are true and within my own knowledge except where otherwise indicated, in which case I have explained the source of my information or belief.

4.   There is now produced and shown to me a bundle consisting of true copies of the documents I will refer to in my witness statements marked 'GG1'.

5.   Bustco Limited was incorporated on 30th October 1996 under the Companies Act 1985.

6.   The registered office of the Company is at Suite 1, 1 Poor Street, London.

7.   The nominal capital of the Company is £1000 divided into 1000 shares of £1 each. The amount of the capital paid up or credited as paid up is £2.

8.   The principal objects for which the Company was established are as follows: To carry on business as a general trading company and other objects stated in the memorandum of association of the Company.

9.   A winding up order was made against Bustco on the petition on 1st March 2009. I refer to page [ ] of 'GG1' which is a true copy of the winding up order.

10. I was appointed as the liquidator of Bustco Limited on 1st April 2009. I refer to page [ ] of 'GG1' which is a true copy of my certificate of appointment.

11. Bustco Limited's last set of accounts dated 31st December 2008 show that it was balance sheet insolvent as at 31st December 2008 with a deficiency in the sum of £2,000,000. I refer to page [ ] of 'GG1' which is a true copy of the accounts of Bustco Limited. Creditors' claims lodged in the liquidation amount to £3,500,000. I refer to page [ ] of 'GG1' which is a true copy of the proofs of debt evidencing the creditors' claims.

12. Following my appointment I began to investigate the affairs of Bustco Limited. The following matters became apparent.

13. On 1st January 2009 there was a bank transfer in the sum of £250,000 from Bustco Limited to Mr Flakey. I refer to page [ ] of 'GG1' which is a true copy of the bank statement of Bustco Limited showing the transfer of £250,000 from Bustco Limited to Mr Flakey. This appears in the accounts as payment for a gobstopper bought from Mr Flakey. I refer to page [ ] of 'GG1' which is a true copy of the accounts of Bustco Limited showing the entry showing the purchase.

14. The true value of the gobstopper (even when not partially sucked) is 5 pence. This is a mere fraction of the £250,000 paid to Mr Flakey for this. I refer to page [ ] of 'GG1' which is a true copy of the price list of Toothy Sweets showing the retail price of their gobstoppers to be 5 pence each.

15. The money paid represented the whole of Bustco Ltd available money in the bank. By making the payment, the monies left in Bustco Limited were dissipated. This meant that creditors in the winding up can hope for a dividend of no more than 1 penny for each £1 owed to them.

16. On 2nd January 2009 a winding up petition was presented by Her Majesty's Revenue and Customs for £1 million in unpaid VAT. I refer to page [ ] of 'GG1' which is a true copy of the petition. The winding up petition had been preceded by a number of letters by HMRC warning that unless they were paid they intended to issue a winding up petition on 2nd January 2009. I refer to page [ ] of 'GG1' which is a true copy of the letters.

17. In the light of the above, the payment to the Respondent was at a significant undervalue to the Company and, given the circumstances and timing of the purchase, it is to be inferred that the payment was made that the payment was made with the sole purpose of putting the Company's money beyond the reach of HMRC and its other creditors.

18. I therefore ask this Honourable Court to make the order in the terms sought.

STATEMENT OF TRUTH

I believe that the facts stated in this Witness Statement are true.

Signed [ ]
Full name [*GILES GRABBER*]
Dated [ ] 20[ ]

26.3 DECLARATION THAT A PAYMENT IS A TRANSACTION DEFRAUDING CREDITORS PURSUANT TO SECTION 423 OF THE INSOLVENCY ACT 1986

IN THE HIGH COURT OF JUSTICE
CHANCERY DIVISION
COMPANIES COURT

NO: [ ] OF 20[ ]

IN THE MATTER OF BUSTCO LIMITED, REGISTERED NUMBER 011111
AND IN THE MATTER OF THE INSOLVENCY ACT 1986

BEFORE MR REGISTRAR WISE
DATED: [ ] 20[ ]

BETWEEN:-

GILES GRABBER

Applicant

-and-

IAN FLAKEY

Respondent

DRAFT MINUTE OF ORDER

UPON THE APPLICATION of Giles Grabber of Grabbers LLP, Liquidator of the above named company, BUSTCO LIMITED ('the Company')

UPON HEARING Counsel for the Applicant and Counsel for Ian Flakey, the Respondent

AND UPON READING the evidence noted as being read

IT IS DECLARED that the payment of £250,000 by Bustco Limited ('the Company') to the Respondent on or around 1st April 2008 is void against the Applicant as liquidator and that the same constituted a transaction at an undervalue within the meaning of section 423 of the Insolvency Act 1986 AND was entered into for the purpose of either putting assets beyond the reach of the Company's creditors or otherwise prejudicing the interests of the company's creditors in relation to the claims which they were or might make.

IT IS ORDERED that the Respondent do pay to the Applicant the sum of £250,000.

IT IS ORDERED that the Respondent do pay to the Applicant the costs of and occasioned by the Applicant such costs to be assessed if not agreed.

CHAPTER 27

APPLICATION UNDER THE SUMMARY PROCEDURE

OBJECTIVE

The court has the power to make a declaration in respect of a company in liquidation that a person who is or was an officer of the company or has acted as liquidator or administrative receiver of the company or who is or was concerned in the formation, promotion and management of the company who has misapplied or retained or become accountable for any money or property of the company or has been guilty of misfeasance or breach of any fiduciary or other duty to the company.[1]

An officer includes a director manager or secretary. An auditor has been held to be an officer of the company for these purposes.[2] Breach of other duty includes a claim for negligence.[3] The section is not however available for the collection of a simple contractual debt.[4]

Equivalent proceedings may be brought against an administrator under paragraph 75 of Schedule B1 to the Insolvency Act 1986.

---

[1]   Section 212 of the Insolvency Act 1986.

[2]   *Re Thomas Gerrard & Sons Ltd* [1968] Ch 455 at 473. The question of whether or not an auditor is properly treated as an officer of the company for these purposes is however, in the author's opinion, not entirely clear cut.

[3]   *Re D'Jan of London Ltd* [1993] BCC 646.

[4]   *Re Etic Ltd* [1928] Ch 861.

The application may be made by the liquidator, the Official Receiver or any creditor or (with the court's permission) any contributory of the company.[5]

Any compensation ordered goes to the general funds in the hands of the liquidator rather than to compensate an individual creditor.

APPLICATION

If there have been existing proceedings, the application is by ordinary application in those proceedings on notice for a declaration and an order restoring the position.

Where there have been no previous proceedings, the application should be made by originating application on notice.

The application must recite nature of the declaration sought and the grounds for bringing the application.[6]

The application should be returnable to the registrar in the Companies Court or to the district judge in a Chancery District Registry or county court with insolvency jurisdiction.

The respondent should be the person against whom relief is sought.

COURT FEES

Where the application is made by originating application a court fee of £130 is payable.[7] Where the application is made by ordinary application on notice to other parties, a court fee of £60 is payable.[8] Where the application is made by consent or without notice in existing proceedings a court fee of £30 is payable.[9]

SERVICE

The application will need to be filed at court and served on the respondent as soon as practicable after it is filed and in any event, unless it is necessary to apply ex parte or on short notice, at least 14 days before the date fixed for the hearing.[10]

The usual rule is that, subject to any other express provision, the application must be served at least 14 days before the date fixed for the hearing.[11] However, the court does have power, in cases of urgency, to hear an application immediately with or without notice to the other parties.[12]

---

[5]   Section 212 of the Insolvency Act 1986.

[6]   Rule 7.3(2) of the Insolvency Rules 1986.

[7]   Paragraph 3.5 of Schedule 1 to the Civil Proceedings Fees Order 2008.

[8]   Paragraph 3.12 of Schedule 1 to the Civil Proceedings Fees Order 2008.

[9]   Paragraph 3.11 of Schedule 1 to the Civil Proceedings Fees Order 2008.

[10]   Rule 7.4(5) of the Insolvency Rules 1986.

[11]   Rule 7.4(5) of the Insolvency Rules 1986.

[12]   Rule 7.4(6) of the Insolvency Rules 1986.

Service may be effected by post provided it is addressed to the person it is to be served on and prepaid for either first or second class post.[13] It may be sent to the last known address of the person to be served.[14]

A document sent by first class post is treated as being served on the 2nd business day after posting, unless the contrary is shown.[15] A document sent by second class post is treated as being served on the 4th business day after posting, unless the contrary is shown.[16] The date of posting is presumed to be the date postmarked on the envelope, unless the contrary is shown.[17]

Where service of any application or any order of the court is to be made to a person outside England and Wales an application must be made to the registrar for directions as to the manner, timing and proof of service.[18]

The application needs to be supported by a witness statement stating:[19]

- the date the company was incorporated;
- the registered office of the company;
- the nominal share capital of the company;
- the issued share capital of the company;
- the objects of the company;
- the grounds upon which the application is made;
- in what place the person to be served is either to be found or presumed to be found.

Subject to these provisions, Part 6 of the CPR is deemed to apply under the Insolvency Rules 1986.[20]

THE FIRST HEARING

At the first hearing, the registrar or district judge will give directions as to whether points of claim are needed and for the filing of evidence. He may also require the application to be served on other people. He may give directions as to whether witnesses are to attend for cross examination. The first hearing is likely to be in chambers and the advocates will not be expected to robe.

EVIDENCE

No evidence needs to be filed before the first hearing. The application will however need in due course to be supported by a witness statement by the applicant. This will need to address:

- the basis upon which the applicant has the right to bring the claim;

---

[13] Rule 12.10(1) of the Insolvency Rules 1986.
[14] Rule 12.10(1A) of the Insolvency Rules 1986.
[15] Rule 12.10(2) of the Insolvency Rules 1986.
[16] Rule 12.10(3) of the Insolvency Rules 1986.
[17] Rule 12.10(4) of the Insolvency Rules 1986.
[18] Rule 12.12(3) of the Insolvency Rules 1986.
[19] Rule 12.12(4) of the Insolvency Rules 1986.
[20] Rule 12.11 of the Insolvency Rules 1986.

- the order he seeks;
- the date the company was incorporated;
- the date upon which the petition to wind up the company was presented;
- the date upon which the company went into liquidation;
- the basis that the respondent falls within the jurisdiction of the court (that he is or was an officer of the company or has acted as liquidator or administrative receiver of the company or who is or was concerned in the formation, promotion and management of the company);
- the nature of the duty he owes to the company;
- particulars of the matters – how and when it is said the respondent has misapplied or retained or become accountable for any money or property of the company or has been guilty of misfeasance or breach of any fiduciary or other duty to the company;
- that the arrangement operated to cause loss to the company and its creditors;
- particulars of the loss caused to the company or its creditors by the respondent (or if more than one, attributable to each respondent).

And exhibit:

- evidence of the locus of the applicant;
- the winding up order;
- evidence showing the respondent has misapplied or retained or become accountable for any money or property of the company or has been guilty of misfeasance or breach of any fiduciary or other duty to the company;
- evidence of the loss caused by the respondent's involvement in the wrongful trading.

KEY STATUTORY PROVISIONS

Section 212 of the Insolvency Act 1986

212 Summary remedy against delinquent directors, liquidators, etc
(1) This section applies if in the course of the winding up of a company it appears that a person who—

(a) is or has been an officer of the company,

(b) has acted as liquidator ... or administrative receiver of the company, or

(c) not being a person falling within paragraph (a) or (b), is or has been concerned, or has taken part, in the promotion, formation or management of the company,

has misapplied or retained, or become accountable for, any money or other property of the company, or been guilty of any misfeasance or breach of any fiduciary or other duty in relation to the company.

(2) The reference in subsection (1) to any misfeasance or breach of any fiduciary or other duty in relation to the company includes, in the case of a person who has acted as liquidator ... of the

company, any misfeasance or breach of any fiduciary or other duty in connection with the carrying out of his functions as liquidator of the company.

(3)   The court may, on the application of the official receiver or the liquidator, or of any creditor or contributory, examine into the conduct of the person falling within subsection (1) and compel him—

    (a)   to repay, restore or account for the money or property or any part of it, with interest at such rate as the court thinks just, or

    (b)   to contribute such sum to the company's assets by way of compensation in respect of the misfeasance or breach of fiduciary or other duty as the court thinks just.

(4)   The power to make an application under subsection (3) in relation to a person who has acted as liquidator of the company is not exercisable, except with the leave of the court, after he has had his release.

(5)   The power of a contributory to make an application under subsection (3) is not exercisable except with the leave of the court, but is exercisable notwithstanding that he will not benefit from any order the court may make on the application.

27.1 ORDINARY APPLICATION FOR A DECLARATION THAT THERE HAS BEEN A BREACH OF DUTY USING THE SUMMARY REMEDY UNDER SECTION 212 OF THE INSOLVENCY ACT 1986

Rule 7.2
Ordinary Application

IN THE HIGH COURT OF JUSTICE
CHANCERY DIVISION
COMPANIES COURT

NO: [ ] OF 20[ ]

IN THE MATTER OF BUSTCO LIMITED, REGISTERED NUMBER 011111
AND IN THE MATTER OF THE INSOLVENCY ACT 1986

BETWEEN:-

GILES GRABBER

Applicant

-and-

IAN FLAKEY

Respondent

TAKE NOTICE that I, Giles Grabber of Grabbers LLP, of 1 Vulture Street, London, as Liquidator of BUSTCO LIMITED, intend to apply to the Registrar on:

Date: [ ] 20[ ]
Time: [ ] am/pm
Place: Royal Courts of Justice, Strand, London WC2A 2LL

For an order in the following terms:

1. A declaration that the Respondent acted in breach of fiduciary duty and/or in breach of trust and/or was guilty of misfeasance within the meaning of section 212 of the Insolvency Act 1986 by causing Bustco Limited ('the Company') to make a payment of £250,000 to Samesburys to pay for the Respondent's grocery shopping on or around 1st April 2008, and /or

2. An order that the Respondent do pay to the Applicant the sum of £250,000 and/or such compensation to the Applicant or make such contribution to the assets of the Company as this Honourable Court thinks fit, and /or

3. An enquiry as to what property in the hands of the Respondent represents the payment of the £250,000.

4. A declaration that the Applicant is entitled to trace into and claim in equity any property known to the Respondent which represents the payment and that the Respondent holds such property on trust for the Applicant.

5. An order that the Respondent delivers up such property to the Applicant.

6. An order for interest, whether or not compounded, on all sums found due to the Applicant at such rates as the Court thinks fit pursuant to the Court's equitable jurisdiction and/or section 35A Supreme Court Act 1981.

7. An order that the Respondent do pay the Applicant's costs of and incidental to this application.

8. Such further and other order and other relief as this Honourable Court thinks fit.

The grounds upon which I seek the above relief are set out in the 1st witness statement of Giles Grabber dated 1st April 2009, a true copy of which is served herewith.

Signed [ ]
Solicitor for the Applicant
Dated [ ] 20[ ]

The names and addresses of the persons upon whom it is intended to serve this application are:

Ian Flakey, 1 Geranium Cottage, London

The Applicant's address for service is:

SILK & CO
2 LAW STREET
LONDON

If you do not attend, the Court may make such order as it thinks fit.

27.2   WITNESS STATEMENT IN SUPPORT OF AN APPLICATION FOR A DECLARATION THAT THERE HAS BEEN A BREACH OF DUTY USING THE SUMMARY REMEDY UNDER SECTION 212 OF THE INSOLVENCY ACT 1986

Applicant: G Grabber: 1st: GG1: [ ] 20[ ]

IN THE HIGH COURT OF JUSTICE
CHANCERY DIVISION
COMPANIES COURT

NO: [ ] OF 20[ ]

IN THE MATTER OF BUSTCO LIMITED, REGISTERED NUMBER 011111
AND IN THE MATTER OF THE INSOLVENCY ACT 1986

1ST WITNESS STATEMENT OF GILES GRABBER

I, Giles Grabber of Grabbers LLP, of 1 Vulture Street, London, as Liquidator of BUSTCO LIMITED, state as follows:

1.   I am the Applicant in this application. I am the Liquidator of Bustco.

2.   I make the application in support of my application for:

    a.   a declaration that the Respondent acted in breach of fiduciary duty and/or in breach of trust and/or was guilty of misfeasance within the meaning of section 212 of the Insolvency Act 1986 by causing Bustco Limited ('the Company') to make a payment of £250,000 to Sameburys to pay for the Respondent's grocery shopping on or around 1st April 2008, and /or

    b.   an order that the Respondent do pay to the Applicant the sum of £250,000 and/or such compensation to the Applicant or make such contribution to the assets of the Company as this Honourable Court thinks fit, and /or

    c.   an enquiry as to what property in the hands of the Respondent represents the payment of the £250,000,

    d.   a declaration that the Applicant is entitled to trace into and claim in equity to any property known to the Respondent which represents the payment and that the Respondent holds such property on trust for the Applicant,

    e.   an order that the Respondent delivers up such property to the Applicant,

f.   an order for interest, whether or not compounded, on all sums found due to the Applicant at such rates as the Court thinks fit pursuant to the Court's equitable jurisdiction and/or section 35A Supreme Court Act 1981,

g.   an order that the Respondent do pay the Applicant's costs of and incidental to this application,

h.   such further and other order and other relief as this Honourable Court thinks fit.

3.   The matters set out in this witness statement are true and within my own knowledge except where otherwise indicated, in which case I have explained the source of my information or belief.

4.   There is now produced and shown to me a bundle consisting of true copies of the documents I will refer to in my witness statements marked 'GG1'.

5.   Bustco Limited was incorporated on 30th October 1996 under the Companies Act 1985.

6.   The registered office of the Company is at Suite 1, 1 Poor Street, London.

7.   The nominal capital of the Company is £1000 divided into 1000 shares of £1 each. The amount of the capital paid up or credited as paid up is £2.

8.   The principal objects for which the Company was established are as follows: To carry on business as a general trading company and other objects stated in the memorandum of association of the Company.

9.   A winding up order was made against Bustco on the petition on 1st March 2009. I refer to page [ ] of 'GG1' which is a true copy of the winding up order.

10.   I was appointed as the liquidator of Bustco Limited on 1st April 2009. I refer to page [ ] of 'GG1' which is a true copy of my certificate of appointment.

11.   Bustco Limited's last set of accounts dated 31st December 2008 show that it was balance sheet insolvent as at 31st December 2008 with a deficiency in the sum of £2,000,000. I refer to page [ ] of 'GG1' which is a true copy of the accounts of Bustco Limited. Creditors' claims lodged in the liquidation amount to £3,500,000. I refer to page [ ] of 'GG1' which is a true copy of the proofs of debt evidencing the creditors' claims.

12.   Following my appointment I began to investigate the affairs of Bustco Limited. The following matters became apparent.

13.   Mr Flakey, the Respondent, is and was at all material times a director of Bustco Limited ('the Company'). Mr Flakey caused the Company to make a payment of £250,000 to Samesburys to pay for Mr Flakey's grocery shopping on or around 1st January 2009. I refer to page [ ] of 'GG1' which is a true copy of the bank statement of Bustco Limited showing the payment of £250,000 from Bustco Limited to Samesburys Supermarket. I further found an order confirmation and delivery note from Samesburys Supermarket confirming the delivery of ½ tonne of rum 'n' raisin ice cream

to Mr Flakey's home address following an order made by Mr Flakey. I refer to page [ ] of 'GG1' which is a true copy of the delivery note and order confirmation.

14.   On 2nd January 2009 a winding up petition was presented by Her Majesty's Revenue and Customs for £1 million in unpaid VAT. I refer to page [ ] of 'GG1' which is a true copy of the petition.

15.   Mr Flakey is and was a director of Bustco Limited at all relevant times and owed Bustco Limited fiduciary duties to act in the best interests of the company and not to make secret profits. As a director he is accountable for his dealings with company's assets.

16.   In the light of the above, I am advised that by procuring the company make the payment to Samesburys Supermarket for his own grocery bill the Respondent acted in breach of his fiduciary duty and/or was in breach of trust and/or was guilty of misfeasance.

17.   In the circumstances Mr Flakey holds the £250,000 or the rum 'n' raisin ice cream he purchased with it on trust for the company and he is liable to account to me for the same. I require an account of what happened to the property of the company received by Mr Flakey.

18.   I therefore ask this Honourable Court to make the order in the terms sought.

STATEMENT OF TRUTH

I believe that the facts stated in this Witness Statement are true.

Signed [ ]
Full name [*GILES GRABBER*]
Dated [ ] 20[ ]

27.3   DECLARATION THAT THERE HAS BEEN A BREACH OF DUTY USING THE SUMMARY REMEDY UNDER SECTION 212 OF THE INSOLVENCY ACT 1986

IN THE HIGH COURT OF JUSTICE
CHANCERY DIVISION
COMPANIES COURT

NO: [ ] OF 20[ ]

IN THE MATTER OF BUSTCO LIMITED, REGISTERED NUMBER 011111
AND IN THE MATTER OF THE INSOLVENCY ACT 1986

BEFORE THE HONOURABLE MR JUSTICE BEAK
DATED: [ ] 20[ ]

BETWEEN:-

GILES GRABBER

Applicant

-and-

IAN FLAKEY

Respondent

DRAFT MINUTE OF ORDER

UPON THE APPLICATION of Giles Grabber of Grabbers LLP, Liquidator of the above named company, BUSTCO LIMITED ('the Company')

UPON HEARING Counsel for the Applicant and Counsel for Ian Flakey, the Respondent

AND UPON READING the evidence noted as being read

IT IS DECLARED THAT the Respondent acted in breach of fiduciary duty and/or in breach of trust and/or was guilty of misfeasance by causing Bustco Limited ('the Company') to make a payment of £250,000 to Samesburys to pay for the Respondent's grocery shopping on or around 1st April 2008 within the meaning of section 212 of the Insolvency Act 1986.

AND IT IS ORDERED that the Respondent do by 4pm on 1st August 2008 pay to the Applicant the sum of £275,000 as being £250,000 in respect of the sum the Respondent in breach of fiduciary duty and/or in breach of trust and/or was guilty of misfeasance caused the Company to pay to Samesburys to pay for the Respondent's grocery shopping on or around 1st April 2008 together with interest in the sum of £25,000 to the date of judgment.

AND IT IS ORDERED that the Respondent do pay the Applicant's costs of and incidental to this application, such costs to be assessed on a standard basis if not agreed.

CHAPTER 28

PRIVATE EXAMINATIONS

OBJECTIVE

The Court has the power to assist a liquidator in his investigations into a company's assets and affairs.[1] The court may, on the application of the office-holder, summon to appear before it:

- any officer of the company;
- any person known or suspected to have in his possession any property of the company or supposed to be indebted to the company; or
- any person whom the court thinks capable of giving information concerning the promotion, formation, business, dealings, affairs or property of the company.

The court can order the respondent to:

- give evidence by witness statement;
- answer interrogatories
- produce documents;
- submit to an oral examination.

---

[1]   Section 236 of the Insolvency Act 1986.

If the respondent fails to attend or there are reasonable grounds for thinking he will abscond, the court can issue a warrant for his arrest, have his books, papers, money or possessions seized and (if he absconds or there is a real likelihood of him absconding) have him held in custody until the hearing.

APPLICATION NOTICE

The liquidator or provisional liquidator or administrator issues an ordinary application in compulsory winding up or subject of an administration order or where other proceedings in which liberty to apply has been given.[2] Otherwise the application should be made by originating application.[3] The application should be returnable to the registrar or district judge. The application must state whether the person:

- is to attend before the court to be examined;
- is to be ordered to clarify any matter which is in dispute in the proceedings or to give additional information in relation to any such matter (and if so whether Part 18 of the CPR applies);
- is to submit evidence by affidavit and the subject matter of such evidence;
- is to produce books, documents or other records, identifying the records sought.

Care should be taken to ensure that the relief sought is specific and clearly identifies what is to be done.

The application must be accompanied by a brief statement of the grounds upon which it is made.[4] The application can be made ex parte,[5] however, this should only be done where there is good reason for doing so.

The respondent should be the person the office holder is seeking relief against.

COURT FEES

Where the application is made by originating application a court fee of £130 is payable.[6] Where the application is made by ordinary application on notice to other parties, a court fee of £60 is payable.[7] Where the application is made by consent or without notice in existing proceedings a court fee of £30 is payable.[8]

SERVICE

The application should be served personally unless the court orders otherwise.[9] Conduct money for any person who is to be examined should be paid.[10]

---

[2]   Rules 7.2 and 7.4 of the Insolvency Rules 1986.
[3]   Rules 7.2 and 7.4 of the Insolvency Rules 1986.
[4]   Rule 9.2 of the Insolvency Rules 1986.
[5]   Rule 9.2(4) of the Insolvency Rules 1986.
[6]   Paragraph 3.5 of Schedule 1 to the Civil Proceedings Fees Order 2008.
[7]   Paragraph 3.12 of Schedule 1 to the Civil Proceedings Fees Order 2008.
[8]   Paragraph 3.11 of Schedule 1 to the Civil Proceedings Fees Order 2008.
[9]   Rule 9.3(5) of the Insolvency Rules 1986.
[10]   Rule 9.6(4) of the Insolvency Rules 1986.

The usual rule is that, subject to any other express provision, the application must be served at least 14 days before the date fixed for the hearing.[11] However, the court does have power, in cases of urgency, to hear an application immediately with or without notice to the other parties.[12]

Service may be effected by post provided it is addressed to the person it is to be served on and prepaid for either first or second class post.[13] It may be sent to the last known address of the person to be served.[14]

A document sent by first class post is treated as being served on the 2nd business day after posting, unless the contrary is shown.[15] A document sent by second class post is treated as being served on the 4th business day after posting, unless the contrary is shown.[16] The date of posting is presumed to be the date postmarked on the envelope, unless the contrary is shown.[17]

Where service of any application or any order of the court is to be made to a person outside England and Wales an application must be made to the registrar for directions as to the manner, timing and proof of service.[18]

The application needs to be supported by a witness statement stating:[19]

- the grounds upon which the application is made;
- in what place the person to be served is either to be found or presumed to be found.

Subject to these provisions, Part 6 of the CPR is deemed to apply under the Insolvency Rules 1986.[20]

WITNESS STATEMENT/GROUNDS

This should state:

- the applicant's capacity (why the applicant has locus to make this application);
- what role the respondent played in the company;
- whether the respondent is under a duty to cooperate;
- precisely what it is sought that the respondent is to do (thus if documents are to be produced identifying those documents);
- why the applicant wishes to have the information or documents sought to assist him in the performance of his functions;
- why it is believed that the respondent has the information or documents sought;

---

[11] Rule 7.4(5) of the Insolvency Rules 1986.
[12] Rule 7.4(6) of the Insolvency Rules 1986.
[13] Rule 12.10(1) of the Insolvency Rules 1986.
[14] Rule 12.10(1A) of the Insolvency Rules 1986.
[15] Rule 12.10(2) of the Insolvency Rules 1986.
[16] Rule 12.10(3) of the Insolvency Rules 1986.
[17] Rule 12.10(4) of the Insolvency Rules 1986.
[18] Rule 12.12(3) of the Insolvency Rules 1986.
[19] Rule 12.12(4) of the Insolvency Rules 1986.
[20] Rule 12.11 of the Insolvency Rules 1986.

- what steps have been taken to encourage the respondent to provide that information and documents voluntarily and why the respondent's reaction to those steps has made the application necessary.

FIRST HEARING

The hearing will be in chambers unless the court directs and will be before a registrar or district judge. The Applicant may be represented by counsel or by solicitors.[21]

Where an order is made for the attendance of the respondent before the court, the order must specify a time, date and place for examination not less than 14 days from the date of the order.[22]

Where affidavit evidence is ordered the court will specify the matters to be addressed. Where documents are to be produced, the documents will be identified and time and manner of compliance will be specified.

RETURN DATE

On the date fixed for the examination, if it appears to the court that any person has property of the company, the court may, on the application of the office holder, order the delivery of the property or money to the office holder.[23]

WARRANT FOR ARREST

If the respondent fails to attend at the appointed time, without reasonable excuse, or there are reasonable grounds for belief that the respondent has or is about to abscond to avoid his attendance, the court may issue a warrant for his arrest and for the seizure of any books, papers records, money or goods in his possession.[24] The court may also authorise him to be kept in custody until he is brought before the court.[25]

KEY STATUTORY PROVISIONS

Sections 235 to 237 of the Insolvency Act 1986

235 Duty to co-operate with office-holder
(1) This section applies as does section 234; and it also applies, in the case of a company in respect of which a winding-up order has been made by the court in England and Wales, as if references to the office-holder included the official receiver, whether or not he is the liquidator.

(2) Each of the persons mentioned in the next subsection shall—

---

[21]   Rule 9.4(5) of the Insolvency Rules 1986.
[22]   Rule 9.3 of the Insolvency Rules 1986.
[23]   Section 237(1), (2) of the Insolvency Act 1986.
[24]   Section 236 of the Insolvency Act 1986.
[25]   Section 236 of the Insolvency Act 1986.

    (a)   give to the office-holder such information concerning the company and its promotion, formation, business, dealings, affairs or property as the office-holder may at any time after the effective date reasonably require, and

    (b)   attend on the office-holder at such times as the latter may reasonably require.

(3)   The persons referred to above are—

    (a)   those who are or have at any time been officers of the company,

    (b)   those who have taken part in the formation of the company at any time within one year before the effective date,

    (c)   those who are in the employment of the company, or have been in its employment (including employment under a contract for services) within that year, and are in the office-holder's opinion capable of giving information which he requires,

    (d)   those who are, or have within that year been, officers of, or in the employment (including employment under a contract for services) of, another company which is, or within that year was, an officer of the company in question, and

    (e)   in the case of a company being wound up by the court, any person who has acted as administrator, administrative receiver or liquidator of the company.

(4)   For the purposes of subsections (2) and (3), 'the effective date' is whichever is applicable of the following dates—

    (a)   the date on which the company entered administration,

    (b)   the date on which the administrative receiver was appointed or, if he was appointed in succession to another administrative receiver, the date on which the first of his predecessors was appointed,

    (c)   the date on which the provisional liquidator was appointed, and

    (d)   the date on which the company went into liquidation.

(5)   If a person without reasonable excuse fails to comply with any obligation imposed by this section, he is liable to a fine and, for contravention, to a daily default fine.

236 Inquiry into company's dealings, etc

(1)   This section applies as does section 234; and it also applies in the case of a company in respect of which a winding-up order has been made by the court in England and Wales as if references to the office-holder included the official receiver, whether or not he is the liquidator.

(2)   The court may, on the application of the office-holder, summon to appear before it—

    (a)   any officer of the company,

(b)   any person known or suspected to have in his possession any property of the company or supposed to be indebted to the company, or

(c)   any person whom the court thinks capable of giving information concerning the promotion, formation, business, dealings, affairs or property of the company.

(3)   The court may require any such person as is mentioned in subsection (2)(a) to (c) to submit an affidavit to the court containing an account of his dealings with the company or to produce any books, papers or other records in his possession or under his control relating to the company or the matters mentioned in paragraph (c) of the subsection.

(4)   The following applies in a case where—

(a)   a person without reasonable excuse fails to appear before the court when he is summoned to do so under this section, or

(b)   there are reasonable grounds for believing that a person has absconded, or is about to abscond, with a view to avoiding his appearance before the court under this section.

(5)   The court may, for the purpose of bringing that person and anything in his possession before the court, cause a warrant to be issued to a constable or prescribed officer of the court—

(a)   for the arrest of that person, and

(b)   for the seizure of any books, papers, records, money or goods in that person's possession.

(6)   The court may authorise a person arrested under such a warrant to be kept in custody, and anything seized under such a warrant to be held, in accordance with the rules, until that person is brought before the court under the warrant or until such other time as the court may order.

237 Court's enforcement powers under s 236

(1)   If it appears to the court, on consideration of any evidence obtained under section 236 or this section, that any person has in his possession any property of the company, the court may, on the application of the office-holder, order that person to deliver the whole or any part of the property to the office-holder at such time, in such manner and on such terms as the court thinks fit.

(2)   If it appears to the court, on consideration of any evidence so obtained, that any person is indebted to the company, the court may, on the application of the office-holder, order that person to pay to the office-holder, at such time and in such manner as the court may direct, the whole or any part of the amount due, whether in full discharge of the debt or otherwise, as the court thinks fit.

(3)   The court may, if it thinks fit, order that any person who if within the jurisdiction of the court would be liable to be summoned to appear before it under section 236 or this section shall be examined in any part of the United Kingdom where he may for the time being be, or in a place outside the United Kingdom.

(4)   Any person who appears or is brought before the court under section 236 or this section may be examined on oath, either orally or (except in Scotland) by interrogatories, concerning the company or the matters mentioned in section 236(2)(c).

28.1 LETTER REQUESTING DOCUMENT BEFORE AN APPLICATION IS MADE FOR A PRIVATE EXAMINATION

Dear Sir,

Re: Bustco Limited (In Liquidation)

As you are aware, we act for Giles Grabbit the liquidator of the Company ('the Liquidator'). We are, together with our client, continuing to investigate the affairs of the Company.

As a former officer of the Company you are under a statutory duty under section 234 of the Insolvency Act 1986 to:

(a) give to the office-holder such information concerning the company and its promotion, formation, business, dealings, affairs or property as the office-holder may at any time after the effective date reasonably require, and

(b) attend on the office-holder at such times as the latter may reasonably require.

1. Review of the Company's books, papers and records

1.1 We have conducted a detailed review ('the 'Review') of all of the company's books, papers and records which have been provided to us to date by the officers and the former officers of the Company (the 'Documents').

1.2 Following the completion of the Review, it is clear that:

1.2.1 the books, papers and records provided to us, which were in no particular order, are incomplete;

1.2.2 certain documentation which we would reasonably expect to form part of the books, papers and records of (i) a private limited company, (ii) a company operating as a widget manufacturer are not contained, or are contained only to a limited extent, within the Documents (see attached Schedule).

1.3 We write to ask you to deliver up to our offices all of these documents in the Schedule relating to the Company in your possession, power and control (by 4pm on 1st April 2009). In so far that such documents are not within your possession, power and control or you are unable to deliver them to us we would ask you to write by 4pm 1st April 2009 to us to tell us where (to the best of your knowledge) each of the documents listed in the Schedule are and who current possesses or controls them.

2. Meeting

2.1 We would be grateful if you could attend for interview at 10am on 1st April 2009 at my offices at 1 Vulture Street, London. A map is enclosed. The nearest tube station is Saint Pools.

2.2 If this appointment is not convenient for you, please could you write back to us by 4pm on 1st February 2009 to suggest three alternative dates and times, within the next three months, that might be convenient for you to attend us.

2.3 Without wishing to limit the agenda of the meeting, we would particularly wish to explore with you at this meeting the following issues:

    2.3.1   your role and duties within the company;

    2.3.2   the corporate structure of the money;

    2.3.3   where all the company's money has disappeared to.

2.4 You may wish to bring any documents you find helpful to assist you. If you wish to be accompanied to the meeting, you may bring someone to accompany you however you will be expected to answer the questions asked yourself without interference or prompting.

3. Formal Notice

3.1 This letter is written under sections 234 to 236 of the Insolvency Act 1986.

3.2 If you fail to attend an appointment, without reasonable excuse, or fail to provide the documents required from you we reserve right to apply to the Court under sections 234 and 236 of the Insolvency Act 1986 to compel you to do so and for an order that you pay our costs of making that application. Failure to co-operate with an office holder without reasonable excuse is a criminal offence under section 235(5) of the Insolvency Act 1986.

Yours faithfully

Wigg & Co

SCHEDULE

LIST OF DOCUMENTS EXPECTED TO FORM PART OF BOOKS, PAPERS AND RECORDS

2. GENERAL COMPANY DOCUMENTATION

(A) CORPORATE

- Company Seal
- Board Minutes
- Shareholder Resolutions
- Register of members
- Register of directors and register of Company Secretary
- Register of charges and Mortgages
- Register of share transfers
- Copies of all Share Certificates issued by the Company
- Shareholders' Agreements (if any)
- Share Subscription Agreements
- Share Purchase Agreements (if any)
- Stock Transfer Forms (if any)
- Resignation letters by Directors/Company Secretary
- Powers of Attorney (if any)

(B) FINANCE

- Loan Agreements
- Details of any mortgages, charges, security granted by the company (if any)
- Documentation evidencing the release of any security (if any)
- Invoices and credit notes
- Any correspondence with auditors of the company
- Complete sets of annual, management and group company accounts
- Budget
- Cash flow projections
- Business plan
- Journals
- Bank statements

(C) TAX

- Returns made to any tax authority (i) of income, profits or gains or of any other amounts; or (ii) in relation to VAT ('Returns')
- All records, claims elections, accounts, computations, invoices or attachments relating to or relevant to any Return
- Returns in respect of PAYE and NIC together with all records, claims, forms, elections, accounts, computations or attachments relating to such returns

- Any notice, demand, assessment, clearance, registration, letter or other document or communication issued by or on behalf of, or addressed to, a tax authority
- Any agreement relating to taxation including group relief agreements, tax covenants, share option or other incentive schemes
- Any professional advice received in relation to taxation

(D) EMPLOYMENT

- Template/standard form employment contracts
- Confirmation that the following documents exist:
  - list of employees
  - payslips
  - working time regulation opt out letters
  - payroll and wage records
  - maternity records
  - annual leave records
  - sickness records
  - staff handbooks
  - policies/manuals/guidance for disciplinary proceedings, grievance, whistle blowing, equal opportunities, data protection, e-mail/internet policies, smoking policy, health & safety manual
  - accident book
  - disciplinary correspondence (if any)
  - details of terminations, redundancies and resignations
  - employment contracts and personnel records
  - details of pensions/benefits

(E) COMMERCIAL

- Leases for the office space of all branches
- Equipment purchase documentation
- Equipment leases (if any)
- Licenses
- IP rights (if any)
  - invoices
  - sales ledger transactions list
  - remittance advices
  - invoice sales daybook
  - credit notes
  - pay advices or payslips
  - P11s and P45s
  - tax documentation
  - insurance documents

28.2   APPLICATION FOR A PRIVATE EXAMINATION

Rule 7.2
Ordinary Application

IN THE HIGH COURT OF JUSTICE
CHANCERY DIVISION
COMPANIES COURT

NO: [ ] OF 20[ ]

IN THE MATTER OF BUSTCO LIMITED
AND IN THE MATTER OF THE INSOLVENCY ACT 1986

BETWEEN:-

GILES GRABBIT

<u>Applicant</u>

-and-

IAN FLAKEY

<u>Respondent</u>

TAKE NOTICE that I, GILES GRABBIT, ('the Applicant') intend to apply to the Registrar on

Date: [ ] 20[ ]
Time: [ ] am/pm
Place: [ ]

For an order pursuant to Sections 236 and 237 of the Insolvency Act 1986 in the following terms:

(1)   That the Respondent do attend court to be examined under oath on a date and time to be fixed and that the Applicant be at liberty to examine the Respondent in respect of the affairs of the Company, and

(2)   That the Respondent be ordered to produce all books, correspondence and documents in his custody or power relating to the Company including the documents set out in the attached Schedule.

(3)   That the Respondent be ordered to pay the costs of and occasioned by this application.

The grounds on which the Applicant claims to be entitled to the Order are set out in the attached Statement of Giles Grabbit.

Signed [ ]
Solicitor for the Applicant
Dated [ ] 20[ ]

My address for service is:

WIGG & CO
I LAW STREET
LONDON

To:
IAN FLAKEY, I GERANIUM COTTAGE, LONDON

If you do not attend, the Court may make such order as it thinks fit.

SCHEDULE ABOVE REFERRED TO

Board minutes
Sales ledgers
Banks statements
Cash books
Invoice sales daybooks
Correspondence files

28.3   WITNESS STATEMENT IN SUPPORT OF AN APPLICATION FOR A PRIVATE EXAMINATION

Applicant: G Grabbit: 1st: GG1: [ ] 20[ ]

IN THE HIGH COURT OF JUSTICE
CHANCERY DIVISION
COMPANIES COURT

NO: [ ] OF 20[ ]

IN THE MATTER OF BUSTCO LIMITED, REGISTERED NUMBER 011111
AND IN THE MATTER OF THE INSOLVENCY ACT 1986

BETWEEN:-

GILES GRABBIT

Applicant

-and-

IAN FLAKEY

Respondent

1ST WITNESS STATEMENT OF GILES GRABBIT

I, Giles Grabbit of Grabbers LLP, of 1 Vulture Street, London, as Liquidator of BUSTCO LIMITED, state as follows:

1.   I am the Applicant in this application. I am the Liquidator of Bustco Limited.

2.   I make the application in support of my application for an order:

(1)   that the Respondent do attend court to be examined under oath on a date and time to be fixed and that the Applicant be at liberty to examine the Respondent in respect of the affairs of the Company, and

(2)   that the Respondent be ordered to produce all books, correspondence and documents in his custody or power relating to the Company including the documents set out in the attached Schedule,

(3)   that the Respondent be ordered to pay the costs of and occasioned by this application.

3.   The matters set out in this witness statement are true and within my own knowledge except where otherwise indicated, in which case I have explained the source of my information or belief.

4.   Bustco Limited was incorporated on 30th October 1996 under the Companies Act 1985.

5.   The registered office of the Company is at Suite 1, 1 Poor Street, London.

6.   The nominal capital of the Company is £1000 divided into 1000 shares of £1 each. The amount of the capital paid up or credited as paid up is £2.

7.   The principal objects for which the Company was established are as follows: To carry on business as a general trading company and other objects stated in the memorandum of association of the Company.

8.   A winding up order was made against Bustco on 1st March 2009. I refer to page [ ] of 'GG1' which is a true copy of the winding up order.

9.   I was appointed as the liquidator of Bustco Limited on 1st April 2009. I refer to page [ ] of 'GG1' which is a true copy of my certificate of appointment.

10. Ian Flakey, the Respondent was the sole director of the Company and dealt exclusively with the Company's creditors and customers. Upon going through the records of the Company the Applicant discovered that the correspondence files were missing as well as the sales ledger and cashbook.

11. The Respondent has made no serious efforts to contact me with a view to discussing the affairs of the Company.

12. There is no other officer of the Company, employee or any other person capable of supplying information concerning sale, cash transactions and transactions other than the Respondent. I have written to the Respondent requesting this information on numerous occasions but have not yet had a response. I refer to page [ ] of 'GG1' which is a true copy of the letters I have sent the Respondent.

13. I need this information to reconstitute a picture of the Company's financial affairs and to identify its assets, liabilities and to form a view of the genuineness (or otherwise) of the claims I have received from those persons asserting to be the Company's creditors.

14. I therefore ask this Honourable Court to make the order in the terms sought.

STATEMENT OF TRUTH

I believe that the facts stated in this Witness Statement are true.

Signed [ ]

Full name [*GILES GRABBIT*]

Dated [ ] 20[ ]

28.4   ORDER FOR PRIVATE EXAMINATION

IN THE HIGH COURT OF JUSTICE
CHANCERY DIVISION
COMPANIES COURT

NO: [ ] OF 20[ ]

BEFORE MR REGISTRAR WISE
DATED: [ ] 20[ ]

IN THE MATTER OF BUSTCO LIMITED
AND IN THE MATTER OF THE INSOLVENCY ACT 1986

BETWEEN:-

GILES GRABBIT

<u>Applicant</u>

-and-

IAN FLAKEY

<u>Respondent</u>

UPON THE APPLICATION OF GILES GRABBIT dated [ ] 20[ ]

AND UPON READING the evidence filed

IT IS ORDERED that Ian Flakey of I Geranium Cottage, London, a former Director of the company do attend at the Chambers of the Registrar, Companies Court, Room No [ ], Thomas More Building, Royal Courts of Justice, Strand, London WC2A 2LL on [ ] 20[ ] at [ ] am/pm to be examined on oath in the above matter

AND IT IS ORDERED that Ian Flakey do deliver up to the Applicant by 4pm on [ ] 20[ ] deliver up to the Applicant all books, papers and records in his possession or under his power or control relating to the Company

Dated: [ ] 20[ ]

NOTE:

IF YOU FAIL TO COMPLY WITH THIS ORDER WITHOUT REASONABLE EXCUSE HAVING BEEN GIVEN TO AND ACCEPTED BY THE COURT A WARRANT MAY BE ISSUED FOR YOU TO BE ARRESTED AND BROUGHT TO THE COURT FOR EXAMINATION.

28.5 WARRANT FOR THE ARREST OF THE EXAMINEE ON HIS FAILURE TO ATTEND A PRIVATE EXAMINATION

IN THE HIGH COURT OF JUSTICE
CHANCERY DIVISION
COMPANIES COURT

NO: [ ] OF 20[ ]

BEFORE MR REGISTRAR WISE
DATED: [ ] 20[ ]

IN THE MATTER OF BUSTCO LIMITED
AND IN THE MATTER OF THE INSOLVENCY ACT 1986

To the Tipstaff and his assistances of this Court and to every constable within his jurisdiction and to the Governor of Brixton Prison.

IAN FLAKEY was required by an order of this Court dated [ ] 20[ ] to attend at this Court to be examined on oath and to produce documents in his possession or under his control namely the books and records of Bustco Limited.

The said Ian Flakey of 1 Geranium Cottage, London has failed to attend at the appointed time and produce the required documents.

You the Tipstaff and his assistances of this Court and others are required to seize any books, papers, records, money or goods in the possession of Ian Flakey and to arrest Ian Flakey and to bring him before this Court for examination at such time and place as the Court directs. In the meantime he shall be detained and delivered to the Governor of Her Majesty's Prison at Brixton. This shall be reported to the Court and its directions sought.

Anything you seize you are required safely to keep in your possession to await the written orders of the Court as to its disposal *or* to deliver to or otherwise deal with as directed by the judge of this Court.

And you, the Governor of Brixton Prison are required to receive Ian Flakey and keep him in custody to await the direction or order of this Court.

Dated: [ ] 20[ ]

CHAPTER 29

APPEAL FROM AN ORDER OF A REGISTRAR

OBJECTIVE

An appeal from a registrar of the companies court or a district judge is to a High Court judge. Permission needs to be sought from the judge being appealed or (if refused) from the appellate judge.

APPEAL NOTICE

The appellant's notice must be filed within 21 days after the date of the decision under appeal using form PDIP 1. The appeal should be filed in the High Court or the Chancery District Registry with jurisdiction for that area. Sufficient copies should be prepared to allow one for the appellant, two for the court and one for each respondent to the appeal.

The appellant should also file:

- a copy of the order under appeal;
- a time estimate;
- a chronology of events;
- an approved transcript or note of judgement; and
- a skeleton argument.

Where it is impractical to serve the skeleton at the same time as the appellant's notice it should be filed within 14 days of filing the notice.

COURT FEES

The court fee to be paid when filing an appeal notice is £200.[1]

SERVICE

The appeal notice will need to be served on the respondents within 7 days of the notice of appeal being filed.

RESPONDENT'S NOTICE

A respondent to an appeal may file a respondent's notice. This should be on form PDIP 2. The respondent's notice must be filed at court no later than 14 days after the date on which the respondent is served with the appellant's notice. The respondent's notice will need to be served on the appellants within 7 days of the respondent's notice being filed.

APPEAL BUNDLE

The appellant needs to prepare, file and serve his appeal bundle not later than 7 days before the hearing of the appeal.

TIME LIMITS

The time limits are strict and can only be extended by order of the court. They cannot be extended by agreement with the other side.

KEY STATUTORY PROVISIONS

Rules 7.2 and 7.49 of the Insolvency Rules 1986

7.2 Interpretation
(1)　In this Chapter, except in so far as the context otherwise requires—

'originating application' means an application to the court which is not an application in pending proceedings before the court; and
'ordinary application' means any other application to the court.

(2)　Every application shall be in the form appropriate to the application concerned.

7.49 Procedure on appeal
(1)　Subject as follows, the procedure and practice of the Supreme Court relating to appeals to the Court of Appeal apply to appeals in insolvency proceedings.

---

[1]　Paragraph 2.4 of Schedule 1 to the Civil Proceedings Fees Order 2008.

(2)   In relation to any appeal to a single judge of the High Court under section 375(2) (individual insolvency) or Rule 7.47(2) above (company insolvency), any reference in the CPR to the Court of Appeal is replaced by a reference to that judge and any reference to the registrar of civil appeals is replaced by a reference to the registrar of the High Court who deals with insolvency proceedings of the kind involved.

(3)   In insolvency proceedings, the procedure under RSC Order 59 (appeals to the Court of Appeal) is by ordinary application and not by application notice.

Paragraph 17 of the CPR Practice Direction – Insolvency Proceedings

17 Appeals in insolvency proceedings

17.1   This Part shall come into effect on 2nd May 2000 and shall replace and revoke Paragraph 17 of, and be read in conjunction with the Practice Direction – Insolvency Proceedings which came into effect on 26th April 1999 as amended.

17.2

(1)   An appeal from a decision of a County Court (whether made by a District Judge or a Circuit Judge) or of a Registrar of the High Court in insolvency proceedings ('a first appeal') lies to a Judge of the High Court pursuant to s. 375(2) of the Act and Insolvency Rules 7.47(2) and 7.48(2) (as amended by s. 55 of the Access to Justice Act 1999).

(2)   The procedure and practice for a first appeal are governed by Insolvency Rule 7.49 which imports the procedure and practice of the Court of Appeal. The procedure and practice of the Court of Appeal is governed by CPR Part 52 and its Practice Direction, which are subject to the provisions of the Act, the Insolvency Rules and this Practice Direction: see CPR Part 52 rule 1(4).

(3)   A first appeal (as defined above) does not include an appeal from a decision of a Judge of the High Court.

17.3

(1)   Section 55 of the Access to Justice Act 1999 has amended s. 375(2) of the Act and Insolvency Rules 7.47(2) and 7.48(2) so that an appeal from a decision of a Judge of the High Court made on a first appeal lies, with the permission of the Court of Appeal, to the Court of Appeal.

(2)   An appeal from a Judge of the High Court in insolvency proceedings which is not a decision on a first appeal lies, with the permission of the Judge or of the Court of Appeal, to the Court of Appeal (see CPR Part 52 rule 3);

(3)   The procedure and practice for appeals from a decision of a Judge of the High Court in insolvency proceedings (whether made on a first appeal or not) are also governed by Insolvency Rule 7.49 which imports the procedure and practice of the Court of Appeal as stated at Paragraph 17.2(2) above.

17.4   CPR Part 52 and its Practice Direction and Forms apply to appeals from a decision of a Judge of the High Court in insolvency proceedings.

17.5   An appeal from a decision of a Judge of the High Court in insolvency proceedings requires permission as set out in Paragraph 17.3(1) and (2) above.

17.6   A first appeal is subject to the permission requirement in CPR Part 52, rule 3.

17.7   Except as provided in this Part, CPR Part 52 and its Practice Direction and Forms do not apply to first appeals, but Paragraphs 17.8 to 17.23 inclusive of this Part apply only to first appeals.

17.8   Interpretation:

   (a)   the expressions 'appeal court', 'lower court', 'appellant', 'respondent' and 'appeal notice' have the meanings given in CPR Part 52.1(3);

   (b)   'Registrar of Appeals' means—

      (i)   in relation to an appeal filed at the Royal Courts of Justice in London, a registrar in bankruptcy; and

      (ii)   in relation to an appeal filed in a district registry, a district judge of that district registry.

   (c)   'appeal date' means the date fixed by the appeal court for the hearing of the appeal or the date fixed by the appeal court upon which the period within which the appeal will be heard commences.

17.9   An appellant's notice and a respondent's notice shall be in Form PDIP 1 and PDIP 2 set out in the Schedule hereto.

17.10

   (1)   An appeal from a decision of a registrar in bankruptcy must be filed at the Royal Courts of Justice in London.

   (2)   An appeal from a decision of a district judge sitting in a district registry may be filed—

      (a)   at the Royal Courts of Justice in London; or

      (b)   in that district registry.

   (3)   An appeal from a decision made in a county court may be filed—

      (a)   at the Royal Courts of Justice in London; or

      (b)   in the Chancery district registry for the area within which the county court exercises jurisdiction.

(There are Chancery district registries of the High Court at Birmingham, Bristol, Caernarfon, Cardiff, Leeds, Liverpool, Manchester, Mold, Newcastle upon Tyne and Preston. The county court districts that each district registry covers are set out in Schedule 1 to the Civil Courts Order 1983.)

17.11

(1) Where a party seeks an extension of time in which to file an appeal notice it must be requested in the appeal notice and the appeal notice should state the reason for the delay and the steps taken prior to the application being made; the court will fix a date for the hearing of the application and notify the parties of the date and place of hearing;

(2) The appellant must file the appellant's notice at the appeal court within—

(a) such period as may be directed by the lower court; or

(b) where the court makes no such direction, 21 days after the date of the decision of the lower court which the appellant wishes to appeal.

(3) Unless the appeal court orders otherwise, an appeal notice must be served by the appellant on each respondent—

(a) as soon as practicable; and

(b) in any event not later than 7 days, after it is filed.

17.12

(1) A respondent may file and serve a respondent's notice.

(2) A respondent who wishes to ask the appeal court to uphold the order of the lower court for reasons different from or additional to those given by the lower court must file a respondent's notice.

(3) A respondent's notice must be filed within—

(a) such period as may be directed by the lower court; or

(b) where the court makes no such direction, 14 days after the date on which the respondent is served with the appellant's notice.

(4) Unless the appeal court orders otherwise a respondent's notice must be served by the respondent on the appellant and any other respondent—

(a) as soon as practicable; and

(b) in any event not later than 7 days, after it is filed.

17.13

(1) An application to vary the time limit for filing an appeal notice must be made to the appeal court.

(2)   The parties may not agree to extend any date or time limit set by—

    (a)   this Practice Direction; or

    (b)   an order of the appeal court or the lower court.

17.14   Unless the appeal court or the lower court orders otherwise an appeal shall not operate as a stay of any order or decision of the lower court.

17.15   An appeal notice may not be amended without the permission of the appeal court.

17.16   A Judge of the appeal court may strike out the whole or part of an appeal notice where there is compelling reason for doing so.

17.17

(1)   In relation to an appeal the appeal court has all the powers of the lower court.

(2)   The appeal court has power to—

    (a)   affirm, set aside or vary any order or judgment made or given by the lower court;

    (b)   refer any claim or issue for determination by the lower court;

    (c)   order a new trial or hearing;

    (d)   make a costs order.

(3)   The appeal court may exercise its powers in relation to the whole or part of an order of the lower court.

17.18

(1)   Every appeal shall be limited to a review of the decision of the lower court.

(2)   Unless it orders otherwise, the appeal court will not receive—

    (a)   oral evidence; or

    (b)   evidence which was not before the lower court.

(3)   The appeal court will allow an appeal where the decision of the lower court was—

    (a)   wrong; or

    (b)   unjust because of a serious procedural or other irregularity in the proceedings in the lower court.

(4)   The appeal court may draw any inference of fact which it considers justified on the evidence.

(5) At the hearing of the appeal a party may not rely on a matter not contained in his appeal notice unless the appeal court gives permission.

17.19 The following applications shall be made to a Judge of the appeal court:

(1) for injunctions pending a substantive hearing of the appeal;

(2) for expedition or vacation of the hearing date of an appeal;

(3) for an order striking out the whole or part of an appeal notice pursuant to Paragraph 17.16 above;

(4) for a final order on paper pursuant to Paragraph 17.22(8) below.

17.20

(1) All other interim applications shall be made to the Registrar of Appeals in the first instance who may in his discretion either hear and determine it himself or refer it to the Judge.

(2) An appeal from a decision of a Registrar of Appeals lies to a Judge of the appeal court and does not require the permission of either the Registrar of Appeals or the Judge.

17.21 The procedure for interim applications is by way of ordinary application (see Insolvency Rule 12.7 and Sch 4, Form 7.2).

17.22 The following practice applies to all first appeals to a Judge of the High Court whether filed at the Royal Courts of Justice in London, or filed at one of the other venues referred to in Paragraph 17.10 above:

(1) on filing an appellant's notice in accordance with Paragraph 17.11(2) above, the appellant must file:

(a) two copies of the appeal notice for the use of the court, one of which must be stamped with the appropriate fee, and a number of additional copies equal to the number of persons who are to be served with it pursuant to Paragraph 17.22(4) below;

(aa) an approved transcript of the judgment of the lower court or, where there is no official record of the judgment, a document referred to in paragraph 5.12 of the Practice Direction supplementing CPR Part 52.

(b) a copy of the order under appeal; and

(c) an estimate of time for the hearing.

(2) the above documents may be lodged personally or by post and shall be lodged at the address of the appropriate venue listed below:

(a)   if the appeal is to be heard at the Royal Courts of Justice in London the documents must be lodged at Room 110, Thomas More Building, The Royal Courts of Justice, Strand, London WC2A 2LL;

(b)   if the appeal is to be heard in Birmingham, the documents must be lodged at the District Registry of the Chancery Division of the High Court, 33 Bull Street, Birmingham B4 6DS;

(c)   if the appeal is to be heard in Bristol the documents must be lodged at the District Registry of the Chancery Division of the High Court, Third Floor, Greyfriars, Lewins Mead, Bristol, BS1 2NR;

(ca)   if the appeal is to be heard in Caernarfon the documents must be lodged at the district registry of the Chancery Division of the High Court, Llanberis Road, Caernarfon, LL55 2DF;

(d)   if the appeal is to be heard in Cardiff the documents must be lodged at the District Registry in the Chancery Division of the High Court, First Floor, 2 Park Street, Cardiff , CF10 1ET;

(e)   if the appeal is to be heard in Leeds the documents must be lodged at the District Registry of the Chancery Division of the High Court, The Court House, 1 Oxford Row, Leeds LS1 3BG;

(f)   if the appeal is to be heard in Liverpool the documents must be lodged at the District Registry of the Chancery Division of the High Court, Liverpool Combined Court Centre, Derby Square, Liverpool L2 1XA;

(g)   if the appeal is to be heard in Manchester the documents must be lodged at the District Registry of the Chancery Division of the High Court, Courts of Justice, Crown Square, Manchester, M60 9DJ;

(ga)   if the appeal is to be heard in Mold the documents must be lodged at the district registry of the Chancery Division of the High Court, Law Courts, Civic Centre, Mold, CH7 1AE;

(h)   if the appeal is to be heard at Newcastle Upon Tyne the documents must be lodged at the District Registry of the Chancery Division of the High Court, The Law Courts, Quayside, Newcastle Upon Tyne NE1 3LA;

(i)   if the appeal is to be heard in Preston the documents must be lodged at the District Registry of the Chancery Division of the High Court, The Combined Court Centre, Ringway, Preston PR1 2LL.

(3)   if the documents are correct and in order the court at which the documents are filed will fix the appeal date and will also fix the place of hearing. That court will send letters to all the parties to the appeal informing them of the appeal date and of the place of hearing and indicating the time estimate given by the appellant. The parties will be invited to notify the court of any alternative or revised time estimates. In the absence of

any such notification the estimate of the appellant will be taken as agreed. The court will also send to the appellant a document setting out the court's requirement concerning the form and content of the bundle of documents for the use of the Judge. Not later than 7 days before the appeal date the bundle of documents must be filed by the appellant at the address of the relevant venue as set out in sub-paragraph 17.22(2) above and a copy of it must be served by the appellant on each respondent.

(4)   the appeal notice must be served on all parties to the proceedings in the lower court who are directly affected by the appeal. This may include the Official Receiver, liquidator or trustee in bankruptcy.

(5)   the appeal notice must be served by the appellant or by the legal representative of the appellant and may be effected by:

(a)   any of the methods referred to in CPR Part 6 rule 2; or

(b)   with permission of the court, an alternative method pursuant to CPR Part 6 rule 8.

(6)   service of an appeal notice shall be proved by a Certificate of Service in accordance with CPR Part 6 rule 10 (CPR Form N215) which must be filed at the relevant venue referred to at Paragraph 17.22(2) above immediately after service.

(7)   Subject to sub-paragraphs (7A) and (7B), the appellant's notice must be accompanied by a skeleton argument and a written chronology of events relevant to the appeal. Alternatively, the skeleton argument and chronology may be included in the appellant's notice. Where the skeleton argument and chronology are so included they do not form part of the notice for the purposes of rule 52.8.

(7A) Where it is impracticable for the appellant's skeleton argument and chronology to accompany the appellant's notice they must be filed and served on all respondents within 14 days of filing the notice.

(7B) An appellant who is not represented need not file a skeleton argument nor a written chronology but is encouraged to do so since these documents may be helpful to the court.

(8)   where an appeal has been settled or where an appellant does not wish to continue with the appeal, the appeal may be disposed of on paper without a hearing. It may be dismissed by consent but the appeal court will not make an order allowing an appeal unless it is satisfied that the decision of the lower court was wrong. Any consent order signed by each party or letters of consent from each party must be lodged not later than 24 hours before the date fixed for the hearing of the appeal at the address of the appropriate venue as set out in sub-paragraph 17.22(2) above and will be dealt with by the Judge of the appeal court. Attention is drawn to paragraph 4.4(4) of the Practice Direction to CPR Part 44 regarding costs where an order is made by consent without attendance.

17.23 Only the following paragraphs of the Practice Direction to CPR Part 52, with any necessary modifications, shall apply to first appeals: 5.10 to 5.20 inclusive.

17.24

(1) Where, under the procedure relating to appeals in insolvency proceedings prior to the coming into effect of this Part of this Practice Direction, an appeal has been set down in the High Court or permission to appeal to the Court of Appeal has been granted before 2nd May 2000, the procedure and practice set out in this Part of this Practice Direction shall apply to such an appeal after that date.

(2) Where, under the procedure relating to appeals in insolvency proceedings prior to the coming into effect of this Part of this Practice Direction, any person has failed before 2nd May 2000 either:

(a) in the case of a first appeal, to set down in the High Court an appeal which relates to an order made (County Court) or sealed (High Court) after 27th March 2000 and before 2nd May 2000, or

(b) in the case of an appeal from a decision of a Judge of the High Court, to obtain any requisite permission to appeal to the Court of Appeal which relates to an order sealed in the same period,

the time for filing an appeal notice is extended to 16th May 2000 and application for any such permission should be made in the appeal notice.

17.25 This paragraph applies where a judge of the High Court has made a Bankruptcy order or a winding-up order or dismissed an appeal against such an order and an application is made for a stay of proceedings pending appeal.

(1) the judge will not normally grant a stay of all proceedings but will confine himself to a stay of advertisement of the proceedings.

(2) where the judge has granted permission to appeal any stay of advertisement will normally be until the hearing of the appeal but on terms that the stay will determine without further order if an appellant's notice is not filed within the period prescribed by the rules.

(3) where the judge has refused permission to appeal any stay of advertisement will normally be for a period not exceeding 28 days. Application for any further stay of advertisement should be made to the Court of Appeal.

29.1 APPELLANT'S NOTICE OF APPEAL

Appellant's notice   **In the High Court of Justice**

For use in connection ONLY with an Appeal from a
decision of the County Court or a Registrar of the High
Court in insolvency proceedings

**Notes for guidance are available which will help
you complete this form. Please read them
carefully before you complete each section**

For Court use only	
Appeal Court Reference No	
Date filed	

Section I	Details of the case

Name of Court | High Court, Companies Court | Case number | 1234 of 2009 |

Case name | Re: Bustco Limited |

Names of claimant/ applicant/ petitioner	Giles Grabbit	Names of defendant(s)/ respondent(s)/ debtor(s)	Ian Flakey

In the case, were you the (tick only one box)

☐ claimant ☐ applicant ☐ petitioner
☐ defendant ☐ respondent ☐ debtor ☐ other (please specify) _____

Section 2	Your (appellant's) name and address

Your (Appellant's) name	Ian Flakey
Your Solicitor's name (*if you are legally represented*)	Duff & Co

Your (your solicitor's) address

I Lost Street London	Reference or contact name	Freddie Fudge
		020 711 1111
	Contact telephone number	111 London
	DX number	

Section 3	Respondent's name and address

First respondent's name Solicitor's name (*if legally represented*)	Giles Grabbit
	Wigg & Co

First respondent's (solicitor's) address

I Law Street, London	Reference or contact name	Sally Solicitor
	Contact telephone number	020 722 2222
	DX number	222 London

Second respondent's name	

Solicitor's name (*if legally represented*)	

Second respondent's (solicitor's) address

	Reference or contact name	
	Contact telephone number	
	DX number	

Details of other respondents are attached ☐ yes ☐ no

Section 4	Permission to appeal and time estimate for appeal hearing

Do you need permission to appeal? ☐ yes ☐ no

Has permission to appeal been granted? ☐ yes ☐ no

Date of order granting permission

Name of Judge granting permission

Duff & Co

the Appellant('s solicitor) seek permission to appeal

	Days	Hours	Minutes
How long do you estimate it will take to put your appeal to the appeal court at the hearing?			Thirty

Who will represent you at the appeal hearing? ☐ Yourself ☐ Solicitor ☐ Counsel

Section 5	Details of the order(s) or part(s) or order(s) you want to appeal

Name of District Judge/Circuit Judge/Registrar

Registrar Wise

Date of order(s)

1.4.09

If only part of an order is appealed, write out that part (or those parts)

Section 6	Grounds for appeal

(the appellant) appeal(s) the order(s) at section 5 because

1.	The Learned Registrar erred on the facts because he found for the Respondent against the weight of evidence.
2.	The Learned Registrar took into account irrelevant material insofar that he gave weight to the fact that the Appellant had ginger hair when making findings of credibility. The Learned Registrar ought to have given no weight at all to this consideration in reaching his conclusion.
3.	The Learned Registrar erred on the law in that he relied on the High Court decision in *Grockle v Gump* in finding against the Appellant. The Learned Registrar ought to have relied on *Snooks v Pookey* in which *Grockle v Gump* was overruled by the Court of Appeal.

Does your appeal include any issues arising from the Human Rights Act 1998   ☐ Yes   ☐ No

Signed: Freddie Fudge   Date 2.4.09
(Appellant's Solicitor)

Section 7	What decision are you asking the appeal court to make?

I am (the appellant is) asking that:

(*tick appropriate box*)

☐ the order(s) at section 5 be set aside

☐ the order(s) at section 5 be varied and the following order(s) substituted:

1.	That the Respondent's application against the Appellant be dismissed.
2.	That the Respondent be ordered to pay the Appellant's costs here and below, to be assessed on a standard basis if not agreed.

☐ a new trial be ordered

☐ the appeal court makes the following additional orders:

Section 8	Application for extension of time for filing Appellant's Notice

I apply (the appellant applies) for an application for extension of time for filing this Appellant's notice.

I wish (the appellant wishes) to reply on the following evidence in support of this application:

Statement of Truth

I believe that the facts stated in Section 8 of this appellant's Notice – Insolvency Proceedings are true.

Full name   Freddie Fudge

Name of appellant's solicitor's firm   Duff & Co

Signed: F Fudge   Position or office held   Partner
              (Appellant's solicitor)   (if signing on behalf of firm or company)

CHAPTER 30

TOOLKIT

ISSUING PROCEEDINGS IN THE ROYAL COURTS OF JUSTICE

Proceedings under the Insolvency Act 1986 are instituted by either a petition, ordinary or originating application. An ordinary application is used where there are existing proceedings to which the application forms part. An originating application is used where there are none.

The Companies Court has a separate administrative procedure. Proceedings are issued in the Companies Court General Office, and they are dealt with by the registrars. Proceedings in the Companies Court under a particular statute should be entitled accordingly, thus: 'In the matter of [*name and registration number of the company*] and in the matter of the [*name of statute as appropriate*]'.

COUNTY COURT OR HIGH COURT?

Petitions can be presented in the Companies Court, Royal Courts of Justice, Thomas More Building, Strand, London or at a Chancery District Registry. The High Court has jurisdiction to wind up any company registered in England and Wales.[1]

---

[1]   Section 117(1) of the Insolvency Act 1986.

County courts also have jurisdiction to wind up a company where the company's paid up or credited as paid up does not exceed £120,000 and the county court is in the district in which the company's registered office is situated.[2] The registered office is the place which is the place which has been the longest been the registered office during the 6 months immediately preceding the presentation of the petition to wind up.[3]

Starting proceedings in the wrong court will not invalidate them[4] and, once proceedings are commenced in a court in England and Wales, they may be continued by that court.[5]

A county court may refer a question by case stated to the High Court if all the parties agree or one party and the judge think it is appropriate.[6]

A county court may also transfer proceedings to the High Court generally just as the High Court similarly has power to transfer proceedings to a county court.[7]

REGISTRAR OR JUDGE?

Most applications should be commenced before a registrar. He, may, if he sees fit remit the matter to a judge. However, the following applications must be made direct to a judge and, unless otherwise ordered, shall be heard in public:[8]

- applications to commit any person to prison for contempt;
- applications for urgent interim relief (eg applications for validation orders before a winding up order is made;
- applications to restrain the presentation or advertisement of a petition to wind up;
- applications for the appointment of a provisional liquidator;
- petitions for administration orders or an interim order upon such a petition;
- applications after an administration order has been made pursuant to section14(3) of the Insolvency Act 1986 (for directions) or section 18(3) of the Insolvency Act 1986 (to vary or discharge the order);
- petitions to discharge administration orders and to wind up;
- applications pursuant to section 5(3) of the Insolvency Act 1986 (to stay a winding up or discharge an administration order or for directions) where a voluntary arrangement has been approved;
- appeals from a decision made by a district judge in a county court or by a registrar of the High Court.

---

[2]   Section 117(2) of the Insolvency Act 1986.
[3]   Section 117(6) of the Insolvency Act 1986.
[4]   Section 118(1) of the Insolvency Act 1986.
[5]   Section 118(2) of the Insolvency Act 1986.
[6]   Section 119(1) and (2) of the Insolvency Act 1986.
[7]   Rule 7.11 of the Insolvency Rules 1986.
[8]   *Practice Note on the Hearing of Insolvency Proceedings of 23 May 2005* [2005] BCC 456, [2005] BPIR 688.

URGENT APPLICATIONS

Urgent applications which are expected to last no more than 15 minutes may be listed by arrangement with the Companies Court clerks to be heard by the registrar at 10.15am and at 2pm each Wednesday during term. A note signed by the party's solicitor or counsel explaining the urgency should be included with the application and the parties asking for an application to be dealt with in the duty registrar's list should arrange for the court file and the application to be put before the duty registrar.

EVIDENCE

Evidence in insolvency proceedings may be given by either a witness statement or affidavit.[9] Indeed, the precedents in this book show the evidence being given by witness statement. Having said this, affidavits must be used where the evidence is given under rules 3.4, 4.33 (statements of affairs), 4.42 (further disclosure), 4.39, 4.40, (accounts), 4.73, 4.77 (claims) and 9.3 and 9.4 (examinations).[10]

The practices for evidence in the High Court are adopted for insolvency proceedings.[11]

The Official Receiver or a deputy official receiver may file his evidence by way of a report.[12] There is a similar exception to allow an administrator, liquidator, trustee in bankruptcy, provisional liquidator or interim receiver, a special manager or an insolvency practitioner appointed under section 273(2) to also file their evidence by way of a report, However, this right is limited to applications which do not involve other parties and even then the court may direct otherwise.[13]

BUNDLES

The applicant will normally be expected to prepare a bundle of documents for use in court whenever the documents involved are more than 25 pages long[14] or where the hearing in front of the registrar is likely to last more than one hour.[15] Failure to properly prepare the bundle may be punished by a special costs order.[16]

The bundle should be arranged in the following order:

- the application notice or statements of case 'chapter' format; any back sheets and superseded documents (eg particulars of claim overtaken by amendments, requests for further information recited in the answers given) should be omitted;

---

[9] Rule 7.57(5) of the Insolvency Rules 1986.
[10] Rule 7.57(6) of the Insolvency Rules 1986.
[11] Rule 7.57(1) of the Insolvency Rules 1986.
[12] Rule 7.9(1)(a) of the Insolvency Rules 1986.
[13] Rule 7.9(1)(a) of the Insolvency Rules 1986.
[14] Paragraph 7.9 of the Chancery Guide.
[15] Paragraph 7.40 of the Chancery Guide.
[16] Paragraph 7.10 of the Chancery Guide.

- witness statements, affidavits and expert reports for the applicant: witness statements should have written on them the page for that document in the bundles in manuscript; exhibits should appear separately; back sheets should be omitted;
- witness statements, affidavits and expert reports for the respondent;
- the documents, arranged in chronological order;
- correspondence: inter solicitor correspondence should be included only if and to the extent it is strictly necessary and should be placed in a separate bundle.

Where the volume of documents is large a separate core bundle should be prepared for the trial, containing only those documents likely to be referred to most frequently.

It is of paramount importance that the preparation of bundles is commenced in good time. A common mistake by solicitors is to fail to allow sufficient time to begin the preparation of the bundles in sufficient time to enable the bundles to be agreed with the other parties, for the references to the bundles to be used in skeleton arguments (the bundle needs to be delivered to counsel in sufficient time for this work to be done and account needs to be taken for this for the time limits for delivery of skeleton arguments) and the bundles to be delivered to the court at the required time. The required time means:

- before a trial or application by order not less than 2 clear days (and not more than 7 days);[17]
- for applications (other than applications by order) by 10am on the morning preceding the day of the hearing.[18]

The bundle should be clearly marked with the name and number of the case and the words 'For hearing on [*date*] before [*registrar/judge*]'.

The bundle should be paginated in bold at the bottom of the document (tabs are also useful):

- the documents wherever possible should be in A4 format;
- no more than one copy of any one document should be included;[19]
- documents should be arranged in date order starting with the earliest document;
- documents in manuscript, or not easily legible, should be transcribed; the transcription should be marked and placed adjacent to the document transcribed;
- documents in a foreign language should be translated; the translation should be marked and placed adjacent to the document translated; the translation should be agreed or, if it cannot be agreed, each party's proposed translation should be included;
- no bundle should contain more than 300 pages;
- binders and files must be strong enough to withstand heavy use;
- all staples, heavy metal clips, etc should be removed.

---

[17]   Paragraph 7.16 of the Chancery Guide.

[18]   Paragraph 7.16 of the Chancery Guide.

[19]   If the same document is included in the chronological bundles and is also an exhibit to an affidavit or witness statement, it should be included in the chronological bundle and where it would otherwise appear as an exhibit a sheet should instead be inserted. This sheet should state the page and bundle number in the chronological bundles where the document can be found.

The bundle should be accompanied by the following documents which should be signed by the parties' advocates:[20]

- an agreed time estimate;
- an agreed reading list;
- an agreed time estimate in respect of that reading list.

In the Royal Courts of Justice, bundles should be delivered to the Companies Court Issue Section.

Failure to lodge bundles on time may result in the matter not being heard on the date in question, the costs of preparation being disallowed or an adverse costs order.[21] A log is maintained in the Royal Courts of Justice of late bundles.

TIME ESTIMATES

Realistic estimates of the length of time a hearing is expected to take must be given. In estimating the length of a hearing, sufficient time must be allowed for reading the documents and for judgment, together with the summary assessment of costs and any application for permission to appeal.[22] The parties must inform the court and each other immediately of any material change in a time estimate.[23] Failure to give an accurate time estimate may result in the hearing being adjourned and the party at fault ordered to pay the costs thrown away.[24]

SKELETON ARGUMENTS

A skeleton might usefully include:

- a *dramatis personae*;
- time estimates for both the hearing and reading time;
- a reading list of documents the judge should read before the hearing;
- the facts of the case;
- a chronology (which should be expressed in neutral terms and agreed if possible);
- a list of issues.

The skeleton should briefly set out on double spaced A4 in numbered paragraphs:

- the nature of the case generally and the background facts;
- the propositions of law relied on with references to the relevant authorities;
- the submissions of fact to be made with reference to the evidence;
- the name (and contact details) of the advocate who prepared it.

---

[20] Paragraph 7.17 of the Chancery Guide.
[21] Paragraph 7.29 of the Chancery Guide.
[22] Paragraph 7.4 of the Chancery Guide.
[23] Paragraph 7.7 of the Chancery Guide.
[24] Paragraph 7.8 of the Chancery Guide.

Skeleton arguments should be delivered:

- on trials and applications by order not less than 2 clear days before the date or first date on which the application or trial is due to come on for hearing[25] (that is to say the 1st day it is to come on the warned list);
- on judge's applications without notice with the papers which the judge is asked to read on the application;[26]
- on all other applications, including interim applications, as soon as possible and not later than 10am on the day preceding the hearing.[27]

Unless photocopies of authorities are provided, lists of authorities should be supplied to the usher by 9am on the 1st day of the hearing Failure to lodge bundles or skeleton arguments on time may result in the matter not being heard on the date in question, the costs of preparation being disallowed or an adverse costs order.[28]

In the Royal Courts of Justice, skeleton arguments should be delivered to the Companies Court Issue Section.

Failure to lodge skeleton arguments on time may result in the matter not being heard on the date in question, the costs of preparation being disallowed or an adverse costs order.[29] A log is maintained in the Royal Courts of Justice of late skeletons.

USEFUL EMAIL ADDRESSES AT THE ROYAL COURTS OF JUSTICE

For lodging skeleton arguments, chronologies, reading lists, list of issues, lists of authorities (but not the authorities themselves):

Judge: rcjchancery.judgeslisting@hmcourts-service.gsi.gov.uk

Registrar: rcjcompanies.orders@hmcourts-service.gsi.gov.uk

For lodging the agreed terms of an Order which is ready to be sealed:

Judge: rcjchancery.ordersandaccounts@hmcourts-service.gsi.gov.uk

Registrar: rcjcompanies.orders@hmcourts-service.gsi.gov.uk

---

[25]   Paragraph 7.21 of the Chancery Guide.
[26]   Paragraph 7.22 of the Chancery Guide.
[27]   Paragraph 7.23 of the Chancery Guide.
[28]   Paragraph 7.32 of the Chancery Guide.
[29]   Paragraph 7.29 of the Chancery Guide.

COURT DRESS

Advocates are expected to robe for trials, appeals, contempt hearings (or any hearing where the liberty of the subject is in issue) and for hearings on a petition (such as a winding up petition). Otherwise, advocates should wear a dark business suit for court hearings.

KEY STATUTORY PROVISIONS

Part One and paragraphs 5 and 6 of Part Two of the CPR Practice Direction – Insolvency Proceedings

Part One
General

1.1 In this Practice Direction:

(1) 'The Act' means the Insolvency Act 1986 and includes the Act as applied to limited liability partnerships by the Limited Liability Partnerships Regulations 2001;

(2) 'The Insolvency Rules' means the rules for the time being in force and made under s.411 and s.412 of the Act in relation to insolvency proceedings;

(3) 'CPR' means the Civil Procedure Rules and 'CPR' followed by a Part or rule by number means the Part or rule with that number in those Rules;

(4) 'RSC' followed by an Order by number means the Order with that number set out in Schedule 1 to the CPR;

(5) 'Insolvency proceedings' means any proceedings under the Act, the Insolvency Rules, the Administration of Insolvent Estates of Deceased Persons Order 1986 (SI 1986/1999), the Insolvent Partnership Order 1986 (SI 1986/2142), the Insolvent Partnerships Order 1994 (SI 1994/2421) or the Limited Liability Partnerships Regulations 2001.

(6) References to a 'company' shall include a limited liability partnership and references to a 'contributory' shall include a member of a limited liability partnership.

1.2 This Practice Direction shall come into effect on 26th April 1999 and shall replace all previous Practice Notes and Practice Directions relating to insolvency proceedings.

1.3 Except where the Insolvency Rules otherwise provide, service of documents in insolvency proceedings in the High Court will be the responsibility of the parties and will not be undertaken by the court.

1.4 Where CPR Part 2.4 provides for the court to perform any act, that act may be performed by a Registrar in Bankruptcy for the purpose of insolvency proceedings in the High Court.

1.5   A writ of execution to enforce any order made in insolvency proceedings in the High Court may
      be issued on the authority of a Registrar.

1.6

(1)   This paragraph applies where an insolvency practitioner ('the outgoing office holder')
      holds office as a liquidator, administrator, trustee or supervisor in more than one case and
      dies, retires from practice as an insolvency practitioner or is otherwise unable or unwilling
      to continue in office.

(2)   A single application may be made to a Judge of the Chancery Division of the High Court
      by way of ordinary application in Form 7.2 for the appointment of a substitute office
      holder or office holders in all cases in which the outgoing office holder holds office, and
      for the transfer of each such case to the High Court for the purpose only of making such an
      order.

(3)   The application may be made by any of the following:

      (i)   the outgoing office holder (if he is able and willing to do so);

      (ii)   any person who holds office jointly with the outgoing office holder;

      (iii)   any person who is proposed to be appointed as a substitute for the outgoing office
              holder; or

      (iv)   any creditor in the cases where the substitution is proposed to be made.

(4)   The outgoing office holder (if he is not the applicant) and every person who holds office
      jointly with the office holder must be made a respondent to the application, but it is not
      necessary to join any other person as a respondent or to serve the application upon any
      other person unless the Judge or Registrar in the High Court so directs.

(5)   The application should contain schedules setting out the nature of the office held, the
      identity of the Court currently having jurisdiction over each case and its name and number.

(6)   The application must be supported by evidence setting out the circumstances which have
      given rise to the need to make a substitution and exhibiting the written consent to act of
      each person who is proposed to be appointed in place of the outgoing office holder.

(7)   The Judge will in the first instance consider the application on paper and make such order
      as he thinks fit. In particular he may do any of the following:

      (i)   make an order directing the transfer to the High Court of those cases not already
              within its jurisdiction for the purpose only of the substantive application;

      (ii)   if he considers that the papers are in order and that the matter is straightforward,
              make an order on the substantive application;

(iii) give any directions which he considers to be necessary including (if appropriate) directions for the joinder of any additional respondents or requiring the service of the application on any person or requiring additional evidence to be provided;

(iv) if he does not himself make an order on the substantive application when the matter is first before him, give directions for the further consideration of the substantive application by himself or another Judge of the Chancery Division or adjourn the substantive application to the Registrar for him to make such order upon it as is appropriate.

(8) An order of the kind referred to in sub-paragraph (6)(i) shall follow the draft order in Form PDIP 3 set out in the Schedule hereto and an order granting the substantive application shall follow the draft order in Form PDIP 4 set out in the schedule hereto (subject in each case to such modifications as may be necessary or appropriate).

(9) It is the duty of the applicant to ensure that a sealed copy of every order transferring any case to the High Court and of every order which is made on a substantive application is lodged with the court having jurisdiction over each case affected by such order for filing on the court file relating to that case.

(10) It will not be necessary for the file relating to any case which is transferred to the High Court in accordance with this paragraph to be sent to the High Court unless a Judge or Registrar so directs.

Part Two
Companies

[Paragraphs 2 to 4 concern Winding Up Petitions and are reproduced in Chapter 1.]

5 Distribution of business
5.1 The following applications shall be made direct to the Judge and, unless otherwise ordered, shall be heard in public—

(1) Applications to commit any person to prison for contempt;

(2) Applications for urgent interim relief (e.g. applications pursuant to s.127 of the Act prior to any winding up order being made);

(3) Applications to restrain the presentation or advertisement of a petition to wind up; or

(4) Applications for the appointment of a provisional liquidator;

(5) Petitions for administration orders or an interim order upon such a Petition;

(6) Applications after an administration order has been made pursuant to s.14(3) of the Act (for directions) or s.18(3) of the Act (to vary or discharge the order);

(7)   Petitions to discharge administration orders and to wind up;

(8)   Applications pursuant to s.5(3) of the Act (to stay a winding up or discharge an administration order or for directions) where a voluntary arrangement has been approved;

(9)   Appeals from a decision made by a County Court or by a Registrar of the High Court.

5.2   Subject to paragraph 5.4 below all other applications shall be made to the Registrar or the District Judge in the first instance who may give any necessary directions and may, in the exercise of his discretion, either hear and determine it himself or refer it to the Judge.

5.3   The following matters will also be heard in public—

(1)   Petitions to wind up;

(2)   Public examinations;

(3)   All matters and applications heard by the Judge, except those referred by the Registrar or the District Judge to be heard in private or so directed by the Judge to be heard.

5.4   In accordance with directions given by the Lord Chancellor the Registrar has authorised certain applications in the High Court to be dealt with by the Court Manager of the Companies Court, pursuant to Insolvency Rule 13.2(2). The applications are:

(1)   To extend or abridge time prescribed by the Insolvency Rules in connection with winding up (Insolvency Rule 4.3 and 12.9);

(2)   For substituted service of winding up petitions (Insolvency Rule 4.8(6));

(3)   To withdraw petitions (Insolvency Rule 4.15);

(4)   For the substitution of a petitioner (Insolvency Rule 4.19);

(5)   By the Official Receiver for limited disclosure of a statement of affairs (Insolvency Rule 4.35);

(6)   By the Official Receiver for relief from duties imposed upon him by the rules (Insolvency Rule 4.47);

(7)   By the Official Receiver for permission to give notice of a meeting by advertisement only (Insolvency Rule 4.59);

(8)   To transfer proceedings from the High Court to a County Court (Insolvency Rule 7.11);

(9)   For permission to amend any originating application.[N.B. In District Registries all such applications must be made to the District Judge].

6 Drawing up of orders

6.1   The Court will draw up all orders except orders on the application of the Official Receiver or for which the Treasury Solicitor is responsible under the existing practice.

[Paragraph 7 concerns rescission of a winding up order and is reproduced at Chapter 7.]

[Paragraph 8 concerns restraint of presentation of a winding-up petition and is reproduced at Chapter 4.]

Practice Note on the Hearing of Insolvency Proceedings

1.   The following statement was issued by the Vice-Chancellor.

2.   This Practice Note supersedes all previous Practice Statements of the Bankruptcy Registrars dealing with jurisdiction and work distribution and the Guidelines issued by the Insolvency Court Users' Committee in November 1988.

3.   As a general rule all petitions, claims and applications (except for those listed in paragraph 4 below) should be listed for initial hearing before a registrar or district judge in accordance with rule 7.6(2) Insolvency Rules 1986.

4.   The following applications should always be listed before a judge:

-   proceedings relating to insolvent companies
-   applications for committal for contempt
-   applications for an administration order
-   applications for an injunction
-   applications for the appointment of a provisional liquidator
-   interim applications and applications for directions or case management after any proceedings have been referred or adjourned to the judge (except where liberty to apply to the registrar or district judge has been given).

30.1   FORM 7.1 ORIGINATING APPLICATION

Rule 7.2
Originating Application

(TITLE)

Between
Applicant .. ..
and
Respondent .. ..

(a) Insert name and address of respondent

Let (a) .. .. attend
before the Judge/Registrar on:—
Date .. ..
Time .. .. hours
Place .. ..

(b) Insert name of applicant

On the hearing of an application by
(b) .. .. the applicant
for an order in the following terms:—

(c) State the terms of the order to which the applicant claims to be entitled

(c)   .. ..

(d) Set out grounds or refer to an affidavit in support

The grounds on which the applicant claims to be entitled to the order are:—
(d)   .. ..

(e) State the names and addresses of the persons intended to be served

The names and addresses of the persons upon whom it is intended to serve this application are:—
(e)   .. ..

OR

It is not intended to serve any person with this application.

(f) State the applicant's address for service

The applicant's address for services is: (f) .. ..
.. ..

Dated .. ..

Signed: .. ..
(SOLICITOR FOR THE) APPLICANT

If you do not attend, the court may make such order as it thinks fit.

30.2   FORM 7.2 ORDINARY APPLICATION

Rule 7.2
Ordinary Application

(TITLE)

Between
Applicant .. ..
and
Respondent .. ..

Take notice that I intend to apply to the Judge/Registrar on:

Date .. ..

Time .. .. hours

Place .. ..

(a) State nature and grounds of application

for (a) .. ..

Signed: .. ..

(SOLICITOR FOR THE) APPLICANT
My/Our address for service is:—
……………………………………..

(b) Give the name(s) and address(es) of the person(s) (including the respondent) on whom it is intended to serve the application

To: (b) .. ..

OR

It is not intended to serve any person with this application

If you do not attend, the Court may make such order as it thinks fit